D0193403

THE EUROPEAN UNION SERIES

General Editors: Neill Nugent, William E. Paterson, Vinc... ...

The European Union series is designed to provide an authoritative library on the European Union, ranging from general introductory texts to definitive assessments of key institutions and actors, policies and policy processes, and the role of member states.

Books in the series are written by leading scholars in their fields and reflect the most up-to-date research and debate. Particular attention is paid to accessibility and clear presentation for a wide audience of students, practitioners and interested general readers. The series consists of four major strands:

- General textbooks
- The major institutions and actors
- The main areas of policy
- The member states and the Union

The series editors are **Neill Nugent**, Professor of Politics and Jean Monnet Professor of European Integration, Manchester Metropolitan University, and **William E. Paterson**, Director of the Institute of German Studies, University of Birmingham.

Their co-editor until his death in July 1999, **Vincent Wright**, was a Fellow of Nuffield College, Oxford University. He played an immensely valuable role in the founding and development of *The European Union Series* and is greatly missed.

Feedback on the series and book proposals are always welcome and should be sent to Steven Kennedy, Palgrave Macmillan, Houndmills, Basingstoke, Hampshire RG21 6XS, UK or by e-mail to s.kennedy@palgrave.com

---

General textbooks

Published

Desmond Dinan **Encyclopedia of the European Union**
[Rights: Europe only]

Desmond Dinan **Ever Closer Union: An Introduction to European Integration (2nd edn)**
[Rights: World excluding North and South America, Philippines and Japan]

Simon Hix **The Political System of the European Union**

John McCormick **Understanding the European Union: A Concise Introduction (2nd edn)**

Brent F. Nelsen and Alexander Stubb **The European Union: Readings on the Theory and Practice of European Integration (3rd edn)**
[Rights: Europe only]

Neill Nugent **The Government and Politics of the European Union (5th edn)**
[Rights: World excluding USA and dependencies and Canada]

John Peterson and Elizabeth Bomberg **Decision-making in the European Union**

Ben Rosamond **Theories of European Integration**

Forthcoming

Laurie Buonanno and Neill Nugent **Policies and Policy Processes of the European Union**

Desmond Dinan **Europe Recast: A History of European Union**

Neill Nugent (ed.) **European Union Enlargement**

Andrew Scott **The Political Economy of the European Union**

Philippa Sherrington **Understanding European Union Governance**

The major institutions and actors

Published

Renaud Dehousse **The European Court of Justice**

Series Standing Order (outside North America only)
ISBN 0–333–71695–7 hardback
ISBN 0–333–69352–3 paperback
Full details from www.palgrave.com

Spain and the European Union

Carlos Closa
and
Paul M. Heywood

© Carlos Closa and Paul M. Heywood 2004

All rights reserved. No reproduction, copy or transmission of this publication may be made without written permission.

No paragraph of this publication may be reproduced, copied or transmitted save with written permission or in accordance with the provisions of the Copyright, Designs and Patents Act 1988, or under the terms of any licence permitting limited copying issued by the Copyright Licensing Agency, 90 Tottenham Court Road, London W1T 4LP.

Any person who does any unauthorized act in relation to this publication may be liable to criminal prosecution and civil claims for damages.

The authors have asserted their rights to be identified as the authors of this work in accordance with the Copyright, Designs and Patents Act 1988.

First published 2004 by
PALGRAVE MACMILLAN
Houndmills, Basingstoke, Hampshire RG21 6XS and
175 Fifth Avenue, New York, N.Y. 10010
Companies and representatives throughout the world

PALGRAVE MACMILLAN is the global academic imprint of the Palgrave Macmillan division of St. Martin's Press, LLC and of Palgrave Macmillan Ltd. Macmillan□ is a registered trademark in the United States, United Kingdom and other countries. Palgrave is a registered trademark in the European Union and other countries.

ISBN 0–333–75338–0 hardback
ISBN 0–333–75339–9 paperback

This book is printed on paper suitable for recycling and made from fully managed and sustained forest sources.

A catalogue record for this book is available from the British Library.

A catalog record for this book is available from the Library of Congress

10   9   8   7   6   5   4   3   2   1
13 12 11 10 09 08 07 06 05 04

Printed in China

For Miguel, Malú and Lucas, and for
Frank, Chris and Nick

Contents

List of Figures and Tables

Figures

Tables

Acknowledgements

It is customary to state that a book has taken much longer to complete than originally anticipated. This one is no exception. The road to publication has been long, frequently interrupted, and not always smooth. In part that is a reflection of the practical challenges of coordination involved in any joint authored work; it also reflects the increasing incursions into research time made by a plethora of assessment mechanisms and accountability exercises. At times it felt that the book would never be finished. But in the end, of course, it was and in the process of completion both authors incurred a number of both academic and personal debts which it is a pleasure to acknowledge here.

The staff at the library of the Faculty of Law at the Universidad de Zaragoza – Sergio, Lola and Esther – proved extremely helpful in providing all kinds of assistance with secondary sources. Mari Lo Usero, from the Centro de Documentación Europea at the same institution, provided some essential primary sources. Martha Peach at the Centro de Estudios Avanzados en Ciencias Sociales in Madrid, was an invaluable source of support and advice whilst Paul Heywood was on research leave there during 2000. A Mobility Grant from the Spanish Ministry of Education allowed Carlos Closa to work on this project at the Center for European Studies, Harvard University, in 2001/02. Faculty, visiting scholars and staff there provided a truly congenial working environment.

Willie Paterson and Neill Nugent, editors of the European Union series of which this volume forms a part, provided much helpful advice and support. Several colleagues read and commented on chapters of the manuscript at various points in its development and furnished us with valuable feedback: Kike Alberola offered helpful comments on Chapter 7 and clarified some of the economic terms; César Colino provided valuable insights into the Spanish system of multilevel governance; and Nacho Torreblanca helped refine our thinking on Spanish European policy. Chapter 4 on the Spanish central administration benefited greatly from discussions with Hussein Kassim. A special debt of gratitude is owed to Nacho Molina, who read most of the manuscript and mercifully kept a copy which proved essential when a computer containing the original version was stolen. He also provided the figure in Chapter 3. Figure 8.2 is reproduced by permission under the terms of the standard EU reproduction licence. Others who provided helpful comments and advice include William Chislett, Erik Jones, John Peterson and Mary Vincent.

Steven Kennedy at Palgrave Macmillan displayed his usual indefatigable patience with our numerous requests for deadline extensions, and Rosemary Williams provided essential assistance in the final stages of completing the manuscript. Our most important acknowledgement is to the late Vincent Wright, who should be credited with the initial stimulus for this book and for bringing together the two authors. This volume is testimony – albeit an inadequate one – to his extraordinary influence.

CARLOS CLOSA
PAUL M. HEYWOOD

List of Abbreviations

AC(s)	Autonomous Community(ies)
ACP	African, Caribbean, Pacific countries (Lomé Covention)
AP	Alianza Popular
ARE	Association of European Regions
BERD	European Bank for Reconstruction and Development
BNG	Bloque Nacionalista Gallego
CAP	Common Agricultural Policy
CDC	Convergència Democrática de Cataluña
CEFSP	Common European Foreign and Security Policy
CEOE	Confederación Española de Organizaciones Empresariales
CFP	Common Fisheries Policy
CFSP	Common Foreign and Security Policy
CiU	Convergència i Unió
CCOO	Comisiones Obreras
CMO	Common Market Organizations
COREPER	Committee of Permanent Representatives
CODA	Coordinadora de Organizaciones de Agricultores
CR	Committee of Regions
CSCE	Conference on Security and Cooperation in Europe
CSCM	Conference on Security and Cooperation in the Mediterranean
CSF	Community Support Framework
DG	Directorate General
EAGGF	European Agriculture Guidance and Guarantee Fund
EC	European Community
ECB	European Central Bank
ECHO	European Community Humanitarian Office
ECJ	European Court of Justice
ECSC	European Coal and Steel Community
ECU	European Currency Unit
EDC	European Defense Community
EEC	European Economic Community
EES	European Economic Space
EEZ	Exclusive Economic Zone

EFTA	European Free Trade Association
EIB	European Investment Bank
ELDR	European Liberal, Democratic and Reformist Party
EMS	European Monetary System
EMU	Economic and Monetary Union
EP	European Parliament
EPP-ED	European People's Party and European Democrats
EPC	European Political Cooperation
ERDF	European Regional Development Fund
ERM	Exchange Rate Mechanism
ESC	Economic and Social Council
ESF	European Social Fund
ETA	Euskadi Ta Askatasuna (Basque Country and Freedom)
ETUC	European Trade Union Confederation
EU	European Union
EUL	European United Left
FCI	Fondo de Compensación Interterritorial
FEMP	Federación Española de Municipios y Provincias General
GATT	General Agreement on Tariffs and Trade
GDP	Gross Domestic Product
GNP	Gross National Product
HAJC	Home Affairs and Judicial Cooperation
HB	Herri Batasuna
ICO	International Olympic Committee
IGC	Intergovernmental Conference
IMF	International Monetary Fund
IMP	Integrated Mediterranean Programmes
IU	lzquierda Unida
MAE	Ministry for Foreign Affairs
MAP	Ministry for Public Administrations
MAPYA	Ministry for Agriculture, Fisheries and Food
MRCE	Ministry for Relations with the European Community
NAFTA	North American Free Trade Agreement
NAFO	North Atlantic Fishing Organization
NATO	North Atlantic Treaty Organization
OECD	Organisation for Economic Co-operation and Development
OSCE	Organisation for Security and Co-operation in Europe
PCE	Partido Comunista de España
PCF	French Communist Party

OSCE	Organization for Security and Cooperation in Europe
PES	European Socialist Party
PHARE	Pologne et Hongrie Assistance à la Reconstruction de l'Economie
PNV	Partido Nacionalista Vasco
PP	Partido Popular
PPE	European People's Party
PSOE	Partido Socialista Obrero Español
RDP	Regional Development Plan
REPER	Permanent Representation
RPR	Assembly for the Republic (France)
RTVE	Radio Televisión Española
SEA	Single European Act
SEAE	Secretaría de Estado de Asuntos Europeos
SEPEUE	Secretaría de Estado de Política Exterior y Unión Europea
SPD	German Social Democratic Party
TAC	Total Admissible Catches
TEU	Treaty of European Union (Maastricht Treaty)
TREVI	Terrorism, Radicalism, Extremism and Violence International
UCD	Unión de Centro Democrático
UDC	Unión Democrática de Cataluña
UGT	Unión General de Trabajadores
UN	United Nations
UNICE	Union of Industrial and Employers' Confederation of Europe
UPA	Unión de Pequeños Agricultores
VAT	Value Added Tax
WEU	Western European Union
WTO	World Trade Organization

Introduction: A Framework for Analysis

This book examines the relationship between Spain and the European Union (EU). Rather than offer simply a detailed empirical account of the case of Spain, we have sought to situate our study within a theory-driven analytical framework. Whilst we emphasize national idiosyncrasy where appropriate, we are more concerned to view Spain's interaction with the EU as a paradigmatic example of a broad, if complex, relationship which allows for comparison with other member states. Thus, the book hopes to make a contribution both to theory-testing and to theory-building.

Some thirty years ago, Donald J. Puchala (1972) famously compared studies of European integration to the fable of the blind men and the elephant: the men could describe only the part they were able to feel, resulting in a series of quite different accounts (a snake, a column, and so forth) and no possibility of providing an accurate picture of the whole beast. The fable served to illustrate the difficulty of developing a comprehensive analysis of all the features which characterize the EU, a problem which also applies to any study of the relationship between the EU and one of its member states. Whilst a range of different approaches – fusion theory, the domestic politics approach, reverse image, Europeanization of policies, and so forth – may offer valuable theoretical insights, they tend to focus on particular aspects of the relationship rather than provide a comprehensive analysis. In seeking to develop such a comprehensive analysis, we need to focus on both poles of the relationship: the *elaboration of national policies* towards the EU, and the *impact of membership* on the domestic system. To analyse these two dimensions, this book adopts a broadly neo-institutionalist approach to understanding the EU.

During the 1980s and 1990s, the prevailing trend in studies of EU integration shifted from neo-functionalist accounts (with their emphasis on processes) towards variants of realist intergovernmentalism, which focus on central governments as the principal agencies with negotiating capacity at EU level. The 'domestic politics' approach

1

(Bulmer, 1983) sees EU integration as offering an enlarged arena in which to pursue domestic political games – effectively, the continuation of domestic politics at a different level. The two central tenets of this approach are that domestic political factors can be employed to explain actions at the EU level, and that national governments act as 'clearing houses' which determine whether domestic political disputes will enter the EU arena (Bulmer, 1986: 26). In this respect, the domestic politics approach partially coincides with 'liberal intergovernmentalism' (Moravscik, 1993, 1998), which emphasizes how states' preferences are determined through domestic political processes which reflect national interests, and how the ability of states to achieve their aims in the international arena depends on the relative intensity of these preferences. Some aspects of the Spanish case studied here support such an approach, notably the leading role played by central government and the preeminence of executive power.

These approaches see national preferences as being formed exogenously to the EU's institutional framework – that is, the domestic arena is presented as being more or less autonomous. But as far back as the 1970s, Peter Gourevitch (1978) stressed the need to move beyond Waltz's 'second image' conception that international institutions simply reflect domestic interests, positing instead the notion of the 'second image reversed': according to this view, international institutions constrain in fundamental ways both the preferences and the decision-making of domestic actors. Such a focus suggests a more structural interpretation of national politics, reflecting both the location and relative strength of a given state within the international arena. Along with theories of state interdependence and the currently fashionable emphasis on 'globalization', this approach questions the autonomy of national policy-making and argues that the international context conditions domestic choices.

Again, the Spanish case offers evidence to support such a view. On the one hand, Spain's desire for membership of the EU was driven by its relative weakness and lack of autonomy in the international trading and economic environment – an underlying theme which runs through many of the chapters which follow. On the other hand, changes in Europe's geopolitical climate since the end of the Cold War have acted as a significant driver in Spain's redefinition of its relationship with the EU. Thus, Spanish attitudes and governmental bargaining stances on such issues as EU reform and enlargement, the negotiation of structural funds after 1989, or changes in foreign and security policy, must be understood in the context of post-Cold War changes which modified Spain's international position. Thus, the theoretical underpinning of this second approach highlights the limited choices available to national actors and the reactive nature of their policy choices.

However, all of the approaches discussed so far privilege one or other of the poles in the relationship between the EU and its member states. The 'logic of two-level games' (Putnam, 1988) represents an attempt to incorporate insights drawn from analyses which emphasize respectively the international environment and domestic political processes. Informed by rational choice theory, 'two-level games' stress the simultaneous influence of domestic and international factors on the bargaining strategies of national executives, whose calculations are therefore 'double-edged': domestic policies may be used to influence international outcomes, just as international moves may be used to achieve domestic ends. Yet, the most influential approach to providing a comprehensive account of the changing relationship between the EU and member states derives from the increasingly influential, if still somewhat amorphous, analytical framework referred to as 'neo-institutionalism'. In practice, neo-institutionalism encompasses a diverse range of variants (Hall and Taylor, 1996; Jupille and Caporaso, 1999: 431; Peters, 1998), including an 'historical' version which emphasizes 'path dependency' (Pierson, 1996, 2000; Bulmer, 1994), a 'political' version which emphasizes networking arrangements between key actors, and a 'sociological' version which has strong overlaps with constructivism. What unites most of these approaches is a greater or lesser degree of opposition to the rational choice paradigm which has assumed such a dominant status in certain fields of social science, and which also informs intergovernmentalist accounts.

In spite of its diversity, neo-institutionalist theory offers some valuable pointers as to how we can bridge the twin focus on the elaboration of national policies on the one hand, and the impact of EU membership on the other. The approach adopted here sees the EU as a 'living institution' (Laffan, 1999), in which the 'logic of appropriateness' (March and Olsen, 1989: 21–38) leads actors to seek to match their actions to the requirements of given situations through rules and practices which act as a form of institutional constraint. These rules and practices are in turn embedded in structures of meaning and schemes of interpretation that both explain and legitimize practices (Olsen, 1997). In regard to the elaboration of national policies towards the EU, a neo-institutionalist approach allows for a more nuanced understanding of the role of exogenous preferences: for instance, we might predict that member states will follow a process of 'path-dependence' in their relationship with the EU, governed by a logic of increased returns. In simple terms, what this means is that early choices (such as deciding to join the EU) ensure that the range of future options (for instance, over forms of cooperation) progressively narrows. Furthermore, path-dependence will promote a continued commitment to the prevailing institutional framework, since cooperation within this framework will lead to increasing returns for each member state.

Neo-institutionalism also provides insights into the impact of EU membership on member states – most notably through the notion of 'Europeanization'. Although, in common with many concepts in the study of politics, there is disagreement over the precise meaning of Europeanization (Börzel and Risse, 2000; Olsen, 2001), it can be broadly seen as a label which covers attempts to analyse how membership of the EU leads to change and/or transformation in national polities. Accordingly, in this book we use the term 'Europeanization' to refer to those changes in the Spanish national and sub-national political systems brought about specifically by processes of European integration through the EU. Although precise quantification of such changes is not possible, studies of Europeanization seek to assess and evaluate the impact of the EU in three specific aspects of national political systems: politics, polity and policy. The weight of research findings suggests that the impact is greatest in the area of policy formulation and implementation, followed by a lesser impact on the structure of national polities, with the smallest impact being seen in the organization of domestic politics.

The structure of this book is designed to offer a wide-ranging overview of the relationship between Spain and the EU, whilst also devoting specific attention to how that relationship has led to changes in the politics, polity and policies of the contemporary Spanish democratic system. Chapter 1 provides a contextual account of the historic links between Spain and Europe, taking as its starting point the traumatic loss in 1898 of the last remnants of Spanish empire at the hands the United States of America, but focusing primarily on the route to eventual membership of the European Community. In Chapter 2, we review the 'input' side of the political process, looking at the role of public opinion, political parties and pressure groups. The next two chapters focus more directly on the political system, both at national level (Chapter 3) and in Spain's 17 regional Autonomous

Communities (Chapter 4). Chapter 5 discusses the influence of Spain and Spanish-designed policies on developments within the EU itself. Finally, in the last four chapters, we provide evidence of how Europeanization has had an impact on core national policies, by looking at agriculture and fisheries (Chapter 6), the single market and economic and monetary union (Chapter 7), budgets and structural funds (Chapter 8), and foreign policy and home affairs (Chapter 9). In these four chapters we also show how the EU can operate as a useful arena for adopting national concerns, either to diffuse them or else to provide additional support for domestic policy initiatives through the paradoxical mechanism of developing EU-level policy.

Finally, we conclude by arguing Spain's relationship with the European Union offers something of a paradox. Whilst the country has become deeply Europeanized in its policies, politics and even its polity – moving gradually from being simply a 'nation state' to becoming a 'member state' – this process has at the same time allowed for the recuperation of a genuinely national project. That project, the realization of Spain's historic destiny in the heartland of Europe, had been effectively put on hold by the country's traumatic history throughout much of the twentieth century. At the start of the twenty-first century, Spain is looking to develop and consolidate a role as one of the major players in an expanded European Union.

Chapter 1

Spain and Europe: Historical Overview

Spain's relationship with Europe over the last century can best be described as one of aloofness, although the country's entire history has been conditioned by links with its European neighbours. Indeed, some analysts have described the relationship between Spain and Europe as an ongoing dialectic between centre and periphery, punctuated by critical moments during which Spain stood apart from major European trends (Abellán, 1988; Ramírez, 1996). However, it remains open to dispute whether Spain's historical evolution should be seen as exceptional in the context of wider European developments, or whether it simply represents one variant of the complex pattern which characterizes the emergence of all modern European nation-states.

The year 1898 represented a decisive moment in Spain's perception of difference from its European neighbours (Balfour, 1997). Although Spain's central role in shaping European history during the sixteenth century had long since disappeared, it was not until 1898 that Spain faced an acute crisis of identity over its international orientation. In that year, Spain lost the last remains of its colonial empire to the United States of America, a devastating blow which severely undermined the pseudo-democratic political system of the Restoration Monarchy (established in 1875). Powell (1995: 12–13) argues that in fact this was not a uniquely Spanish experience, since it formed part of the transition from a European state system towards a new global system symbolized by the defeat of two peripheral powers (Spain and Russia) at the hands of two emerging non-European powers (USA and Japan).

The military and political defeat, though, had the effect of throwing the country into a paroxysm of self-doubt, which in turn gave rise to the so-called 'Generation of 98', a group of intellectuals who scrutinized the defects of Spain's cultural, economic and political organization and sought to prescribe remedies. Two opposed views emerged, which were to permeate Spanish attitudes towards Europe throughout much of the twentieth century. On the one hand, thinkers such as Miguel de Unamuno promoted introspection into Spain's supposed idiosyncrasy and distinctive values, which he argued should be defended against imported notions. For others, however, Spain itself was the 'problem' and Europe the solution: in order to overcome its growing marginalization, Spain needed to incorporate European values. The most prominent of these thinkers, Joaquín Costa, coined the term 'Europeanization' precisely in this sense of incorporating liberal, democratic and progressive values instead of falling back on Spanish tradition. What both trends had in common is that they clearly believed Spain was different from the rest of Europe. Thereafter, Spain's non-belligerence in both the First and the Second World Wars further emphasized the perception of both difference and aloofness – reflected in its non-involvement in postwar European reconstruction. Spain's relationship with Europe thus has to be understood in the context of its isolation from the early institutional development of the community of European states.

The Franco dictatorship and Europe

Following the defeat of the Axis powers in 1945, Spain – whose dictator, General Francisco Franco had received significant material support from both Hitler and Mussolini – became a pariah state in a continent won back for democracy. The Franco dictatorship underlined the idea of Spanish exceptionalism and also led to the country's absence from such major initiatives as the Marshall Plan, the 1951 Treaty of Paris which established the European Coal and Steel Community (ECSC), or the creation in 1952 of the European Defence Community. Instead, European states sent clear signals of support to Spain's exiled democratic leaders. Thus, the organizers of the so-called Congress of Europe in The Hague (1948) invited prominent Spanish republicans such as Salvador de Madariaga, an intellectual linked to the European Movement, but blocked an invitation to Spain's Francoist government. Moreover, the Assembly of the Council of Europe, set up after the Congress of Europe, adopted a resolution calling for democratic elections in Spain and the establishment of a democratic regime.

The Franco regime faced a situation in which European organizations served as constant reminders of its lack of democracy, and in response it adopted a distinctly suspicious attitude towards them. The regime reacted with hostility to the creation of the ECSC and then the European Economic Community (EEC) at the end of the 1950s. Franco criticized any attempt to establish unions based on economic logic and appealed instead to what he identified as 'essential' European values, such as Christianity and anti-communism, in which Spain participated fully (Moreno, 1998: 26–7). The dictator believed that two further factors which should also be taken into account were respect for the state's autonomy and sovereignty, and friendship with Latin American countries (Franco, 1975: 1287). European rejection, together with international pressures, helped crystallize the regime's predominant ideological characteristics between 1939 and the mid-1960s: a pronounced nationalism, scorn for European democracies (and for democracy itself) and a rhetorical appeal to pan-Hispanism, but with a distinctly imperial flavour (Ramírez, 1996: 29–53).

Ideological and political preferences, however, did not override economic imperatives. During the 1940s, the combination of enforced international isolation (which affected the trade in raw materials and food) and Franco's own economic doctrine resulted in a policy of autarky, based on economic protectionism via high tariffs, restrictions on imports and state intervention in developing industrial structures (Richards, 1998: 91–169). Autarky, though, resulted in an absolute failure to stimulate economic development and instead led to the further impoverishment of the country. Just when the situation threatened to become wholly untenable, the USA provided vital breathing space for Franco's regime through the Defence Pacts, a bilateral agreement signed in 1953 (Liedtke, 1998). The USA's interest lay in exploiting the geo-strategic advantages provided by Spain in the context of the developing Cold War and, in spite of the distaste of its European allies, integrated Franco's regime under North America's protective political umbrella. Specifically, the 1953 agreement provided economic aid (1 billion US dollars over eight years) in exchange for establishing US bases on Spanish territory. More importantly, however, the agreement opened the gateway to Spain's international recognition: in 1955 Spain joined the United Nations and by 1959 it had also joined the International Monetary Fund (IMF), the World Bank and the Organisation for European Economic Co-operation (OEEC), originally formed to administer Marshall Aid and the precursor of the Organisation for Economic Co-operation and Development (OECD).

In line with this changed international standing, Spain's obsolete policy of economic autarky was also abandoned. By the end of the

1950s, so-called 'technocrats' associated with *Opus Dei* (a hierarchic and strict Catholic order) had assumed leading positions in the government and in 1959 they drafted a Stabilization Plan. The Plan, endorsed by the IMF, sought to liberalize and modernize the Spanish economy by opening its markets to international penetration. Although the change in economic policy did lead to long overdue modernization during the 1960s, it was unable to eliminate some important structural weaknesses. First, the process of industrialization was led by industries such as shipbuilding and steel, which were state-owned and heavily dependent on public capital. Secondly, and in parallel, agriculture saw its importance within the Spanish economy decline, leading to large-scale unemployment of land workers who could not be absorbed by the new industries. Given Spain's lack of an effective social policy, emigration was the only available option to most of these workers. Thus, the manpower surplus that would later surface as the structural problem of unemployment was initially directed towards other European countries (10 per cent of the active population by 1975). Thirdly, industrialization in the area of consumer-oriented goods was led by foreign investment and technology.

All these features reappeared in the 1970s serving as both the background to Spain's bid for accession, and also the main obstacles to it. However, even in the 1960s some form of relationship with the EEC had been seen as essential to accomplish the objectives of the Stabilization and later Development plans. As Powell (1995: 23) observes, Spain was paying a high price for its exclusion because of the increasingly important economic role played by foreign investment, tourism and emigration. Hence, the 1960s saw Spain turn towards 'economic Europeanism' (Ramírez, 1996: 50).

The government realized that remaining aloof from the integration process would deepen Spain's political isolation. Rather than full membership, however, the option sought in 1962, following the example of Turkey and Greece, was associate status (Oyarzun, 1961). The government wanted to negotiate an association agreement that could provide the basis for full integration after the structural adaptation of the Spanish economy. Spain's trade deficit with the EC was rapidly deteriorating since agricultural exports were limited because of the Common Agricultural Policy (CAP), whilst economic growth during the 1960s was stimulating a huge rise in imports from EC countries. The options were either to improve the terms of trade or freeze the policy of economic liberalization.

The Community in turn adopted a policy of 'conditionality' towards Spain. Indeed, EC authorities rejected the Spanish application outright because of the host of adverse reactions it provoked, all of them demanding democracy as a prerequisite for Spanish association. Immediately before Spain's application, the explicit link between democratization and accession to the EC had been established in the Birkelbach Report, approved by the European Parliament (EP) in January 1962. This report laid out the political conditions to be fulfilled by applicant countries. The existence of a democratic government was established as a precondition for membership and countries seeking to join the EC were required to recognize the principles for membership established by the Council of Europe: the rule of law, democracy and respect for human rights and liberties. Association was conceived as a future possibility for these countries which fulfilled the political conditions for membership, but which were not economically ready for full membership. When the EP debated the Spanish application, it made clear that Spain could not qualify because of its lack of democratic freedoms. Moreover, in the opinion of the EP, even purely economic agreements could have a counter-productive effect since they might assist the survival of the Franco regime.

Reactions to the Spanish application for associate status varied amongst European institutions and governments. The Council of Europe – effectively the watchdog of democratic values and human rights in the European Community – also examined the option of some form of economic association between Spain and the EC. Following the main conclusions of the report to the General Assembly of the Council (the MacMillan Report of 1962), the Council took a milder view than the EP: whilst closer political cooperation was ruled out, it argued that practical reasons such as promoting political stability or strengthening opposition democratic forces within Spain justified some lesser form of association. The Council of Europe thus proposed exploring the possibility of a long adaptation period for associate status, providing time for an eventual change in Spanish politics. By contrast, the strongest reaction – and one that mobilised both European and Spanish governments – came from the federalist European Movement. The presence of some Spanish democrats within the Movement probably contributed to its tougher attitude. In a meeting in Munich in June 1962, the IV Congress of the European Movement drafted a '*Note on Spain*' which stated: '. . .integration, either as association or membership, requires democratic institutions'. In the case of Spain, this meant the establishment of genuinely democratic and representative institutions based on popular consent, the guarantee of fundamental rights and freedoms, the recognition of trades unions, and the right to create political parties. The declaration caused outrage within the Spanish government, which dubbed the meeting a conspiracy (*contubernio*) and blamed the anti-Spanish stance on a Marxist, Masonic and atheistic conspiracy (Preston, 1993: 702–5).

But attitudes within the European Community were not uniform, with a division between those countries which regarded any concession as a further boost to dictatorship, and those which thought that some form of relationship with Spain would enhance the likelihood of political change. De Gaulle, in particular, fuelled the second trend. In his idea of a looser confederation of states from the Atlantic to the Urals, there was a place for a dictatorship such as Spain. On the other hand, French politicians were more prone to use the carrot rather than the stick with the Franco regime. Aware of these internal divergences, the Spanish government reiterated its petition for associate status in 1964, pointing out that its new instrument for economic policy, the Development Programme, had been drafted following basic criteria in the Treaty of Rome. Whilst Italy and the Benelux countries rejected any possibility of association, West Germany and France were slightly more positive (Alonso, 1985: 29). This time, the Council of Ministers offered an ambiguous response, agreeing to examine the economic problems posed for Spain by the development of the EC and to look for solutions. But the Spanish aim of association was not even mentioned, as opposed to a so-called Preferential Agreement on commercial trade. Developments within the Community (notably, the rejection of the British application for membership and the 'crisis of the empty chair' provoked by the French government) affected negotiations and the Agreement was ultimately signed only in 1970.

By the time the Preferential Agreement came into force, circumstances had changed so much that it was of very limited value to Spain. The EC's first enlargement in 1973 – described as the nightmare scenario for the agreement (Bassols, 1995: 79) – together with prospects for a free-trade agreement with EFTA countries, left Spain in a comparatively disadvantageous situation. The EC deemed that many industrial products had an 'exceptional' character and were therefore either excluded from the Agreement or covered by a limited reduction of 40 per cent, which hurt Spanish exports. Overall, the system of Generalized Preferences granted more favourable treatment to African, Caribbean and Pacific (ACP) countries and again placed

Spain at a comparative disadvantage. More importantly, Common Agricultural Policy (CAP) rules were applied with immediate effect to Spain's agricultural exports to the new member states (Denmark, Ireland and the United Kingdom), whilst agreements with Morocco, Tunis and Greece were more favourable to agricultural exports from these countries (Tamames, 1978: 125–7). As a result, relations between the EC and Spain soon entered an unstable phase, with the latter seeking to renegotiate the Agreement.

Once more, Spanish options were dependent on the country's political evolution, but there were ominous signs that the dictatorship was reverting to a more hard-line stance. During the first half of the 1970s, opposition within Spain grew, involving not just increased militancy by trades unions but also the use of terror by Basque separatists (Jáuregui and Vega, 1985). Three events in particular tested to the limit Community tolerance of the Franco regime's repressive response to such opposition. In 1970, a military court sentenced to death several members of the Basque separatist organization, Euzkadi Ta Askatasuna (ETA). The use of a military trial and the sentences handed down sparked protests throughout Europe. The European Commission warned of the possible consequences for Spain's relationship with the Community, and ultimately international pressure proved effective as the sentences were commuted to life imprisonment (Preston, 1986: 30–6). However, in 1973 similar strong reactions were provoked by a show trial (known as '*proceso 1001*') which resulted in the sentencing of 10 union leaders to a total of 162 years in prison for illegal association. The start of the trial coincided with the assassination by ETA of the prime minister, Admiral Luis Carrero Blanco, an act which in turn provoked still further repression by the Franco regime. In a series of trials which sparked international outrage and indignation, courts martial in Burgos, Barcelona and Madrid between August and September 1975 sentenced 11 people to death. In spite of the worldwide protests, which also represented the most serious confrontation between the European Community and the Spanish dictatorship (Bassols, 1995: 121), Franco personally confirmed five of the death sentences (Preston, 1993: 775–6).

Reactions were strong (and occasionally violent) throughout Europe. All EC member states except Ireland recalled their ambassadors. The European Parliament approved a resolution which called for a stop to negotiations with the Spanish government. The Commission in turn deplored the executions and also asked the Council to stop ongoing negotiations. However, the declaration adopted by EPC ministers was mildly worded, merely expressing reprobation and the wish that Spain should democratize. More specifically, the Council of Ministers declared that negotiations to revive the Preferential Agreement should not continue. Thus, whilst anticommunism may have worked to the benefit of former enemy states such as West Germany and Italy in helping them become integrated into Western institutions, in the Spanish case dictatorship in the 1970s proved a greater political stumbling block than neutralized anticommunism had been in the 1940s.

The Franco regime's relations with the European Community helped cultivate underlying trends in Spanish perceptions of Europe, and also established the emotional and cultural basis of democratic Spain's relationship with the EC. The reluctance of the EC to engage in forms of cooperation with a dictatorship and the Community's discourse on the link between accession and democratization, reflected its policy of promoting democracy. This stance in turn enormously increased the legitimacy of the new civilian power within Spain. Yet, in regard to Franco, the EC had manifested the innate contradiction which characterized its dealings with third parties: its rhetoric on human rights and democratization was repeatedly undermined by the political and economic interests of its member states, thereby providing the Franco regime some (albeit limited) room for manoeuvre.

The Spanish transition to democracy and EC membership

General Franco's death in November 1975 opened up the prospect of re-democratization in Spain. In a remarkably short space of time, the transition brought about the establishment of internationally recognized democratic institutions and standards. In 1976, the Francoist parliament, the *Cortes*, passed the Law on Political Reform which initiated the formal dissolution of the dictatorship, and in June 1977 the first democratic elections were held. Spain immediately pushed for further international acceptance through membership of European organizations: in July 1977, the new Spanish government applied for EC membership, followed in October by an application to join the Council of Europe, of which Spain became the twentieth member in 1979. In the meantime, the new Spanish democratic constitution was approved in 1978. Apart from the link between democratization and membership, there was an additional reason for the speed of the Spanish application. The Spanish government was fully aware that a delay in lodging the application could provide grounds for the Community to concentrate on the Greek and Portuguese bids for membership and to postpone consideration of Spain's case until these were resolved (Bassols, 1995).

A host of political, social and economic reasons supported the logic of seeking membership of the EC. Occasional mention was also made of more minor factors, such as concern for the almost one million Spanish emigrants in EC countries (Bassols, 1995: 169). But it was economic arguments that carried most weight, reflecting a twin dynamic: first, Spain's economy required further modernization and liberalization; second, the economy was highly dependent on EC markets (Payno, 1984: 144). In regard to the first of these dynamics, the Spanish economy had grown significantly between 1960 and 1975, but the engines of this growth (migrant remittances, tourism income, foreign investment and technological imports) were all but exhausted by 1975. They had also been badly affected by the 1973 oil crisis. Moreover, the basis of Spain's industrialization model (protectionism, tariff barriers, state intervention) had become rigidities that limited further economic development. Members of the political and economic elite saw EC membership as an instrument for the elimination of old economic habits that stood in the way of economic rationalization. In addition, it would expose the historically protected Spanish economy to much-needed open market discipline.

However, it was Spain's asymmetric economic relationship with the European Community which was the decisive factor for seeking membership. In spite of its economic development since the early 1960s, Spain remained a peripheral economy within Europe. This was particularly evident in commercial terms. In 1977, 48 per cent of Spanish exports went to the EC (57 per cent in agriculture, including 80 per cent of fruits and vegetables), compared with 30 per cent of Spain's imports and 41 per cent of foreign investment (Bassols, 1995: 169). These exports were, of course, affected by Community rules. Significantly, the two leading European states in the accession negotiations, France and West Germany, were also Spain's main trading partners. By 1984, they accounted for 54.3 per cent of Spanish imports (25.7 per cent from France and 29.6 per cent from West Germany) and 50.1 per cent of exports (30.6 per cent to France and 19.5 per cent to West Germany). Financial trade followed a similar trend, with EC countries providing 51 per cent of foreign investment in 1983, of which half came from France and West Germany (Payno, 1984). It was easy to draw the conclusion that isolation from the EC would severely limit the prospects for developing Spain's economy. In instrumental terms, the cost of not being a member of the EC was (and remains) so high for the Spanish economy that it outweighed any potential losses deriving from membership (Fuentes Quintana, 1995: 64).

As would occur later on with EFTA and the East European enlargements, the EC had offered alternatives to full membership. The already mentioned Preferential Agreement fulfilled this purpose, even though it was of less value. Although some diplomats argued that the agreement was favourable to Spain (Bassols, 1995: 148, 157), economists were able to demonstrate that the balance sheet was not so positive. Benefits in the industrial sector were outweighed four or five times over by the costs, whilst the figure in agriculture was around 75 per cent (Tamames, 1978: 125–7). And the trend was likely to have continued, since the EC's strategy in revising the agreement was to phase out industrial tariffs in exchange for access to agricultural markets. Against this background, it was clear that any option – a generalized preference agreement, association or full membership – was better than maintaining the status quo. In addition, Community structural funds acted as a further powerful incentive. Thus, one lesson from the process of Spanish accession is that the Community failed to offer stable economic regimes as an alternative to full membership. Once the process of informal integration is underway, countries seek to assert control over the process through developing formal integration.

The importance of economic issues, however, should not overshadow the essentially political motivations for accession. Indeed, membership was primarily a political option: integration into the EC generated a complex system of (symbolic and material) incentives and guarantees that favoured democratization. EC rejection of the Franco regime transformed Europe into a symbol of democracy and, in parallel, contributed to the legitimization of democracy among the Spanish elite and public opinion. The aspiration to identify with Europe and the EC became a central element of the political culture and discourse of democratization. Ultimately, it became one of the elements of political consensus upon which the Spanish transition was built, as demonstrated by the fact that the Spanish application was unanimously supported by all political parties represented in the Spanish parliament. Membership was viewed as an anchor for democracy, a means to end Spain's isolation of the previous two centuries, and a framework for the restoration of human rights and political liberties (Bassols, 1995; Closa, 1995a; Morata, 1998; Ortega, 1994; Barbé, 1999). In the words of the socialist minister who negotiated the final stage of the process, accession had a meta-political value (Morán, 1980: 289).

Membership also served a useful purpose for other political actors. Thus, some remaining Francoists and economic elites – alarmed by developments in neighbouring Portugal – saw the EC as a guarantee of private property, capitalism and as a bulwark against socialism. The prospect of EC membership thus contributed to their embracing of democracy (Pridham, 1991). Several other more specific reasons could be added. For instance, European integration could cushion the impact of the regional issue and related demands for independence; it was also a central element in justifying economic and social modernization; and it provided a framework for defining Spain's international position (Moreno, 1998: 79). The primacy of political considerations may go a long way towards explaining acceptance of the tough accession conditions, and indeed led subsequently to the widespread view that it actually weakened Spain's negotiating position.

The European Community itself, as well as its member states, endorsed the democratizing role of membership and saw it as a means to boost stability in the area (Tsoukalis, 1981: 145). In its communiqué on the planned enlargement, the Commission argued that the three new applicants (Greece, Portugal and Spain) had entrusted to the EC a political responsibility that it could not avoid without denying its very foundational principles. Enlargement would also reflect the wishes of the three new democracies to consolidate and defend themselves against the return of dictatorship. In the words of the Commission President, Roy Jenkins, a straight refusal would be a severe blow to the fragile democratic regimes that had emerged with the open encouragement of the Community (Commission, 1977: 67–8). The European Parliament (EP) and the Economic and Social Council (ESC) voiced similar concerns.

Thus, although Community negotiations were guided by the need to defend the interests of its member states, the association between membership and democratic consolidation was always in the background. On 23 February 1981, the incipient Spanish democracy faced its greatest challenge to date when Lieutenant Colonel Antonio Tejero launched an attempted coup (Agüero, 1995: 161–80). The Community response was to condemn the coup, and its institutions reaffirmed their desire to see a democratic Spain become a member state. The EP in particular issued a reminder that respect for human rights and a democratic form of government were essential elements for EC membership. But the EP also underlined the EC's own responsibility in maintaining and reinforcing Spanish democracy and, consequently, called for an acceleration in accession negotiations that had stalled owing to the French government's lack of flexibility on the agricultural issue. Indeed, most of the EC member states felt a new sense of urgency to complete the negotiations – although this did not in practice make the process any easier or even quicker.

The importance of the EC has led some to conclude that European integration was the principal catalyst to democratization in Spain, since it provided standards and safeguards which both secured and provided impetus to the evolution of domestic developments. Similar observations have been made in regard to Eastern Europe (Agh, 1993: 233). Clearly, the EC did act as a facilitator of democratic establishment, as it also did in the cases of Greece and Portugal. In a country used to national projects being framed in the rhetoric of dictatorship, the European ideal – embracing the rule of law, participatory democracy, a market economy, constitutional order and so forth – offered an alternative overarching political project. But such ideals, as well as the goal of accession, worked more in symbolic or aspirational terms than as material facilitators of democratization. There is widespread agreement on the generally indirect and marginal role of external actors in transition processes (Schmitter, 1993), although this is an issue which is receiving more attention in the light of post–communist transitions and it may well be that the pressure of rules and structures designed abroad shaped the domestic calculus and pay-off matrices (Whitehead, 1991; 1996: 261; Crespo MacLennan, 2000: 1, 181).

The EC, through its control of symbolic and rhetorical resources, provided a complex system of incentives and guarantees (Powell, 1993: 49). Explicit reinforcement of democratization took the form of statements praising reforms and warnings over backtracking, whereas implicit reinforcement came through the carrot of accession. As has been argued elsewhere, EC rhetoric on incorporating new members takes a back seat to the concrete national interests of member states when decisions need to be taken (Closa, 1995). And these interests may run counter to those of applicant states. This is what occurred in the Spanish case, but the key difference to the forthcoming Eastern enlargement was the geo-strategic environment, which was highly important in the conclusion of negotiations.

During the 1970s and 1980s, whilst the Cold War was still at its peak, Spain did not belong to any western security organizations. Moreover, during a brief period at the beginning of the transition, the Spanish government flirted with a non-aligned position. Although consensus on EC membership spread across the political spectrum, NATO membership provoked widespread opposition among leftist parties. For the left, NATO was inseparable from the USA. Unlike other European countries, Spain had not been liberated from fascism by US troops, nor had it enjoyed the benefits of the Marshall Plan. More important, though, was that Franco had received support from USA, which had signed a security agreement with him in 1953 and also endorsed Spain's application for UN membership. This stance reinforced traditional anti-Americanism, which originally stemmed from the military defeat of 1898. Furthermore, sympathy with Latin American anti-imperialist ideology further provoked anti-US feeling on the left. Since NATO was generally perceived in Spanish public opinion as a result of the Second World War and as one of the causes of the Cold War, the identification between NATO and war was widespread. Strategic perceptions strengthened such a view, given Spain's physical distance from the Soviet Union, NATO's main adversary. Instead, Spanish threat perceptions were focused on the Mediterranean rim to its south, a secondary region in NATO planning (Viñas, 1999; Núñez Villaverde, 2001).

Against this background, the cleavage between Spanish parties on the NATO issue became an unanticipated long-term negotiation instrument. Some Spanish politicians and the conservative UCD government thought that NATO membership could serve as leverage with EC governments. They were fully aware that some member states – particularly West Germany and the United Kingdom – might not be receptive to the idea of a new unaligned entrant to the EC. In this way, EC membership became intimately linked to incorporation into Western security organizations in the view both of Spain and existing member states (Heywood, 1995: 264–72). Spain joined NATO in 1981, at a point when accession negotiations were stalled by the French, partly to show Spanish commitment to the defence of Western institutions.

The decision to join NATO undermined the political consensus on foreign policy which had characterized the transition. The Socialist Party (PSOE) strongly opposed NATO membership and promised that if it won the next elections, a referendum on the issue would be held, with the expectation that Spain would withdraw. But following the PSOE's crushing victory in the October 1982 general election, the new government was quickly made to understand that West German support for EC entry was contingent upon Spain's continued membership of NATO. This factor is crucial in explaining the PSOE leadership's change of attitude on the NATO issue. Prime Minister Felipe González in particular developed a policy of proximity towards the West German government, exemplified by his endorsement of the latter's deployment of Euro-missiles. González's changed stance took place after one of his first bilateral meetings with the West German Chancellor, Helmut Kohl, and although little is known about the precise details of their conversations, it is highly likely that the issue of NATO membership was a central topic.

The referendum card was very useful for the PSOE government, which argued that Spanish public opinion would accept NATO membership only if it was presented as a prerequisite for EC membership and, more important, only when membership was confirmed. These arguments influenced EC member states. When EC foreign ministers met in Dublin in 1984, shortly before the PSOE Congress that was due to discuss the referendum on Spain's NATO membership, they agreed that the future of accession negotiations would be decisive for the PSOE's attitude on the referendum. It was after this meeting that commitment to Spain's membership became unequivocal (Pollack, 1987: 140). The PSOE government eventually scheduled the NATO referendum for March 1986, only after Spain had formally become member of the EC on 1 January that year. The González government's pro-NATO campaign sought to conflate three issues in order to appeal to a wide range of voters: Europeanism in the security arena; mild anti-Americanism; and the defence of national interests in regard to the terms of NATO membership, including non-integration into the military structure (Barbé, 1999: 33). In some senses, the Spanish position on NATO closely paralleled that of France and this may help explain Spain's subsequent approach towards the EU's common foreign and security policy (see Chapter 9).

Becoming a member

Accession negotiations started in 1978 and lasted until March 1985, when agreement was finally reached on all the chapters. Spain became a full member state of the European Community on 1 January 1986, the same date on which the Single European Act (SEA) came into force. Negotiations had been protracted and difficult, with setbacks and delays against a background of economic crisis and, in the early stages, Community stagnation. The negotiating parties had very different needs and expectations, which were also asymmetrical. Any perceived gains were smaller for current members than for Spain, which was thus placed in the situation of supplicant. It quickly became evident to the Spanish negotiators that the need to support 'democratic transition', a vital factor in kick-starting the negotiations, would not serve to smooth accession negotiations (Barbé, 1999: 22; Elorza, 1997). The political importance attached to membership by virtually all sectors of Spanish society further weakened the country's bargaining position. In contrast to earlier negotiations with the United Kingdom and Denmark, or subsequent ones with Austria and Sweden, for instance, Spain revealed from the outset its wholehearted acceptance of the EC's political aims.

Obstacles did not derive from the conception of European integration or its potential impact on Spain. Rather, substantive problems focused on concrete sectors and policies: agriculture, industrial goods, fishing, free movement of workers and financial and budgetary matters. Whilst the last of these issues was essentially a matter of concern for governments and EC institutions, in the others there were domestic constellations of interests both within Spain and the member states. Industrial and agricultural issues dominated the negotiations. Indeed, the substance of Spain's accession has been described as granting EC industrial goods access to Spanish markets in exchange for Spanish agricultural products gaining access to Community markets (Story and Grugel, 1991: 25). Importantly, Spanish agricultural products did not have a meaningful alternative to EC markets and thus, in this equation, it was clear that likely losers would be Spanish industrialists, who unsurprisingly reacted to the perceived threat.

In 1980, the employers' association, the Confederación Española de Organizaciones Empresariales (CEOE), published a document on Spanish accession that took a critical stance on this sensitive issue. The CEOE argued that Spain's half-closed economy had reached the limit of its development, and that an opening up through membership of the EC was essential. The question for the CEOE, therefore, centred on the conditions for adaptation. Given that its main concern was with the process of industrial liberalization, the CEOE called for the same transitional period to be applied to both industrial and agricultural goods, thereby hoping to create a trade-off between the two sectors. The employers feared that the elimination of industrial tariffs would mean facing devastating competition in industrial goods from more modern and efficient European firms. In this respect, the Greek precedent suggested that the longest possible transitional period (seven years) should be sought (Elorza, 1997: 15). Moreover, the CEOE argued that value added tax (VAT) should be applied only after the transitional period, whereas the Commission wanted the tax to be introduced from the outset of membership. The CEOE kept a close watch on negotiations during the following years, putting pressure on Spanish negotiators, as did trade unions, farmers and fishing sector associations (Jones, 2000). The common fear was that Spanish politicians were so eager for membership that they would pay too high a price for accession. This continuing tension between government and employers has been referred to as the Spanish–Spanish negotiations (Bassols, 1995) and, in a classic example of a two-level game (Putnam, 1988), actually reinforced the bargaining position of Spanish representatives in the EC.

Regardless of Spain's domestic interests, it was the Community's internal problems which determined the pace and rhythm of negotiations. The behaviour of EC member states mirrored that of members of a select club who, when faced with newcomers, seek to protect their position by transferring any cost onto the new members. To do so, they have recourse to two mechanisms: first, members may force the applicant to bear the costs; or, secondly, they may change the internal rules to their own advantage. In the Spanish case, member states prioritized reducing costs and protecting their own interests. At the same time, the SEA saw a rule change, but even this was not directly caused by the Iberian accessions.

Spain's accession presented a real challenge for existing EC members, on account not just of the size, but also the lack of complementarity between its economy and their own. The problems of accommodating a large economy with major structural problems came to the fore once rhetorical declarations on reinforcing stability and democracy had exhausted their negotiation value. In contrast to Greece's entry, the European Commission's statements on Spain emphasized openly the adjustment problems for both sides. In particular, the following areas were underlined: agriculture, where transitional periods for pricing and free circulation of products would be required; industry, where the elimination of tariffs was necessary; fiscal and financial assistance; industrial restructuring measures; and social and regional issues. The Commission warned of the likely effects deriving from a more competitive environment and the process of industrial restructuring, and as early as April 1978 had indicated that Spain should participate in EC industrial restructuring policies (Story, 1995: 36). The two pillars of negotiation and the basis for Spanish membership would be full acceptance of the *acquis* and the introduction of long transitional periods with different durations between sectors.

The various positions could be summarized schematically under four headings: relative losses, relative gains, log-rolling, and political and strategic interests.

- *Relative losses.* These derive from the negative economic impact of accession on particular sectors and/or countries. Costs for existing members were mainly in primary sectors, especially agriculture. Italian and French producers, for instance, feared competition in their European markets from Spanish products. However, their respective responses differed. In Italy, all parties agreed on the desirability of accession despite the economic costs for Italian agriculture. In France, by contrast, enlargement became a major issue in the 1978 parliamentary elections, with both the Gaullist Jacques Chirac (RPR) and the Communist Georges Marchais (PCF) strongly opposing the accession of any of the three Mediterranean applicants, but most especially Spain. The French government did not want to see the country's share of CAP income reduced. But it is also true that the French position was influenced by vocal and assertive lobbying by farmers, who were seen to have a significant influence on the rural vote. Ultimately, France's attitude paralysed negotiations for almost two years. Some have suggested that François Mitterrand adopted a more obstructive attitude towards the right-of-centre government of Adolfo Suárez, in anticipation of imminent political change in Spain (Bassols, 1995: 273–5). However, there is little evidence to support this view, which also runs counter to the conventional wisdom on EC politics as non-partisan.

  Accession costs also had an important impact on the budgetary equilibrium among member states. The West German government was fully aware of the economic costs of enlargement deriving particularly from the incorporation of Mediterranean products into the CAP – and, more important, its likely role in footing the bill. But, unlike in France, Spain's accession never became a contentious issue in West German domestic politics.

- *Relative gains.* These derive from the positive economic impact of accession, but are less evident because private actors are the main beneficiaries. More significantly, these actors are less visible in expressing their particular interests, which can often be incorporated within a more general discourse in favour of accession. Spanish markets were very tempting for West German industrial products and West Germany also had large investment interests in Spain. Membership was thus seen as a guarantee for the future. A similar case applies to France and the UK. Story (1995: 36) argues that France sought a deal whereby Spain would open up its military, nuclear and electronic markets to France, the implication being that agreement could then be reached on agriculture. In the case of the UK, the British government had sought even before Spanish accession an increased quota for car imports into the Spanish market, which resulted in 1984 in an agreement between Spain and the EC. Finally, net food importers, such as UK and West Germany, were interested in offering cheaper supplies to domestic markets.

- *Log-rolling.* Accession should not be seen just as a bilateral settlement of issues raised by the applicant state. Rather, it also offers a convenient excuse for existing member states to link various outstanding issues within a global solution. Thus, accession became linked to certain member states finding solutions to problems which derived from the EC's existing internal agenda. And the solutions implied not only short-term pay-offs, but also some changes to the rules that made up the *acquis communautaire*. During the Spanish accession negotiations, member states faced two other major issues: the reform of the CAP and the structure of the Community budget, both of which stood to be profoundly affected by Spain's entry. In 1980, the French President, Valéry Giscard d'Estaing, warned that Spanish accession should not be discussed before resolution of the EC's budgetary structure and clarification of the place of agriculture. In regard to agriculture, the 'precondition' (*préalable*) set out by Giscard in 1977 had stated that France would ask for a reform of the EC's 1972 regulations concerning French and Italian fruit, vegetable and wine growers: the implication was that these matters had to be settled before negotiations on entry could proceed (Story; 1995: 35). Fears by French and Italian agricultural producers derived as much from Spanish competition as from the market organization of most Mediterranean products. As a prerequisite for unlocking the stalemate in negotiations, the French government pressed for a prior reform in the regulations on fruits and vegetables, as well as wine, which were to be protected from future Spanish competition.

The second issue that provided an opportunity for log-rolling was the budgetary dispute with the UK. The British government had long pressed for a revision of its budgetary contribution, but it was not until 1984 that member states were able to reach a settlement. Further log-rolling efforts concerned the UK's insistence on Spain lifting the Gibraltar blockade which had been imposed in 1969, leading to the border being reopened in 1984. That same year, at the Dublin summit, the Greek socialist Prime Minister, Andreas Papandreou, threatened to veto Spanish and Portuguese entry unless adequate funds were allocated to Greece under the Integrated Mediterranean Programmes (IMP).

- *Political and strategic interests.* These refer to existing member states' vested political interests in promoting the membership of a new state. In a context where the accession of a new state points to relative losses outweighing gains, and where the demands of log-rollers require extensive additional commitments, the key factor in determining whether to proceed with accession is the attitude of political sponsors. In the Spanish case, France and West Germany provided the strongest support. French advocacy of Spanish membership originally derived from de Gaulle, who saw Spain's accession as a means to shift the EC's centre of gravity southwards and thereby convert France into the political axis of the Community (Tsoukalis, 1981: 147). But France also faced a dilemma between long-term political goals and short-term economic costs deriving from Spanish accession. In response, the French adopted the tactic of attempting to delay economic costs whilst gaining some concessions through log-rolling. Domestic politics played an important role. Given the opposition of the Gaullist RPR and the PCF, the attitude of the Socialists was critical. After their initially cool stance in the 1970s, it was only after Mitterrand was elected president in 1981 that the picture began to change in favour of Spanish interests.

West Germany, on the other hand, provided the most consistent support for Spanish entry. The Spanish application came at a time when West German governments were playing a more active role and French governments were moving away from Gaullist policies (Tsoukalis, 1981: 145). Germany wanted a peaceful and stable security environment across the continent, which entailed avoiding any revolutionary temptation in the southern periphery. That in turn implied using the web of western organizations to bind in the new democracies. As already indicated, the West German government was keen to link Spanish entry to the EC to full NATO membership. Like the United Kingdom, it saw enlargement as an instrument for political stability and the strengthening of NATO.

In this context, enlargement depended also upon West German willingness to settle the budgetary issue. Once the West German government obtained full assurance about Spain's engagement in western defence, it became an overt supporter of Spanish accession. At the 1983 Stuttgart summit, the West German presidency unblocked the impasse by securing a commitment to a new budgetary increase that would serve both to finance enlargement as well as other outstanding financial problems. The source of financing would be an increase of the 1 per cent ceiling on national VAT contributions which would be mainly shouldered by West Germany itself. But the West German government also changed the chronology of enlargement: it would no longer be conditional upon internal budgetary reform, but instead the reverse would hold. The reform would come into force only after Spanish and Portuguese accession.

Accession thus entailed finding a resolution to the equation whereby political and strategic interests plus the relative gains deriving from accession could successfully construct a compensation package for relative losers and log-rollers. Ultimately, accession depended on the resolution of two main issues and the basic agreement of two major countries (Alonso, 1985: 167). First, the outstanding budgetary question depended upon West German willingness to foot the bill for accession. Second, the agriculture question depended on French acceptance of any deal reached. Awareness of this double dependency conditioned an essential element of Spain's European policy: alignment with the French and West German positions on the development of the EC.

The impact of a new member on the European Community

One of the underlying themes of this volume is an assessment of the impact of Spain's membership on the European Community/Union, so this section simply seeks to provide a broad-brush overview. The accession of Spain (and Portugal) substantially changed the EC's economic and social structure: the total population within the Community increased by 18 per cent whilst GDP grew by just 8 per cent; unemployment, meanwhile, rose 36 per cent in agriculture and 14 per cent in industry. Population in poorer regions was doubled to reach 20 per cent of the total. Community worries deriving from Spanish accession fell into three broad categories (Bassols, 1995: 168).

- *Policy-related.* Without question, Spanish accession had a profound impact on French and Italian agriculture. Competition from Spanish products continues to provoke strong responses from French farmers and the full accommodation of Spanish agriculture within the CAP has yet to be achieved. In addition, other southern Mediterranean countries have seen their farming exports to the EC damaged by Spanish membership. In this sense, fears of EC protectionism *vis-à-vis* third countries have proved well-founded, but this does not reflect a specifically Spanish attitude. Rather, it exemplifies how a new member state will seek to use existing Community instruments for its own benefit. However, fears of a possible dilution of the commitment to free-trade as a result of government intervention or huge inflows of Spanish migrant workers have proved unfounded.

  The accession of a new member state also provides an opportunity for log-rolling either through changes to existing policies or the development of new ones. In the case of Spain, in addition to changes to the CAP, membership served as the catalyst for the development of the Common Fisheries Policy (CFP). In fact, negotiations with Spain on this issue were delayed until the EC had completed the design of its new policy in 1983, precisely on account of the perceived threat from the Spanish fishing fleet. Transitional periods were used to accommodate the policy anxieties of both Spain and the EC member states. As shown in Figure 1.1, the periods in question ran between 6 and 17 years, although by 1996 they had all been effectively completed.

- *Financial.* In any enlargement, a main concern of existing members is to maintain or improve their own budgetary position. There was a clear perception that Spain (and Portugal) would become, under existing Community policies, net recipients of funds. Moreover, once they had joined, the new entrants were able to seek a revision of policies and resource allocation under the integration process to lessen inequalities between centre and periphery (Featherstone, 1989: 199). The Delors I package can be seen as a result of this trend, as was also the Edinburgh settlement of the Delors II package.

Figure 1.1   *Transitory periods for Spain's full accession to the EU*

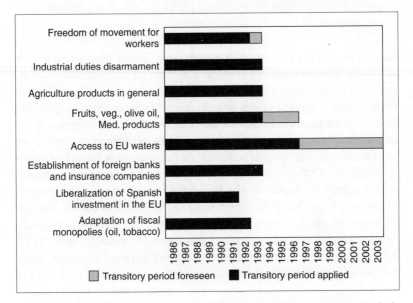

Source: Data from Secretaría General del Portavoz del Gobierno, Ministerio de la Presidencia España en la Unión Europea. *Diez años de la firma del Tratado de Adhesión* (Madrid, 1995).

Indeed, Spain has been a leading actor in developing the Community's constitutional principles for redistribution, for instance in regard to economic and social cohesion (see Chapter 8).

• *Institutional and political.* Fears focused explicitly on how an institutional setting designed for six member states would operate with double that number. This fear fed into a broader stimulus to intensify the integration process launched with the SEA. In particular, concern over the practical operation of the EC led to the more widespread use of qualified majority voting (QMV). When Spain joined in 1986, it was offered either 10 Council votes and 1 Commissioner, or 8 votes and 2 Commissioners. Spanish negotiators chose the second option. In general terms, the Spanish government felt quite satisfied with the degree of institutional representation achieved. Moreover, Spain has sought to avoid appealing to the Luxembourg compromise as the foundational basis for its Community membership. This does not mean that Spanish governments have not been ready to use their veto power, but threatened vetoes have been used to defend specific national interests rather than to resist the political aim of integration (ever closer union).

Indeed, during the first years of membership, Spain adopted an openly pro-integrationist attitude, as evidenced through such initiatives as the statute of European citizenship. In addition, Spain placed on the Community's agenda some new areas of concern in which it had vested interests, such as the Mediterranean and Latin America. Such initiatives, alongside perceptions of membership as being an emotional reaction and/or solution to the country's historical problems (Barbé, 1999: 20), in fact masked a tougher negotiating attitude which sought to maximize the benefits of membership. In the words of one top Spanish official, Spain used any available occasion after the signature of the accession act in 1985 to improve its accession conditions without ever asking for a formal renegotiation (Elorza, 1997: 15). It was widely felt that the price of membership was high: Spain had very long transitional periods in the most competitive sectors (10 years in agriculture and 15 in fisheries). Also, it shared the burden of the Community's internal settlements and pay-offs deriving from enlargement. Thus, Spain contributed to the British cheque agreed at Fontainebleau and also the Integrated Mediterranean Programmes (IMP) (Elorza, 1997: 16). Moreover, Spain had to accept the free trade agreements with EFTA countries as part of the *acquis*. In the opinion of Felipe González, these implied an unbalanced economic penetration since they dealt with industrial products and excluded liberalization in agriculture and food sectors (González, 1988: 13). The fact that accession coincided with the SEA programme further deepened the challenge of economic liberalization.

Conventional wisdom has it that Spain's accession conditions were very tough and that renegotiation could be justified as an attempt to redress that situation. Spain did seek a reduction of the transitional periods in agriculture and fisheries, free movement of workers, and the elimination of the external tariff, as well as continually seeking budgetary returns. It also blocked negotiations for the creation of the European Economic Space (EES) in 1991. In short, Spain seemed to be attempting to renegotiate its accession terms using economic criteria (Barbé, 1999: 82). A strong commitment to Europeanism and the country's successful economic performance following membership allowed these demands to pass relatively unnoticed. Whilst the transition to democracy had taken place during a deep economic recession,

EC membership coincided with the start of an economic boom. The economic crisis of the early 1990s, however, and the radical change of political and strategic context following the collapse of communism, transformed Spain's position within the EC.

Globally, Spanish attitudes towards Europe assumed a more gradualist tenor, the result both of internal socio-economic difficulties deriving from convergence policies, and also changes in the international system which had placed Spain in the periphery of a Community looking north and east (Barbé, 1999: 34,42). Barbé (1999: 36) refers to a normalization of Spanish membership, characterized by the loss of naivety plus a reevaluation of specific national self-interest, but this conveys a misleading impression. Spain has always been prepared to defend its own self-interest, a stance which became more visible once pro-integrationist rhetoric started to lose its appeal in European discourse, and also once the priority of dealing with new Eastern democracies overshadowed the attractiveness of the most recent EC member.

At the beginning of the 1990s and during the negotiation of the Maastricht Treaty of the European Union (TEU), Spain was still able to capitalize on its positive attitude towards German reunification, which did not pose the same kind of psychological problems as for other member states. Indeed, Spain viewed the new situation as a unique opportunity to create a political Europe, a top Spanish priority, and as the best way to reduce the risk of being left on the periphery (Ortega, 1995: 180). Spain's enthusiasm for a united Germany and the economic generosity of German chancellor Helmut Kohl ultimately resulted in the cohesion funds approved at the TEU. But the TEU also opened a new stage in Spain's policy towards the European Union. Internally, the demands implied by a commitment to economic and monetary union (EMU) led to political divergence on European integration for the first time in contemporary Spain. Externally, Spain faced a new geopolitical challenge. There were particular fears about political and economic demands from Central and Eastern Europe (Ortega, 1995; Barbé, 1999), the most concrete of which was a reorientation of economic efforts towards the East at the expense of Southern Europe, the Mediterranean and Latin America. But there was also an implicit fear of a change in German priorities within Europe.

Spanish governments had to redefine their European policy. In regard to discourse, Spain moved from support for federalism towards a strong defence of the *acquis*. The minimalist idea of Europe as a market was rejected (Barbé, 1999: 52) and 'variable geometry' was also opposed for fear that it would lead to indirect marginalization. Spanish interests coincided with the emerging EU orthodoxy, particularly the emphasis on European identity and values that underpinned official discourse during the 1990s (Barbé, 1999: 31). Thus, the beginning of the EFTA enlargement negotiations was made conditional on ratification of the TEU and the approval of the Delors II package. Similarly, Eastern enlargement has been made conditional upon the maintenance of the *acquis*, to ensure that it should not imply costs for cohesion countries, or for agriculture. A second change concerns Spain's structural position. The reorientation of Community construction northwards and eastwards led Spain to defend priorities and geopolitical space within the European project in order to become the 'Leading Force in the South' (Barbé, 1999: 57). But it has also implied a stronger defence of its institutional presence and voting power. Above all, there has been a change in the traditional pattern of alliances. The Mediterranean group has recovered a sense of purpose and, impelled by domestic political changes, Spanish governments have sought a more pluralistic approach to alliances than their traditional support for the Franco–German axis.

Chapter 2

The Internal Sources of EU Policy: Public Opinion, Political Parties and Pressure Groups

The historical overview presented in Chapter 1 of Spain's relationship with the EU provides an account that stresses structural factors. Spain's long-term economic, political and cultural links all pointed logically towards membership. Moreover, these structural factors helped shape perceptions of the EU within Spain which were widely shared by political actors. This is not to suggest, however, that Spain's EU policy has been driven solely by structural factors; on the contrary, this chapter seeks to illustrate how domestic politics have also shaped policy.

National identity and European integration

Any interpretation of Spanish public opinion about the EU must take into account certain elements of the country's political culture. Since the 1898 war against the USA, Europe has been a contradictory point of reference for Spain. On the one hand, there has been a tendency towards introspection and a feeling of being different to the rest of Europe, a sense that still permeates much of Spanish society. However, 40 years of dictatorship under General Franco helped to promote an alternative viewpoint. Thus, Europe (in the sense of non-Spanish) came to be perceived as the repository of those modernizing and liberalizing values which were lacking in Spanish public life. Many saw the adoption of these values as necessary to overcome the country's lack of political and economic development. In fact, Spanish intellectuals had already adopted the term 'Europeanization' at the start of the twentieth century to indicate an openness towards the assimilation of European political, economic, social and cultural trends (Marichal, 1988).

Political isolation under the Franco regime and its particular relationship with the European Community strengthened this positive

Figure 2.1   *European and national identity*

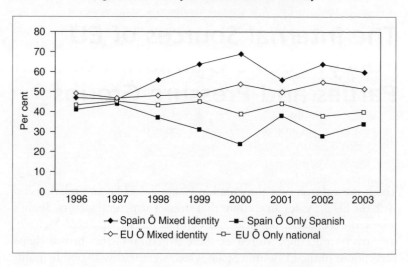

Source: compiled from Eurobarometer Standard Polls, 45–58 (1996–2003).

perception to such a point that the 'myth of Europe' has become an essential element in the reinvention of national identity in democratic Spain (Morán, 1995: 104–7). As a result, since the 1970s European integration has not represented a source of political cleavage, despite differences over specific issues and the overall rhythm of progress. The relationship between national and European identities is covered in some standard Eurobarometer questions. Respondents are asked whether they feel European only, European and Spanish (or another EU nationality), Spanish and European, or Spanish only. Results since 1996 are shown in Figure 2.1.

Data for those years in which this question has been systematically addressed in Eurobarometer polls show that Spanish public opinion has mirrored the European trend. The proportion who claim a dual identity (that is, both Spanish and European or European and Spanish) has increased, although there was a marked falling-off in 2001 – but there is an overwhelming tendency to place Spanish identity ahead of European: of those who claim a mixed identity, barely 6 per cent see themselves as European first. By the same token, the number who see themselves as exclusively Spanish has steadily declined until 2000, since when the total has hovered around 30 per cent. In comparison with average figures across the EU, Spaniards have a much more positive attitude towards shared identities (generally about 10 per cent above the EU average) and a lower propensity towards exclusive identity (between 5 and 10 per cent below the EU average). In their analysis of similar data, Llamazares and Reinares (1998) concluded that there is a positive association between Spanish and European identities, rather than any contradiction or trade-off between them.

There are two possible explanations for these trends. First, in contrast to the situation in many other EU countries, a large majority of Spaniards do not see European integration as a threat to their language, identity or culture (Eurobarometer Mega, 1996). Rather, worries for Spanish public opinion derive from specific issues, such as farmers fearing lower EU subsidies and a loss of social benefits (Eurobarometer, 1999). Occasionally, particular issues that generate conflict give rise to concern about Spain's compatibility within the EU. This happened, for instance, when it was believed that the EU wanted to suppress the 'ñ' from the Spanish alphabet, or to ban bull-fighting. Such issues have a strong mobilizing appeal for public opinion. And some more important issues, such as the 'Halibut conflict' with Canada, have also acted as catalysts for more strongly nationalistic feelings.

Second, Spanish and European identity can actually complement each other: Spain's success in achieving long-sought membership has served to reinforce national self-esteem. It could be argued that, paradoxically, the EU has acted as an instrument to build an inclusive and collective national project that had been lacking for over a century. Such a feeling might best be portrayed as an 'accommodation of differences', or being Spanish as a particular form of being European. In answer to the 1998 Eurobarometer question about whether there was a distinctive European cultural identity, Spanish responses indicated a clear distinction between the existence of such an identity and feeling European: just 38 per cent of Spaniards, the second lowest figure in the EU, agreed that there is a distinct European identity. Other empirical research confirms this perception. Europe (generally conflated with the EU) is seen as a source of identification, but primarily through its role as a resource for Spanish national identity (Rosa *et al.*, 1998: 127). Spanish citizens view the European project as part of their national project, rather than a project with its own specific purpose. Moreover, Europe is seen as a paradigm of success and progress for Spain: it is seen simultaneously as both a cause of, and a target for, development (ibid.: 118).

When considering the link between a national and supranational identity, the existence of alternative epistemic communities should also be borne in mind. In the Spanish case, Latin America remains a powerful reference point in terms of identity. In a 1997 poll, 41 per cent of Spaniards thought that Spain has as many links in terms of identity with Europe as with Latin America, with slightly more seeing links with the latter as being the stronger of the two (Barómetro Demoscopia, 1997: 19). Llamazares and Reinares (1998) have shown that, contrary to expectations, there is a positive association between European identification and identification with Latin-American Spanish speaking countries. These two types of overlapping identities are not necessarily contradictory; instead, attachment to one supranational community may also favour attachments towards another.

The European project has also contributed to the reconfiguration of identities within Spain. Since the 1970s, regional nationalism has seen a significant expansion. In terms of identity, this has meant the need to accommodate attachments at several levels and within alternative frames of reference. Research has underlined the viability of multilevel identities. Whilst people with *non-exclusive* identities (that is, neither solely Spanish nor regional) are more likely to have strong European identities, there is a negative relationship between *exclusive* regional identities and European identity. The association between Spanish and European identities is stronger than that between regional and European identities. The association with European identity is lower when the predominant identity is either exclusively regional or else regional nested with national (Llamazares and Reinares, 1998). Thus, people with balanced nested identities (as much Spanish as regional) or predominantly Spanish identities (more Spanish than regional) or else exclusively Spanish identities have a stronger attachment to the idea of a European identity than people with predominantly or, especially, exclusively regional identities.

However, this conclusion requires some qualification. It is not the case that regional nationalism is always inimical to supranational identification: for instance, voters for Catalan nationalist parties have a higher identification with Europe than the Spanish mean. On the other hand, nationalist party voters in Galicia and the Canary Islands are below the Spanish mean: in these two regions, the negative economic effects of European integration have been felt sharply (fishing and milk quota problems in Galicia, and a feeling of being marginalized on the periphery in the case of the Canary Islands). Similarly, Basque nationalist party voters (particularly supporters of Herri Batasuna) are below the Spanish mean. These differences may be explained by the interaction between nationalist feelings and the perception of the EU either as a political facilitator or as the source of specific regional problems, reflecting the differential impact of membership across Spain's regions.

In short, it can be argued that the EU provides an additional institutional point of reference that reinforces those multilevel identities which derive essentially from the regional/national cleavage. In such cases, European identity is almost always listed as the third preference. In practice, though, European identity has been highly instrumental for the articulation of joint regional and national identities. People with an exclusively territorial identity (either Spanish or regional) are more prone to support centralism or separatism respectively. European identities are higher among people who support the existing territorial structure of both national and regional institutions. There is thus a relationship between European identification and views on the territorial structure of the Spanish state.

The instrumental character of attachment to a European identity can be seen through such issues as European citizenship. Whilst more than half of all Spaniards think European citizenship is necessary in order for integration to progress, a commitment to national and regional 'citizenships' remains predominant (Eurobarometer Mega; 1996). Asked about the future, only 10 per cent of Spaniards saw themselves as likely to feel predominantly EU citizens (compared to an EU average of 16 per cent) and 51 per cent thought they would still see themselves as Spanish citizens (compared to an EU average of 61 per cent favouring national citizenship). On the issues of regional citizenship, however, 38 per cent of Spaniards saw themselves in the future as regional citizens against an EU average of 22 per cent. Again, attitudes towards European citizenship do not depend solely on identities but also on political-institutional preferences and the available political alternatives. The commitment to European citizenship is higher amongst those who support the eventual independence of Autonomous Communities, and higher for regional nationalists than the Spanish average.

Specific and diffuse support for the EU in Spanish public opinion

Easton's (1965) distinction between *specific support* and *diffuse support* is useful when interpreting public opinion data. Specific support derives mainly from the evaluation of system outcomes (such

Figure 2.2   *Indices of net support, net evaluation and net benefits of EU membership*

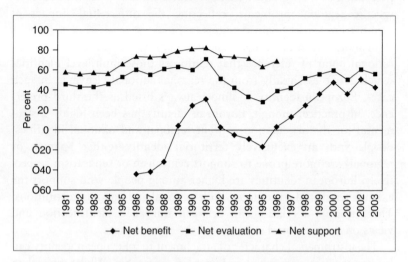

Source: Data from Eurobarometer Standard Polls, 15–58 (1981–2003). Data cover: EU-10 since 15/1981; EU-12 since 25/1986 and including ex-GDR since 34/1990; EU-15 since 43/1995.

as particular EU policies) whilst diffuse support refers to a reserve of positive attitudes that is independent of specific outcomes. Diffuse support allows for the acceptance or tolerance of outcomes that can be seen as negative (ibid.: 273). Some Eurobarometer questions tap attitudes that can be related to these two different modes of support. Thus, an affective dimension (close to the notion of diffuse support) is expressed in responses to questions such as '*Are you in favour of European unification?*,' '*Are you in favour of the integration process*' or '*Are you in favour of a federal Europe?*'. Questions implying an instrumental evaluation can be seen as eliciting a sense of specific support: for instance, '*Do you think that your country's membership of the EU is a good thing?*' or '*Do you think that your country has benefited from EU membership?*' Following Niedemayer (1995) and Barreiro and Sánchez Cuenca (2001), we can construct an index that shows the difference between positive and negative responses. For example, in 1999, 48 per cent of Spaniards questioned thought that Spain had benefited from membership against 21 per cent who thought it had not, resulting in a 'net' positive level of 27 per cent.

Three indices have been constructed from the above questions and are shown in Figure 2.2. A measure of diffuse support (labelled 'net

Figure 2.3   *Net support for European integration (Spain and EU average, 1981–96)*

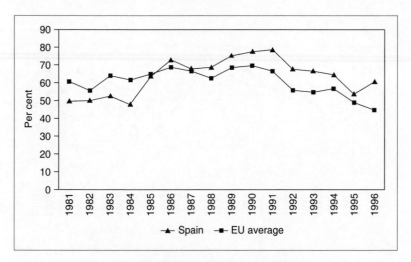

Source: Data from Eurobarometer Standard Polls, 15–45 (1981–2003).

support') is derived from responses to the question, '*Are you in favour of European unification?*', which was included in Eurobarometer surveys until 1996. Measures of specific support draw respectively on responses to the questions '*Do you think that your country's membership of the EU is a good thing*' ('net evaluation') and '*Do you think that your country has benefited from EU membership?*' ('net benefit'). The responses show a parallel evolution in all three: an incremental trend until 1991, a decrease from 1991 to 1995, and a steady rise thereafter until 2000. Of the three, it is diffuse support which has the highest values, consistently above the EU average (Figure 2.2), although oscillations in diffuse support have generally been similar in both the EU and Spain.

Specific support reveals different outcomes, depending on the question asked. When membership is considered in overall terms, the trend closely mirrors support for integration (Figure 2.3). But, in contrast to the former index, Spanish scores since 1986 have on occasion been below the EU average, at least until 1996. After that date, perceptions of membership as a good thing have run ahead of the EU average (Figure 2.4). The peak of positive evaluations was reached in 1990, when it stood at 80 per cent, but by 1996 the difference between positive and

Figure 2.4   *Net evaluation of membership (Spain and EU average, 1981–2003)*

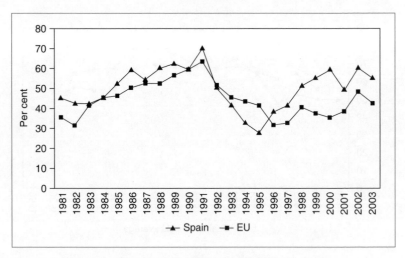

Source: Data from Eurobarometer Standard Polls, 15–59 (1981–2003).

negative evaluations had reached their lowest point. Nonetheless, 65 per cent of Spaniards remained in favour of ratifying EU membership should this become the subject of a referendum (Eurobarometer 45 Mega, 1996). Since 1992, though, the 'neutral' response (neither good nor bad) has increased significantly.

When instrumental evaluation is specified more precisely and respondents are asked about costs and benefits, the results change substantially (Figure 2.5). The number of those saying that Spain benefited from EU membership grew progressively from 1986 to 1991 when it reached a peak of 58 per cent (compared with 25 per cent who thought the opposite). After 1991, the number who thought EU membership did not benefit Spain grew significantly, to the point that they reached a majority. The figures show there were net positive evaluations of membership between 1989 and 1993 and again after 1996. It is striking, given Spanish pro-European sentiments, that net positive evaluations of membership were consistently lower than the EU average until 1997, whereupon the trend changed; since then assessments of net positive benefit of membership to Spain have been higher than the EU average. More significantly, the change of trend was so deep that negative evaluations fell below the EU average (Eurobarometer Trends, 1974–1992).

Figure 2.5   *Net benefit of membership (Spain and EU average, 1986–2003)*

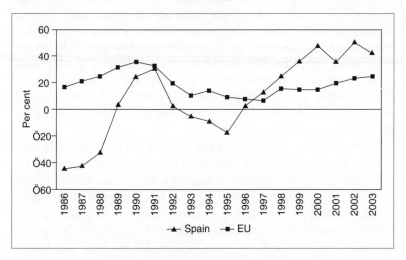

Source: Data from Eurobarometer Standard Polls, 25–59 (1986–2003).

Thus, Spanish support for integration (equivalent to diffuse support) has been above the European average, yet perceptions of membership benefits (equivalent to specific support) have been below the European average. How can we explain these differences? On the one hand, it is possible that the deep-rooted underlying support for EU membership ran counter to judgements when instrumental considerations were at stake. In this respect, Spanish public opinion shows some degree of incoherence (Barreiro and Sánchez Cuenca, 2001): in spite of being in favour of the EU, citizens are less prepared to accept the consequences of an open market where goods and workers circulate freely. On the other hand, there appears to be a particularly strong correlation between the economic cycle and instrumental evaluation of EU membership. Although this is a common trend for all EU countries, in the Spanish case the oscillations in levels of support have been much larger.

There is also a correlation, empirically demonstrated by Barreiro and Sánchez Cuenca (2001), between feelings of support for Europe and such domestic factors as the unemployment rate or general satisfaction with democracy. Essentially, in Spain as in other member states, perceptions of the EU are mediated by national priorities. Thus, the Spanish public lists as priority issues for the EU: tackling unemployment (90 per cent), solving problems in agriculture and fisheries (87 per cent) and peace-keeping (85 per cent) (Eurobarometer Mega 45, 1996). But when these priorities are compared to Spanish public opinion on areas of legitimate EU authority, a contradictory picture emerges. In regard to unemployment, less than half (48 per cent) think that the EU should have competences in this area. Significantly, in both 1996 and 1997, some half of Spanish respondents thought agriculture and fisheries should be wholly national concerns, reflecting some highly visible clashes between Spain and the EU (Eurobarometer 46, 1996).

To summarize, a majority of the Spanish public expresses diffuse support for the integration process. However, perceptions of the EU have also been significantly influenced by more instrumental considerations. Thus, Spanish public opinion has moved from a wholehearted acceptance of the integration process towards a more questioning attitude which reflects considered evaluation of the potential costs. In this regard, the role of the media has been very important. In 1996, 66 per cent of Spaniards thought they were not well-informed about the EU and its policies (Eurobarometer Mega 45, 1996). However, media coverage of EU-related issues has increased significantly since Spain became a member. To a large extent, media reporting understandably concentrates on areas of conflict, such as the fisheries disputes with Morocco and Canada, the penalties imposed on Spain for surplus milk production, agricultural reforms covering wine and olive oil, or difficult budgetary negotiations. It is noteworthy that in 1992, a poll showed that 85 per cent of Spaniards thought indigenous products should be protected from competition by other EU member states (CIRES, 1993). Commenting on these data, Barreiro and Sánchez Cuenca (2001) concluded that Spaniards are highly protectionist and that this protectionism does not seem to be associated with a lack of information. In short, it may be that many Spaniards hold to some long-established attitudes and values which clash with the inherent logic of European integration.

Spanish political parties

The role of Spanish political parties in regard to European integration not only helps to explain, but also tends to mirror, shifts in public attitudes. The Spanish party system has not been affected substantially by any significant cleavage over Europe, nor has the issue led to significant

Table 2.1   *Spanish parties in European Parliament political groups*

	European political group	*Spanish member parties*
EPP-ED	Group of the European People's Party and European Democrats	Partido Popular (PP) Partido Nacionalista Vasco (PNV) Unió Democrático de Catalunya (UDC)
PES	Group of the Party of European Socialists	Partido Socialista Obrero Español (PSOE)
ELDR	Group of the European Liberal, Democratic and Reformist Party	Convergència Democrática de Catalunya (CDC)
Greens/EFA	Group of the Greens/ European Free Alliance	
EUL/NGL	Confederal Group of the European United Left/ Nordic Green Left	Izquierda Unida (United Left)
UEN	Group of the Union for a Europe of Nations	
EDD	Europe of Democracies and Diversities Group	

Source: Data adapted from http://www.europarl.eu.int (accessed October 2003).

internal splits within parties. Of the three classical dimensions of party activity (electoral, organizational and ideological-programmatic), the influence of Europe is felt only on the third. In regard to the first dimension, it is national cleavages, conflicts and policies which dictate electoral tactics and guide voting behaviour. In terms of organization, internal party changes have essentially been restricted either to an enlargement of the international affairs department or the creation of *ad hoc* secretaries for European policy. Parties have also joined European party groups (see Table 2.1)

At the programmatic level, all Spanish parties have wholeheartedly embraced EU accession and membership. Indeed, Spain is the only non-founding member whose accession to the EU has been unanimously supported by all political parties, with continued support evident on such issues as enlargement, reform and so forth. Two issues symbolize consensus. First, political parties usually agree on basic reforms required by European integration: thus, the Spanish *Cortes* ratified the Treaty of Maastricht (TEU) with 314 votes in favour, 8 abstentions and only 3 votes against (those of the Basque HB). The required constitutional reform resulted from a pact between the PSOE, the PP and CiU, with the agreement of the remaining parties. Similar majorities supported the ratification of the Treaty of Amsterdam. Second, consensus has helped governments to present their negotiating stance in terms of 'matters of state'. For instance, the unanimous approval in November 1991 of a parliamentary resolution endorsing the government's stance on the TEU strengthened its negotiating position on social and economic Cohesion Funds. Similarly, the government's position in negotiations over enlargement and the EFTA countries enjoyed unanimous parliamentary support.

Consensus has been helped by both the relatively limited fragmentation of the Spanish party system and infrequent changes of government, with just three parties holding office between 1977 and 2003: the UCD (1977–82), the PSOE (1982–96) and the PP (since 1996). Politicians have sought to underline the continuity of Spain's European policy. The PSOE, for example, argued that European integration represented the clearest line of continuity in Spanish foreign policy since 1977, in turn reflecting the huge support that EU accession enjoyed within Spanish society (Yáñez and Viñas, 1992: 95). When the PP took office in 1996, Christian Democrat elements within the party sought to emphasize continuity with the preceding PSOE and UCD governments, arguing that the Socialists had merely carried through the foreign policy designed and initiated by an earlier centrist administration (Rupérez, 1996).

Throughout much of the 1980s, basic agreement combined with large government majorities allowed EU policies to be presented as being virtually 'above' party. However, since the start of the 1990s, EU issues have increasingly become a focus of party competition. The change is explained by both external and internal factors. Externally, the reconfiguration of geopolitical space within Europe also led to shifts in the traditional pay-off matrices. Internally, there was a significant shift in public opinion as EU symbols ceased to have such positive connotations for politicians and public alike. Moreover, the prospect grew of a change in government, especially as in the 1993 elections the PSOE fell short of an absolute majority for the first time since 1982. Against this background, EU issues became more contentious, and clashes between party leaders on European issues increased significantly. The PP, for instance, criticized the Cohesion

Fund agreement on various grounds, including its very terms and conditions. Once in government, though, the PP changed its stance, demonstrating that its original criticism had been mainly tactical. Yet the growing differentiation between parties on programmatic and ideological grounds, even if sometimes more apparent than real, did represent a normalization of party stances on EU issues, as parties sought to root their differences within deeper party identities.

The Socialist Party (PSOE)

The Socialist Party (PSOE) has traditionally been seen as holding the most orthodox view on the integration process. According to Gillespie (1996: 160), the PSOE's federalist stance reflected the idealism of a generation which identified with the pro-European views originally expressed by Spanish intellectuals such as Ortega y Gasset. In fact, the PSOE has moved a long way in its view of integration, from a somewhat ambiguous stance prior to 1976, through seeing the EC as a vehicle for the advancement of socialism, towards the adoption of a modernizing discourse (Álvarez-Miranda, 1994: 164). The PSOE dropped its objections to the 'capitalist' integration process early in the 1970s, and the responsibilities of assuming political office in 1982 led to further moderation. In 1983, the Socialist Parliamentary Group unanimously ratified the Agreement of Friendship, Defence and Cooperation with the USA, followed by an official expression of support for the deployment of Euro-missiles in West Germany and, ultimately, the endorsement in 1986 of Spain's NATO membership.

Two factors help explain this progressive moderation in the PSOE's stance on Europe. The first relates to its links with other socialist parties. During the transition to democracy, the West German SPD in particular closely monitored the PSOE's activities, and support from the Socialist International further boosted the party's pro-Europe position. The SPD was interested in a stable southern Europe, and therefore sought to promote a programmatic shift towards moderation within the PSOE similar to its own historic conversion at Bad Godesberg. Moreover, the SPD sponsored the view of West German readiness materially to support Spanish accession to the EC. But, once in office, the PSOE was able to develop its independence from SPD tutelage. In the face of poor electoral results for other socialist parties in Europe during the 1980s, the PSOE skilfully exploited its role within Europe, and in particular the party's strength within the European Parliament's Socialist Group, where it was for a period the largest single party (Gillespie, 1996). The PSOE's former minister of transport, Enrique Barón Crespo, was elected President of the European Parliament between 1989 and 1992 and in 1999 became Chair of the Socialist Group.

The second factor is more important. The PSOE led the final phase of accession negotiations and was in power during the first 10 years of Spanish membership of the European Union. The PSOE's European policy was therefore shaped by the demands of holding governmental office. Official PSOE policies were often party policies only to the extent that party organs endorsed decisions taken within the administration. Gillespie (1996: 157) comments that, particularly after 1986, the party as such played no role in the formulation of Spain's EU policy whereas, in contrast, the personal style and tastes of Felipe González were probably decisive. Critics have described the PSOE government's policy on Europe as part of its 'hegemonic project', whereby all aspects of domestic, social and economic policy were presented and legitimized by reference to the necessity of adjusting Spanish socio-economic and political structures to meet the demands of membership of the European Community (Holman, 1996).

The tenor of the PSOE's EU policy can thus be explained by a combination of the demands of being in government together with an idealistic heritage of support for Europe. Broadly, it could be described as cloaking national interest within a federalist discourse and a commitment to Community orthodoxy (Closa, 1999). According to Felipe González (1988), Community debates have been characterized by a false dichotomy between national interest and community interest – but the way forward lies not in pitting relative advantages against each other, but rather through the joint exploitation of collective advantages. For González (1992: 22), political union implies both cohesion and citizenship: hence some of the main Spanish contributions to the integration process, such as the proposal for European citizenship or the cohesion funds policy. González's strong leadership in European affairs was characterized by a combination of high-level pro-European statesmanship with less visible hard-edged bargaining.

The PSOE's European policy produced a clear political pay-off whilst the Spanish economy performed well. The PSOE deliberately sought to capitalize on the popularity of EU membership to introduce its programme of modernization through political and social transformation (Boix, 1999: 13; Holman, 1996). Modernization involved a mix of macroeconomic stability and state interventionism, characterized by the abandonment of systematic Keynesian demand policies, the development of active industrial policies in order to restructure the public sector and to compete internationally, and the construction of a fully fledged welfare state to compensate the unemployed and others who lost out as the Spanish economy was transformed (Boix, 1999). Central to the PSOE's view of Europe was the existence of a 'European social model', shared with many Christian democrats and based on three essential elements: health protection, public education and a comprehensive pension system. In essence, the public sector should play a key role in the provision of a welfare infrastructure (Solana, 1993). Problems began to appear, though, when the economic cycle hit a downturn and a strong recession had set in by 1992. Pro-European rhetoric started to lose its domestic appeal and some European symbols even acquired a negative connotation. Some have argued that, after 1993, the PSOE encouraged a stronger defence of national interests (Gillespie, 1996: 155; Barbé, 1999).

Externally, the economic crisis and the climate of austerity introduced by the EMU programme, together with new EU priorities, made González's federalizing discourse, based on economic redistribution, look less persuasive. Given this context, and the growing electoral threat of the PP, a more nationalistic stance proved very useful for the PSOE. But this did not mean it renounced its federalist stance. Rather, González (1992: 21) argued that the real risks in Europe derived precisely from such tendencies towards the renationalisation of policies. Even during the harshest period of economic recession (with strong anti-European feeling provoked by ratification of the Maastricht Treaty) the government's response to Spanish problems was described as 'more Europe' (Barbé, 1996: 12). González's leadership was essential to this stance, since some critical elements within the PSOE were pressing for a renegotiation of the EMU programme, or at least greater flexibility in applying its terms. González became a defender of EU orthodoxy. In his address to the European Parliament at the end of the 1995 Spanish presidency, the PSOE leader appealed for a continued commitment to European integration and the avoidance of short-sighted attitudes, defensive nationalism or destructive rivalries.

Since going into opposition in 1996, the PSOE has proclaimed its Europeanism as a distinctive feature to set it apart from the more nationalist discourse of the PP. Even in 1999, PSOE leaders such as Josep Borrell called explicitly for a federal EU, yet at the same time lobbied German chancellor Gerhard Schröder in support of the PP government's thesis on Agenda 2000. But, in contrast to their former appeals for consensus, the PSOE has brought its political conflicts with the PP into the European arena. The Socialists favoured, for instance, the employment policy promoted by Lionel Jospin and have also sought to exploit specific issues, such as payments by the PP government to the electrical utilities, which contravened EU regulations.

The People's Party (PP)

The People's Party (PP) is, despite its name and claim to be part of the Christian Democratic family, the end result of long process of reorganization of a series of groups and organizations on the political right. The heterogeneity of its make-up militated against the emergence of a clearly defined position on the issue of Europe. Whilst Christian Democrats, such as Marcelino Oreja and others who had been members of the UCD government, share the traditional views of Adenauer or De Gasperi, ex-Francoists and conservatives originally associated with the far-right Alianza Popular (AP), do not view Spain's twentieth-century history as being traumatic. Moreover, their interpretation of Francoism sees it more in terms of economic modernization than as being marked by isolation and so they do not subscribe to the 'myth of Europe' (Torreblanca, 1999).

The transformation of the PP from its right-wing origins as the AP to becoming a member of the European People's Party Group (EPP) in the European Parliament dates from the late 1980s. The party's admission to the EPP was a tense affair. Some of the more established European Christian Democratic parties, as well as the smaller nationalist parties in Catalonia and the Basque Country that were already members of EPP, saw the Partido Popular as a straightforwardly conservative party with links to a Francoist past (Hanley, 1996). The PP therefore sought to present itself as similar to other moderate European parties, by renewing its image and abandoning certain ideological positions. These were necessary steps en route to becoming a credible alternative to the PSOE. Accession to the EPP was finally achieved on the eve of 1989 European elections. None the less, the PP encompasses a wide spectrum of ideological viewpoints (liberals, Christian democrats, conservatives and some nostalgic ex-Francoists) which has rendered more difficult the elaboration of a single stance on the issue of Europe. The result has been a certain confusion in the PP's European policy.

For the first 10 years of Spain's EU membership (1986–96), the PP was in opposition. As a result, the PP was unconstrained in its discourse on EU matters by the political realities imposed by holding office. There was also a felt need to distance itself from the ruling PSOE's stance on the integration process. Historically, the right had stressed the link between membership of Europe and being in NATO (Álvarez-Miranda, 1994: 164), but the PSOE's u-turn on the NATO issue had undermined that element of differentiation. The PP thus sought to develop a more nationalistic stance. After the 1992 Edinburgh summit, Aznar criticized González for his defence of Cohesion Funds, describing him as the Union's 'beggar'. Aznar argued that the excessive pro-European enthusiasm of the Socialists had weakened Spain's negotiating position. The PP repeatedly complained throughout Spain's 1995 presidency of the EU that insufficient attention was being paid to real Spanish concerns: agriculture, fisheries and unemployment. In the 1996 election campaign, Aznar made much play of the assertion that the PSOE government had failed to defend Spanish interests, claiming that González had been a good President for Europe but a bad one for Spain (Grasa, 1997: 35).

A second element of differentiation concerns the PP's commitment to the nation-state. At a meeting in Spring 1995 of the EPP Inter-Parliamentary Conference, Aznar outlined his concept of a '*Europa de las patrias*', in which sovereign nation-states are – and must remain – the basic elements of the integration process (Bernárdez, 1995: 309). The PP's more nationalistic discourse, centred on the defence of Spanish self-interest, reflected a pragmatic approach based on growing public scepticism about European integration, together with the view that there was no longer any need to appeal to the EU to legitimize restrictive macroeconomic policies (Torreblanca, 1999). The defence of 'national interests' was expected to provide an electoral pay-off (Grasa, 1997: 38). In fact, during the 1993 election campaign, the PP had initially argued in favour of leaving the Exchange Rate Mechanism of the European Monetary System (EMS), but the stance was dropped once the prospect of gaining office became more realistic. Thereafter, agreement on the broad outlines of the commitment to Europe was coupled with fierce criticism of PSOE management of Spanish interests within the EU.

The PP's discourse clearly put Spain's national interests at the forefront of the party's European policy. Yet, in seeking to differentiate the PP's commitment to Europe from that of the PSOE, Aznar also sought to square the circle by calling for a Europe of sovereign nation-states alongside a quasi-federalist cohesion policy. The commitment to cohesion led to the adoption of some inconsistent policies: whilst criticizing the PSOE's stance on Cohesion Funds and claiming that such funds did not reduce income disparities between regions, the PP none the less supported financial transfers in order to defend Spanish interests (Arias Salgado, 1997: 63).

When the PP eventually came to power in 1996, the new government's European policy reflected dual characteristics. On the one hand, the Ministry for Foreign Affairs was committed to a continuation in broad outline of the PSOE's European policy, reflecting the views of the Christian democratic element within the PP and those more conservative members with experience within Europe. Some in the PP called for a non-partisan national project for the EU, exemplified by agreement on the objectives of Spanish EU presidency under the PSOE (Méndez de Vigo, 1997). More significantly, several members of the new government explicitly endorsed the continuity thesis: Rafael Arias Salgado, for instance, argued that differences with the Socialists were matters of emphasis rather than substance (Arias Salgado, 1997: 62). Similarly, Abel Matutes, the PP Foreign Minister, had endorsed as chairman of the EPP group the conclusions of the Spanish presidency of 1995 (in contrast to fierce domestic criticism). Finally, Defence Minister Eduardo Serra reiterated the thesis that the Spanish national project had to be framed within an EU context (Serra, 2000), a line of continuity shared even by Prime Minister Aznar (at least in terms of rhetoric) (Barbé, 1999: 123).

However, party political considerations ensured that a more nationalistic line would prevail. Orthodox Christian Democrats found their views on Europe relegated to a secondary plane, not helped by the somewhat lacklustre performance of Matutes, a former EU commissioner whose sympathies lay with Christian Democratic thinking on Europe. In practice, the PP's European policy was primarily informed by Aznar's personal views, as had happened previously under González. In contrast to the PSOE leader, however, Aznar appeared less comfortable on the international arena, exhibiting a more stilted diplomatic style and a tendency towards introspection which was more suited to the national stage. In consequence, at least initially, the combination of ideologically-inspired nationalism and the real day-to-day demands of being in the EU led to an erratic series of policies, lacking a sense of overall coherence (Grasa, 1997). On the issue of integration, for instance, the PP pursued an inconsistent policy: at first, Aznar went against Community orthodoxy by supporting an increase in the powers of the European Council as against the Commission (Aznar, 1994). Yet, five years later, during the fraud crisis under Jacques Santer, Aznar supported the Commission against the European Parliament and dismissed the report by the Committee of Wise Men which led to its resignation en masse. Aznar's changed stance reflected his growing awareness of how important the Commission could be for a medium-sized country such as Spain (Sahagún, 2000: 40).

Aznar's personal influence was also apparent in Spain's bilateral links with other EU member states. The PP's strategy in regard to developing allies within the EU was initially driven by ideology rather than by strategic considerations. The British Conservative Party exerted a certain fascination for the PP, which shared – at least whilst in opposition – its views over issues such as the EMS, the need to defend the role of national parliaments, and to curb the Commission's powers (Barbé, 999: 69). Similarly, once in power, the PP looked to the French conservative government as an important point of reference, whilst relations were tense with Spain's traditional allies, Germany and Italy (paymaster and Mediterranean partner respectively). Spain's relations with Germany went through a cool phase, despite apparent ideological proximity. There was speculation about a lack of personal empathy between Aznar and Kohl, but the reality was that the interests of the two countries were progressively diverging. Spain's main objectives were to ensure that it was in the first wave of membership of EMU and that it would not be prejudiced in any new EU financial arrangements, but on both issues Germany presented some obstacles. Equally, Spain's relations with Italy reflected an excess of self-confidence together with some naivety. Over time, the PP government was able to correct these 'positioning' errors, which were mainly due to a lack of experience in EU affairs amongst its leading figures. Changes of government in the UK and France also contributed to a revised assessment of the political landscape. Indeed, the most salient change in the PP's international (and European) politics was its growing proximity to the UK after the election of Tony Blair – even to the point of accepting this would lead to a distancing from the Franco–German axis (Barbé, 1999: 140).

Inexperience was also evident in the PP's initial stance on a number of EU issues. Thus, Aznar adopted a pragmatic view of the 1996 reform programme, proposing gradualism, a single institutional framework and common objectives (although with different speeds), and political and financial support for those states which faced difficulties in achieving such objectives (Aznar, 1995: 173). But Aznar's selection of top priorities for the 1996 Inter-Governmental Conference revealed that he was not yet fully attuned to EU politics. He called, firstly, for a more precise definition of the subsidiarity principle, which Spanish governments had traditionally seen (with good reason) as a UK-inspired attempt to weaken the Commission, one of Spain's most important institutional allies. Aznar's second topic was reform of the EU budget, which lay outside the IGC agenda. Finally, he called for the creation of a common police and judicial space, a long-standing Spanish priority, but did not handle the issue effectively during the IGC (Closa, 1998).

Paradoxically, though, Aznar was able to benefit from a factor which had earlier helped González: just as the PSOE had been virtually the only socialist government in the EU between 1986 and 1996, by 1999 the situation had been reversed and the PP was now the only conservative government in the EU. Such isolation provided clear pay-offs in institutional and political terms: institutionally, José María Gil-Robles was elected President of the European Parliament; politically, Aznar was given the opportunity to exercise leadership within the European right. Spain's successful economic performance and entry into EMU, as well as the PP's overwhelming electoral victory in 2000, also helped boost Aznar's role, as did his agreement with Tony Blair on specific EU policies as well as the integration process. These views were reflected in the Declaration of Chequers, signed by both leaders in April 1999. Subsequently, Aznar and Blair jointly presented to the March 2000 Lisbon European Council an ambitious programme to define 'a new strategic goal for the EU [which would combine] economic dynamism and social justice to build a successful knowledge-based economy . . . able to offer jobs and prosperity to all' (Blair and Aznar, 2000). This was followed up by a joint article in *The Financial Times* in June 2000, and marked a radical departure from Spain's former close partnerships with France and Germany.

The United Left (IU)

The third nationally based political force in Spain is the United Left (IU), a broad-ranging coalition whose main element is the Communist Party (PCE). The PCE had been one of the lead players in the development of Euro-communism during the 1970s (Carrillo, 1977) and had accordingly distanced itself from the views of the Soviet Union on European integration. Instead, the PCE had enthusiastically endorsed

Spanish membership of the European Community, which was associated with federalist principles. As early as at its 1972 Congress, the PCE had proclaimed itself in favour of Spanish accession. However, the electoral fortunes of the PCE following the restoration of democracy, particularly after 1982, condemned it to a relatively marginal role in Spanish politics.

The PCE was able to stage some form of recovery after the NATO referendum in 1986 under the banner of a new coalition, United Left (IU). The widespread opposition to Spanish membership of NATO served as a catalyst for various social groups on the left to join together against what was perceived as the PSOE's betrayal of a leftist programme whose distinctive feature had been precisely its attempt to detach European integration from NATO membership. IU initially called, without much conviction, for a renegotiation of the accession Treaty on the grounds that the costs in agriculture and fisheries were excessive. Their attitude reflected a fear of 'peripheralization' of the Spanish economy within the EU (Álvarez-Miranda, 1994: 164). Over time, IU became increasingly concerned to defend the social dimension of EU membership, which led to criticism of the EMU programme for creating an unfettered capitalist market. The macroeconomic policy which underpinned EMU was seen as representing neo-liberal orthodoxy, whilst the Convergence Programmes were seen as a tool to dismantle the welfare state. As a result, IU formally opposed ratification of the Maastricht Treaty and, for the first time, consensus on Europe amongst Spain's major parties broke down.

However, IU was divided over its policy on Europe, and one of its organized factions, New Left, remained in favour of the Treaty. IU discourse has subsequently sought to combine support for a more socially oriented integration process with a strong defence of Spanish interests, a position which reflected the concerns of a public becoming more sensitive towards the costs deriving from membership. A somewhat shambolic electoral and programmatic agreement with the PSOE in the run-up to the 2000 general election led to further moderation in IU discourse, specifically over the Stability Pact and wider EU macroeconomic policy.

Regional parties

Three factors determine the attitude of Spain's regional parties towards the EU. First, an assessment of the how the process of European integration may help re-shape the Spanish state influences views on the benefits of membership. Secondly, regional parties are also affected by their position of the left-right spectrum, with the more leftist ones sharing the IU perspective against capitalist Europe or market Europe. Finally, the differential impact of EU policies in the various regions encourages a more instrumental evaluation of membership.

In regard to the first of these factors, the EU represents a powerful image and resource for the regionalist discourse (Closa, 2001b). Both for the Basque PNV and the Catalan CiU, the EU offers a new arena for political action – both through associations and institutions. The concept of a *Europe of the Regions* as a form of political organization that replaces nation-states has been highly functional for the discourse of both parties. Moreover, their links with transnational parties and federations (the PNV with EPP and CiU with both the EPP and the ELDR) follow more logically than those of the PP: as genuine Christian Democrats and Liberals, their views on Europe largely coincide with their partner parties despite their regional status.

Regional parties do manifest differences in the way in which calls for self-determination and/or independence are linked to Europe. Thus, for CiU leaders, Europe and Catalonia are powerful and mutually reinforcing images, which serve a twofold ideological purpose. First, the Catalan discourse can be linked to a wider political entity that is democratic and modern, hoping thereby to undermine the suggestion that the promotion of the region's language is narrow, autocratic or provincial (Laitin, 1997: 291). Second, Europe provides an example of a growing political authority which is not a state, thereby reinforcing Catalan claims for a regional autonomy which does not rely on the socio-political configurations of statehood (Laitin, 1997: 293). CiU has also utilized the discourse of reintegration in Europe. Thus, CiU has supported both PSOE and PP minority governments on condition (among other domestic pay-offs) that convergence programmes be applied.

The Basque PNV, on the other hand, has been more assertive on the issue of self-determination and the ultimate aim of independence. More openly than Catalans, the PNV has called for the eventual membership of an independent Basque State in the European Union, symbolized by their addition of a 'thirteenth star' on the European flag. The PNV's withdrawal from the EPP (in protest at the admission of the PP) reflected a shift towards a more assertive attitude in which EU membership now forms part of the future project of independence.

The second factor conditioning regionalist discourse on the EU is the parties' location on the right–left cleavage and their analysis of the costs and benefits of membership for their own regions. In both the Basque Country and in Catalonia, the negative impacts of membership have been limited, and the PNV and CiU have not sought to capitalize on any popular dissatisfaction with the EU. Moreover, the free-market focus of the integration process fits easily with the parties' ideological preferences.

The Galician BNG, on the other hand, represents a rather different view. More left-leaning, it has criticized neo-liberal policies in the EU, but also feels that Galicia has suffered as a peripheral region from EU policies. The BNG's official stance is therefore very critical (although the party is somewhat divided on the issue of Europe) since the effects the CAP and the CFP on Galicia have been particularly negative. Similarly, the Canary Islands nationalists sought to defend their statutes against perceived threats from the EU.

Interest articulation: Spanish lobbies

The development of a more pluralistic civil society in which interest groups can establish roots came about in Spain in parallel with accession to the EU. Spain's civil society is relatively weak in terms of networks of organized groups and institutions outside the state apparatus, with a small number of interest groups and low levels of associational activity compared to other European countries (Keating, 1993: 337; Molins and Morata; 1993: 117; Molins and Casademunt, 1999; Torcal and Montero, 1999).

The first years of transition witnessed the emergence of many groups which were highly politicized. Over time, two main trends emerged. First, groups representing employers and labour have assumed a position of dominance over all other interest groups, particularly during the 1980s and 1990s. Second, EU policies in particular sectors have stimulated the emergence of specific interest groups seeking to exploit new opportunity structures to lobby for their members.

Broadly, both the trade unions and the employers' organizations benefited from an effective vacuum within a weakly organized civil society. Moreover, they derived an enhanced role from their *political* involvement in the transition to democracy, in which they supported what were virtually consociational agreements. The employers' association (the CEOE), and the trade unions (the socialist UGT and the communist CCOO plus some smaller organizations) were involved in negotiating with government a series of agreements whose principal aim was to provide the social calm required for a peaceful transition. The *Pactos de la Moncloa* in 1977 linked both employers and unions in the short-term management of macroeconomic policy. Thus, whereas social concertation in some parts of northern Europe was the centrepiece of the industrial relations regime, in Spain it acted as the vehicle through which the broader democratic political regime was established (Boix, 1999; Molins and Casademunt, 1999: 133).

The domestic arena was the priority for both employers and unions. However, CEOE closely monitored accession negotiations, to such an extent that an official involved in negotiations described CEOE's monitoring as 'the Spanish–Spanish negotiations' (Bassols, 1996). Industrialists were acutely aware and fearful of the effects of competition on the heavily protected market in which they had grown. Immediately after accession in 1986, the CEOE opened an office in Brussels with the objective of lobbying on behalf of its members, and it joined the Union of Industrial and Employers' Confederation of Europe (UNICE). However, the CEOE has not been effective at lobbying in Brussels, reflecting poorly developed bargaining strategies in the EU arena (Jones, 2000). Such ineffectiveness is probably best explained by the CEOE's structure, which is based on sectoral and territorial groups ranging from agriculture to industry and commerce, but which is poorly suited for the highly specialized and fragmented policy-making process of the EU. Thus, companies and interest groups have sought more specifically focused lobbying routes.

The trade unions, in turn, were initially more directly interested in the domestic arena. This reflected the fact that they enjoyed very high salience as political actors as a result of the consociational management of the transition. Although the unions saw some potential costs from European integration, they shared the general consensus on membership and had always supported Spanish accession. Thus, the unions paid relatively little attention to EU affairs: the UGT became a member of the European Trade Union Confederation (ETUC) only in 1988, and the CCOO joined two years later (the Basque ELA-STV is also a member of ETUC). This relatively late entry underlines the priority accorded by Spanish unions to national issues.

In addition, the structure of industrial relations in the EU did not seem to provide an appropriate model for Spain's unions. It has been suggested that social dialogue in the EU has had only a limited impact in Spain, particularly in employment market regulation. On the other hand, the philosophy of consensus which underpins the European approach has offered a more positive example (Herrador, 2000). Spanish unions are, at least rhetorically, committed to the idea of a European industrial relations space. During the IX Congress of ETUC in Helsinki (1999), Spain's major unions adopted a joint strategy and submitted joint proposals, seeking to strengthen ETUC with a larger budget, and improved decision-making and coordination capacity. Specifically, the Spanish unions favoured the delegation of powers to allow European-level coordination of union claims in support of a reduction in the working day (Moreno and Bonmati, 1999).

The unions' interest in the EU as a political arena grew after 1988, when they clashed with the Socialist government over macroeconomic policy. Following the Spanish peseta's entry to the Exchange Rate Mechanism of the EMS, the UGT and CCOO launched a joint plat-form (*Propuesta Sindical Prioritaria*) demanding higher social expen-diture, increased government planning of the economy, an extensive housing policy and a fairer tax system. Although the PSOE govern-ment sought to legitimize its macroeconomic policies by reference to the demands of EU membership, the unions in turn sought to mobi-lize through the EU against such policies (see Chapter 6). It should be noted that the unions' criticism of specific EU policies (particularly, EMU) has not reflected general hostility to the EU, and has been coupled with positive discourse on the construction of a social Europe.

Sectoral lobbying presents a different picture. When Spain joined the Community, the lobbying process was still at an embryonic stage (Jones, 2000). Democratization and EU membership, together with the emergence of the Autonomous Communities, coincided to create a more open, multilevel and permeable political structure in Spain. The emergence of lobbying in Spain could be characterized by the follow-ing (and, occasionally, opposed) trends. First, there has been a predom-inance of public lobbying. The lack of a pluralistic tradition in Spain has meant that networks of key actors have been slow to develop, thus enhancing the role of the state as national gatekeeper and autonomous actor – a situation reinforced by the fact that private-sector participa-tion in decision-making is still seen as representing an obstacle to the so-called 'public interest' (in this respect, Spain resembles the French tradition) (Molins and Morata, 1993: 128). Thus, the new political structure in Spain has been particularly favourable for those public institutions with the capacity to act as autonomous lobbies, such as the

Autonomous Communities. The traditional function of interest articulation relies mainly on public lobbying.

In parallel, the EU has offered a strong incentive to develop lobbying opportunities in particular policy arenas, notably agriculture. Before 1982, Spanish agricultural organizations exhibited their corporatist inheritance in terms of organization and operating style. This inheritance, together with a rather ambiguous relationship with the Socialist government, resulted in an informal approach to events at the European level, and a certain lack of coordination in Brussels (Molins and Morata, 1993: 127). Functional and territorial fragmentation characterized agriculture lobbies. Among these, the CNAG (*Confederación Nacional de Agricultores y Ganaderos*), which grouped together large landowners in Andalucía and Extremadura, was distinctive among European agriculture organizations in that it belonged to the employers' federation, the CEOE. The CNJA (*Centro Nacional de Jóvenes Agricultores*) sought to unite all sectors that relied on land as their main source of income. Its territorial base was Castile and Valencia. The COAG (*Coordinadora de Organizaciones de Agricultores y Ganaderos*) also belonged to the CEOE and coexisted with regional organizations. Finally, UPA (*Unión de Pequeños Agricultores*) belonged to the socialist union UGT, and operated mainly in Galicia and Extremadura. The EU provided an incentive to reorganize, as agricultural organizations saw the need to develop permanent, professional central structures with the capacity to negotiate in Brussels. The most significant result has been the creation of ASAJA (*Asociación Agraria–Jóvenes Agricultores*) in 1988, representing more than 200,000 agricultural workers. The European arena offers a number of opportunities: negotiation with the government to determine the Spanish position on the European stage, participation in consultation committees, and timely mobilization which almost always coincides with decisive meetings in Brussels (Molins and Casademunt, 1998: 139).

Two factors have conditioned Spanish agricultural lobbying: low membership in comparison to other member states (Moyano, 1997: 787) and organizational weakness (Sumpsi, 1994). In consequence, agricultural lobbying has tended to be reactive, with a limited capacity to exert real influence. In spite of this, the Common Agricultural Policy (CAP) has contributed to the emergence of at least three types of discourses (Moyano, 1997: 789–92):

1 *Entrepreneur discourse.* Predominant in ASAJA, this approach sees agricultural production in terms of a modern profit-seeking

enterprise, and is therefore opposed, for instance, to aid measures which might make farmers mere harvesters of EU subsidies.

2 *Neo-rural discourse.* Associated with COAG and UPA, this discourse sees agricultural production as a particular way of life that must be protected, and therefore rejects any reform of the CAP.

3 *Agricultural fundamentalist discourse.* A strand within all organizations, this discourse seeks a return to a more autarkic conception of agriculture and its traditional values, seeking to protect it from market competition, which is seen as the source of all evils.

A further feature of Spanish lobbying concerns ownership in the industrial, banking and utilities sectors. Historically, publicly-owned companies accounted for a large proportion of Spain's industrial structure. Such companies have thus been very active, since they stood to be most affected by competition rules. Thus, former monopolies such as the oil company, CAMPSA, made huge efforts to stave off competition, and other publicly-owned companies in the mining, ship-building or aviation sectors sought to maintain state subsidies. In general, these companies were more reactive than proactive. The extensive process of privatization has given rise to a new elite of managers of formerly public companies with strong links with politicians and officials, helping to forge a style of mediation in which personal contacts are decisive (Molins and Casademunt, 1999: 124).

Nonetheless, some authors argue that business organizations have been hesitant about becoming involved with government, which has hindered joint action in Brussels. Instead, the pattern of interaction between public officials and private organizations has been more informal than institutionally entrenched, and the coordination of positions with regard to new EU policies has sometimes been lacking. The 'national position' defined by public officials in Brussels has thus not always coincided with the wishes of the private sector (Molins and Morata, 1993: 129).

To sum up, it can be concluded that Spain's EU policy has become progressively more influenced by domestic sources. Public opinion still maintains a large reserve of diffuse support in favour of European integration, although there is growing evidence of a more pragmatic response to the issue. As a result, political parties and public opinion have mutually influenced each other: the emergence of a more nationally focused discourse by parties (particularly in the PP) in response to the public's increasingly pragmatic responses to Europe has in turn further influenced public opinion. National lobbying within the EU has been weak, with unions and employers lacking a sufficiently consolidated institutional framework to make a significant impact within Europe. In contrast, highly specialized sectoral lobbies (for instance, agriculture and fisheries) have been highly visible and more able to influence government policy. As will be seen in the next chapter, formal institutional structures have been decisive in the definition of Spain's EU policy.

Chapter 3

Institutional Adaptation: Reshaping Political Structures

Membership of the European Union has naturally led to some change and adaptation within the Spanish executive, legislature and judiciary. However, institutional transformation and modification has been much more limited than actual policy changes. Where it has taken place, such institutional reorganization has tended to be reactive rather than proactive, and most frequent in those areas which deal with specific policy sectors. In the executive, the key player in EU decision-making, membership has prompted organizational as well as procedural changes. In regard to the legislature, EU membership has generated attitudinal rather than specific practical changes. The judiciary, meanwhile, has been obliged to make significant adaptations to ensure consistency of interpretation and application of laws emanating from EU institutions.

Morata (1996: 153) has argued that the integration process has had a negative impact on both the horizontal and the vertical division of powers. According to Molina (2001a), integration has served to reinforce the role of the core executive within the Spanish political system, placing it above parliament, parties and civil society, and has further bolstered the 'presidentialization' of Spain's policy style (see also, Heywood and Molina, 2000). Any overall assessment requires caution, however: on the one hand, it is the social and political context of membership (as described in Chapter 2), rather than the direct impact of EU membership, which has mainly accounted for the nature and scope of institutional transformation. On the other hand, as the example of Germany demonstrates, the process of European integration may stimulate institutional convergence, but at the same time may also reinforce distinctive national trends (Goetz, 1995).

The executive and national administration

Changes in Spain's national executive and administrative structure have had an impact in three domains. First, membership has prompted the creation of new bodies charged with directing Spanish European policy. Second, the scale and range of European policy initiatives have required all government departments to focus on EU issues and in turn underlined the need to establish some mechanism to ensure coordination between them. Finally, some government departments have introduced specific changes in order to adapt their internal structure to EU policies and processes. Overall, Europeanization has had an important impact on government and administration alike, yet it has not diluted the characteristic features of the Spanish system, such as the high level of departmentalization (Molina, 2001a). Figure 3.1 outlines the machinery and process of Spanish administration in EU affairs.

Central government and EU policy

The Spanish constitution assigns the government full responsibility over the direction of foreign policy, reflecting the fact that Spain's political structure is characterized by executive dominance (Heywood, 1999). The Lower House of the *Cortes*, the Congress, elects the prime minister (formally, the President of the Council of Ministers), but has no say in the appointment of ministers. The prime minister has the final responsibility for policies, including EU policy, a role that has been greatly enhanced by the salience of the European Council as a site of top-level bargaining since the early 1980s. In practice, Spain's European policy has often reflected the personal tastes of the premier (both Felipe González and José María Aznar) rather than any deep ideological or theoretical reflection (see Chapter 2). For instance, the close personal bond between Aznar and Tony Blair – based on shared conceptions of Europe and the Atlantic, reform of the welfare state, and a generational affinity (Barbé, 1999: 146) – has followed González's special relationships with Helmut Kohl and François Mitterrand. For a long time, these informal contacts lacked any institutional framework of support, with advice on foreign policy mainly channelled through the International and Defence Department in the Prime Minister's Office (Heywood and Molina, 2000). In 2000, Aznar created the Council of Foreign Affairs, an interdepartmental committee that he himself chaired. Its creation – which further underlined the presidentialization of EU policy – reflected the need both to coordinate the foreign activities of several ministries and also to enhance Spain's international standing.

Within the government, day-to-day dealing with EU affairs is

Figure 3.1 *The Spanish administration in EU policy-making*

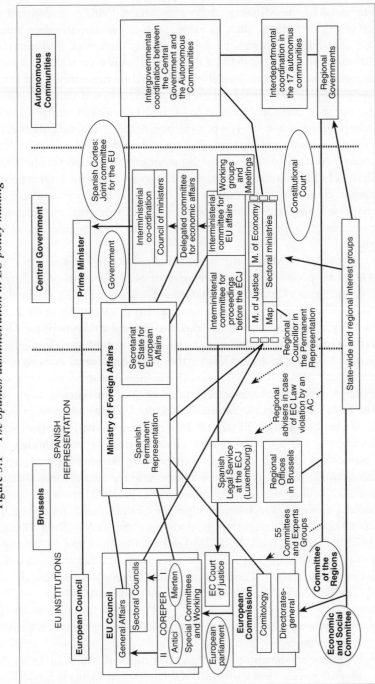

entrusted to the Ministry of Foreign Affairs (MAE). In contrast to other member states, such as France, there is no specific department for EU affairs, although in the late 1970s there was a Ministry of Relations with the EC (MRCE). The MRCE oversaw initial accession negotiations, following guidelines approved by the cabinet, but in the early 1980s it was dissolved and the MAE assumed the lead role in European affairs. In fact, the MAE had been dealing with Europe-related affairs since 1971, when the post of departmental under-secretary for European integration was created, with Raimundo Bassols as its first incumbent. The reestablishment of the primacy of the MAE derives both from the perception of European policy as 'international' rather than domestic politics (a feature which was particularly marked during accession negotiations), and from the constitutional principle of supporting a unified approach to the foreign policy of the state.

Within the MAE, the two principal bodies responsible for European policy are the Secretariat of State for European Affairs (*Secretaría de Estado para Asuntos Europeos*, SEAE), located in Madrid, and the Permanent Representation (REPER) in Brussels. Under the Socialist administrations, the internal structure of the MAE remained essentially unchanged. However, the PP governments of Aznar have made alterations to the MAE on several occasions. In 1996, the SEAE was merged with the Secretariat of the State for Foreign Affairs to create the Secretariat of State for Foreign Policy and the European Union (*Secretaría de Estado de Política Exterior y para la Unión Europea*, SEPEUE). Within this new body, EU affairs were handled at the lower level of a General Directorate. Although the justification offered for these changes was improved coordination between EU pillars, the merger in fact reflected an electoral commitment to reduce top-level administration. In 1998, the PP added a second General Directorate within the SEPEUE and, following the 2000 elections, brought them both into the SEAE (Real Decreto 557/2000 of 27 April. BOE 28 April 2000). Thus, the MAE saw a return to its traditional model of three secretaries of state, covering foreign affairs, the EU and international cooperation respectively.

The SEAE has the following functions (Molina, 2001a):

- To follow-up sectoral and general policies through the two General Directorates.
- To take decisions on judicial and institutional issues. In 1996, the new PP government disbanded the Directorate General for Judicial

and Institutional Coordination and transferred its activities to the Technical General Secretariat until, in 2000, a new sub-directorate was established.

- To maintain a permanent (and, in theory, exclusive) relationship with the REPER and Spanish administrative bodies, thereby acting as a mediating body.
- To participate in interdepartmental coordination mechanisms, as described below.

Below the SEAE are two further administrative levels which deal with the three 'pillars' of European co-operation established in the Maastricht Treaty. The General Secretariat for EU Affairs covers issues such as staffing, material support and so forth, and in turn comprises three General Directorates which generally deal with Pillar One (European Community, including the single market and single currency) issues. The first is the DG for Coordination of EU General Technical Affairs, and broadly deals with general affairs, trade and customs affairs and economic affairs respectively. The second is the DG for Coordination of the Internal Market and other Community Policies, which deals with issues of Agriculture and Fisheries; Transport, Communications and the Environment; Social, Cultural, Education, Health and Consumer affairs; and Judicial affairs. Finally, the third DG, created as part of the 2000 reform, covers European Foreign Policy. It aims to offer an institutional and strategic framework for Spain's 'European policy', comprising relations both with the EU and with each of the member states singly or in groups (Barbé, 1999; Ortega, 1995). There have been occasional initiatives to flesh out such a European policy: for instance, on the eve of the 1996 IGC, a seminar was held for 30 Spanish ambassadors (covering EU member states, EU applicant states, NATO members, as well as the EU itself, NATO, the OSCE, the WEU and Moscow). The seminar was conceived as an exercise in policy definition up to the year 2000, covering EU reform and enlargement, NATO reform, and financial reform.

The existence of separate General Directorates, outside the SEAE, which deal with Pillar Two (Common Foreign and Security Policy) and Pillar Three (Justice and Home Affairs) issues appears to run counter to policy coordination attempts. Nonetheless, the main impact of EU membership on Spain's executive and administrative structure has been the creation of coordination mechanisms. A number of factors, including the wide range of issues on which the EU engages its member states and the need to act at both national and EU levels, have reinforced demands for coordination (Kassim, Peters and Wright, 2000: 6). The MAE and the SEAE in particular have assumed the lead role in coordination (Dastis, 1995: 323). Yet, there is widespread agreement that poorly developed coordination capabilities of the SEAE represent a main weakness in Spain's administrative structure. The SEAE's lack of hierarchical authority over the units it has to coordinate, together with departmental fragmentation, has led to overload (Dastis, 1995; Zapico, 1995; MAP, 1997; Molina, 1999; Ordóñez, 1994). Against this background, informal coordination mechanisms assume greater importance than formal channels and processes. Such informal mechanisms (essentially, personal contacts) have been reinforced by the ethos of the SEAE itself, which has been staffed since its inception by a small team of officials who share a vocational attitude towards EU issues.

The second main body involved in the definition of Spain's European policy is the Permanent Representation (REPER), formally linked to the MAE since it has the status of an embassy. Its origins go back to a joint embassy in Belgium and the EC, held by the Count of Casa Miranda. In 1965, Alberto Ullastres was appointed as the first Spanish Ambassador solely to the EC. The Spanish REPER was established following accession in 1986, and its importance is underlined by the fact that it is the largest Spanish embassy (and indeed one of the largest among EU member states in Brussels). By 2002, all national ministries had officials located at the REPER. The size of the REPER derives from coordination requirements together with the desire of all ministries to have a large number of negotiators in Brussels. Other factors, such as the length of membership or geographical distance may also contribute to the scale of Spain's REPER (Kassim and Peters, 2001). The structure of the REPER mirrors ministerial organization in Spain, rather than mapping onto the EU's internal organization. Officials in Brussels operate within a culture that is inspired more by unity than by sectoral interests, and working patterns reflect this: there is a daily coordination meeting between the Permanent Representative, the Vice-Representative and the representatives of each ministerial department. Unity is further supported by the relative autonomy of REPER officials, who have on occasion engaged in negotiations (without reference to Madrid) with the Working Groups organized by the Commission (Zapico, 1995: 57). The officials' specialist knowledge of the Community machinery enables them to advise central government, even to the point of sometimes having to issue instructions to themselves either through a lack of any lead from Madrid or because of the need to be flexible during negotiations.

Although the REPER and the SEAE have assumed the lead role as promoters and negotiators of Spain's EU policies, the policy process still reflects a certain lack of coordination. The EU's decision-making structure has been seen by some as reinforcing a tendency towards departmentalization in the Spanish administration (Molina, 1997; Dastis, 1995). Moreover, Dastis (1995: 349) has argued that practical operation and efficacy have been steadily eroded, to the point where the utility of some coordinating mechanisms can be called into question. The main defect lies in the unsatisfactory procedures for the circulation of information.

A number of reasons account for such shortcomings. First, the functional specialization implicit in the enormous range of Community policies has been built upon by each ministerial department following its own criteria. Sectoral departments have progressively abandoned the status quo created during the long accession negotiations, which consolidated the role of both the SEAE and the REPER as the key interpreters of Spanish national interest. During those negotiations, Spain's bargaining position was tightly controlled, involving a small group of senior civil servants whose authority was enhanced by the predominant role played by the executive in the Spanish policy-making process (Heywood, 1999). Moreover, the principle of an exclusive vertical relationship between the Ministry for EC Relations (MRCE) and the REPER was well-established, and only exceptionally was direct communication allowed between the REPER members and their respective ministries. The disappearance of the MRCE (whose *raison d'être* was precisely the centralisation of EU affairs) made it more difficult for the remaining departments to accept the leadership of the MAE, which historically has not been one of the powerful departments within Spanish government.

Following accession, the different ministries gradually began to develop sufficient experience and confidence to act by themselves in the EU arena, without feeling the need for external orientation or coordination. The direct involvement of ministerial negotiators from the early stages of community policy initiatives (for instance, within the Working Groups) gave rise to vertical networks rather than horizontal ones. It should be noted that the final decision on Spain's position usually lies in the hands of the minister with functional

Table 3.1   *The Spanish network for EU policy-making*

Party in office	Ministry of Foreign Affairs	Ministry for Relations with the EC (1978–81)	Secretary of State for the EU
UCD (1976–82)	Marcelino Oreja (1976–80)	Leopoldo Calvo Sotelo (1978–80)	
		Eduardo Punset (1980–81)	
PSOE (1982–96)	José Pedro Pérez Llorca (1980–82)		Raimundo Bassols (1981–82)
	Fernando Morán (1982–85)		Manuel Marín (1982–86)
	Francisco Fernández Ordóñez (1985–92) Javier Solana (1992–95) Carlos Westendorp (1995–96)		Pedro Solbes (1985–1991) Carlos Westendorp (1991–94) Emilio Fernández-Castaño (1995–96)
PP (1996–present)	Abel Matutes (1996–2000) Josep Piqúe (2000–2002) Ana Palacio (2002–)		Ramón de Miguel (1996–2000)

Source: Authors' own adaptation of various newspaper and government sources.

competence on the issue in question, thereby underlining the importance of coordination mechanisms.

In spite of the obstacles to vertical coordination, some administrative features have been introduced to help ameliorate the situation. Thus, public officials from almost all ministerial departments staff the SEAE and the REPER, imparting to both of them (particularly the former) a special character as islands of efficiency and horizontal communication rarely found in Spanish public administration. One of the most salient features of Spain's EU administration has been the consolidation of a policy network of top-level officials and other key actors. A thick web of personal links and professional relationships supports a relatively small group of people responsible for Spanish EU policy. Continuity and rotation between top posts related to EU affairs has been essential for the development of this network (see Table 3.1), as well as an ethos of a highly technocratic policy function somewhat removed from day-to-day political struggles. The defence of Spain's national interest (as well as a deep understanding of the process of European integration) serves as the *leitmotif* of the

Table 3.1 cont.

Permanent Representative	Commissioners	Director Generals
Raimundo Bassols (1976–81)		
Gabriel Ferrán (1981–82)		
Carlos Westendorp (1985–91)	**Membership commenced 1 January 1986**	
Camilo Barcia (1991–94)	Manuel Marín (1986–99) Abel Matutes (1986–95) Marcelino Oreja (1995–99)	Eneko Landáburu (1987–96) Eduardo Peña Abizanda (1990–91) Segismundo Crespo (1992–93) Ramón de Miguel (1995–96)
Javier Elorza (1994–2000) Francisco Javier Conde de Saro (2000–02) Carlos Bastarreche (2002–)	Pedro Solbes (1999–) Loyola de Palacio (1999–)	Eneko Landáburu (1996–) Pablo Benavides (1996–2000) José Manuel Silva (2000–) Luis Romero (2002–)

network (thereby contributing to the sense of a Trojan horse, discussed in Chapter 5). However, relations have not always been marked by perfect harmony and differences have occasionally emerged on important issues. For instance, there were disagreements between Spaniards within the Commission and national officials over the budgetary package accompanying EMU. Those in Brussels preferred a reduction in VAT contributions, whilst those in Madrid favoured instead a larger share of Community funds (Bernárdez, 1995: 228).

Intra-administrative coordinating mechanisms

There are two different dimensions to Spain's intra-administrative coordinating mechanisms. One involves the relationship between the centre and the 17 Autonomous Communities (described in Chapter 4). The other relates to the coordination between different departments within the central administration. The coordination model adopted relies on standing committees of ministerial rank, three of which have functions related to EU affairs: two are policy-oriented committees and the third deals exclusively with EU judicial affairs.

The only horizontal or intra-administrative committee specialized in EU affairs is the *Comisión Interministerial para la Unión Europea*, whose function is to coordinate the Spanish position when the interests of several departments are involved. The Secretary of State for the EU (that is, the head of the SEAE) chairs the committee, which has two vice-chairs drawn from the Ministry of the Economy and the Ministry of Foreign Affairs, and is composed of senior representatives from all ministerial departments. In practice, the committee has been characterized by a high degree of delegation, which – together with the large membership – reduces its political relevance and efficiency as well as increasing coordination problems (Dastis, 1995: 325; MAP, 1997: 168; Molina, 1999). Moreover, the committee has tended to focus on discussion of topical issues of immediate moment rather than long-term strategic ones (Morata, 1998: 389; Ordóñez, 1994: 378).

A second committee is the *Comisión Delegada del Gobierno para Asuntos Económicos*, which does not specialize in EU affairs, but is nonetheless powerful as it deals with economic policy in general. The Ministry of the Economy (MEH) plays the lead role in this committee, both providing the chair and also setting the agenda, but the presence of two top officials provides for an informal link with the *Comisión Interministerial para la Unión Europea*. Standing members of the *Comisión Delegada* include the Head of the Prime Minister's Private Office, the General Secretaries of Finance, of Trade, and of Fisheries, and the Under-Secretaries of Agriculture, Fisheries and Food, of Industry and Energy, and of Employment and Social Security. Representatives from other government departments can attend meetings when issues of relevance to them are being discussed. The importance of the Ministry of the Economy in EU matters has grown in parallel to the implementation of the EU's and Spain's own liberalization programmes. Indeed, the MEH has on occasion had to defend its line against other departments which have sought to negotiate delays in liberalization measures (Fernández Ordóñez, 1999: 647).

The elaborately titled *Comisión Interministerial de Seguimiento y Coordinación de las Actuaciones Relacionadas con la Defensa del Estado Español ante el Tribunal de Justicia de las Comunidades Europeas* (Monitoring and Coordinating Committee for Defence of the Spanish State in relation to the European Court of Justice) specializes in EU judicial affairs. The Committee is staffed by representatives from the Prime Minister's Office, the Ministries of Justice and of the Economy, and also other concerned departments on an *ad hoc* basis. It examines all proceedings brought against Spain, as well as any others that could affect Spanish interests. Again, coordination is complicated by the artificial separation between the initial phase, which involves Commission notices of infringement of EU legislation, and the formal judicial phase, which involves the Spanish state acting as such. The first phase is handled by the relevant department with the SEAE, while the latter falls within the remit of the Attorney General, located in the Ministry of Justice.

On occasion, governments have created *ad hoc* committees for specific tasks. In 1993, an inter-ministerial committee was set up to prepare and coordinate the Spanish position during the accession negotiations of the Nordic members and Austria. Its proposals were submitted to the two standing committees referred to above (Elorza, 1995). Another committee, established in 1997 and chaired by the Minister of the Economy, was tasked with coordinating the introduction of the euro. That same year, a further committee was entrusted with drafting Spain's position in the Agenda 2000 negotiations. Inter-ministerial committees have also prepared Spanish presidencies of the EU, and a Support Unit, headed by Alfonso Dastis, was established to support the January–June 2002 Presidency.

High-level coordination may also be carried out, of course, within the Council of Ministers (and the preparatory meetings of the Committee of Under-Secretaries). Within the Council of Ministers, the Minister of Foreign Affairs plays a secondary role compared more powerful colleagues, or when there are other political imperatives. For instance, in 1996 the Aznar government approved a decree on digital television for political reasons, in spite of warnings from Foreign Affairs that it may contravene European rules.

Vincent Wright (1996: 165) argued that, given the difficulties of coordination, it is surprising how much actually seems to take place. Yet, whilst coordination may be important in some respects, its absence does not appear to be overly disruptive or dysfunctional. Indeed, Wright suggests that a lack of coordination, or inadequate coordination, may even be functional – not just in ensuring latitude at the bargaining table, but also in terms of policy adjustment, allowing legal compliance or street-level implementation to be phased in over a more prolonged and politically palatable period.

Internal changes in ministerial departments

Spain's administrative structure has gone through a process of change that has made it resemble other member states much more than was the case in 1986. This process has been influenced both by EU membership itself and, in parallel, the introduction of new public management techniques (Molina, 1997). The influence of EU membership can be seen through Spanish administrative structures being shaped in line with EU policies, although there has not been such an obvious impact on working procedures and processes. A low level of specialization on EU affairs is still seen to be a general characteristic of Spain's bureaucracy. Moreover, administrative recruitment and training has not incorporated any requirement of familiarity with EU matters (such as Community law) or command of other European languages. A Ministry of Public Administration document recognized explicitly that Spanish bureaucrats have a low level of foreign language skills, scant training in negotiation techniques, limited experience of network organizations and an unwillingness to leave home (MAP, 1997: 176).

Nonetheless, EU membership has prompted the creation and design of government portfolios which are more consistent with EU policies. For instance, Commission pressure was a key factor in the eventual establishment of a Ministry of the Environment in 1996, a portfolio which had been absent in Spain up to that point. However, the Commission insisted on being able to deal with a relevant counterpart in the Spanish government and this led first to the creation in 1990 of a Secretary General for the Environment within the Ministry of Public Works (MOPU), upgraded subsequently to Secretary of State for Water and Environmental Policy. In 1993, environment was accorded ministerial rank within the Ministry of Public Works and Urban Policy and, finally, in 1996, it was established as a separate ministerial department.

The EU also exercised some influence on the 1991 merger of the Ministry of Public Works with the Ministry of Transport and Telecommunications. This merger aimed at promoting a consistent policy on regional and territorial development, and at improving efficiency in the coordination of EU structural funds by centralizing them within a single department, the renamed Ministry of Development (*Fomento*). A third case of EU influence can be seen with the creation in April 2000 of the Ministry of Science and Technology, which replaced the historic Ministry of Industry and Energy, and reflected a shift from economic *dirigisme* towards the promotion of the so-called new economy based on the knowledge society.

The second, and perhaps more obvious, impact of EU membership has been the internal reorganization of ministerial departments, usually involving an adaptation of functions to match specific EU policies. Although there are no specific units within each department which manage EU related affairs, which have instead been handled by Technical General Secretariats (*Secretarías Generales Técnicas*), many departments have set up new bodies to monitor specific EU policies. Thus, for instance, a unit in charge of managing infrastructure investments was created within the Ministry of Public Works (MOPU), reflecting the importance of Community funds in this area. In the former Ministry of Industry and Energy, directorates shifted from mirroring public-owned corporations, such as shipbuilding and steel, to adopting more functionally derived roles, such as R&D, or small and medium enterprises. By the same token, the Ministry of Agriculture and Fisheries was reorganized in 1991 to match the structure of the Common Agricultural Policy (CAP), with four new functional general secretariats created to cover food policy, agricultural structure and production, agricultural markets, and fisheries. The PP government merged the first three of these, as part of its policy of streamlining top offices. Elsewhere, EU membership prompted the creation of *ad hoc* units, such as the State Secretariat for Budgets and Public Expenditure (*Secretaría de Estado de Presupuestos y Gasto Público*) set up by the PP in 1996 within the Ministry of the Economy to ensure that Spain's budgetary and fiscal policy remained in line with the convergence criteria for EMU.

Finally, a third clear impact of EU membership is that certain aspects traditionally within the domain of the Ministry of the Economy have assumed greater autonomy. An obvious example, resulting from EMU, is the Bank of Spain, but there have also been new agencies created – for instance, in defence of competition, reflecting a need to modernize and adapt Spain's administrative structures.

Implementation

When Spain joined the EU, doubts were cast over the commitment and capacity of the Spanish authorities to implement EU legislation. Yet, indicators from the Commission's General Secretariat convey a somewhat different picture. First, Spain has an impressive record on the implementation of directives, at least in recent years: between

2000 and 2002, the implementation rate ranged between 90 and 98 per cent. In comparative terms, Spain over this period usually ranked second behind Denmark and, on occasion, third. However, if we look at a second indicator, the number of cases under examination by the Commission for presumed non-compliance, the picture changes substantially. In July 2001, for instance, Spain had the highest number of cases. Significantly, of the three possible sources for Commission scrutiny (its own initiative, complaints by others, or a failure to communicate implementation of directives), a large proportion of the Spanish cases stem from complaints – of which a disproportionate number (66.5 per cent) concern the environment. Investigations into environmental cases are not uncommon in the EU, but the proportion in Spain is noteworthy. The third indicator concerns actual infringement procedures initiated by the Commission. Here, once more the picture changes substantially: as of July 2001, Spain had the lowest rate of investigated cases which had led to formal infringement procedures (31 per cent) and also one of the lowest rates of cases referred to the European Court of Justice (4.74 per cent) as a proportion of the total number. Table 3.2 confirms this trend: in spite of receiving around 10 per cent of the EU's letters of formal notice, Spain accounts for a far smaller proportion of cases actually brought to the ECJ. It appears that Spanish authorities may require Commission warnings to implement EU legislation, but they then opt for implementation rather than face judicial procedures in the ECJ.

The role of the Cortes (the Spanish Parliament)

EU membership has an immediate impact on national parliaments, given the need to transfer legislative autonomy over a wide range of issues. Such transfers are mainly to the European Council and, to a lesser extent, the European Parliament; they usually entail a strengthening of national executives *vis-à-vis* their national parliaments, thereby contributing to concerns about the so-called democratic deficit. In the Spanish case, the democratic deficit is more marked because the members of the Council do not need to be elected representatives. However, evidence suggests that, despite the transfer of powers to the EU, the existing equilibrium between executive and parliament in Spain has not been substantially altered by EU membership, since the system was already strongly biased in favour of the executive (Pérez Tremps, 1991: 93–104; Heywood, 1999).

Table 3.2 *Infringement procedures against Spain compared with EU total*

		1986	1987	1988	1989	1990	1991	1992	1993
Letters of formal notice	Spain	22	32	31	53	114	79	129	107
	EU	–				962	853	1271	1209
Reasoned opinions	Spain	–	8	11	8	15	30	39	28
	EU					279	411	248	352
Referrals to the ECJ	Spain	–	1	1	5	3	2	5	5
	EU					78	65	64	44

		1994	1995	1996	1997	1998	1999	2000	2001
Letters of formal notice	Spain	86	81	59	104	78	72	93	65
	EU	974	1016	1142	1461	1101	1075	1317	1050
Reasoned opinions	Spain	53	15	30	23	36	21	32	32
	EU	546	192	435	334	675	460	460	460
Referrals to the ECJ	Spain	9	6	9	7	6	7	8	14
	EU	89	72	92	121	123	178	172	162

Source: Data from EU Commission, Annual Reports on the Application of Community Law in Member States (4th – 19th Reports).

The Spanish Constitution does specify a role for the *Cortes* in foreign affairs, assigning it jointly with the government the task of guaranteeing the fulfilment of international obligations. In practical terms, though, most commentators agree that the role of the Spanish parliament in the adoption of EU rules and directives has been insufficient and barely visible to the public (Molina del Pozo, 1995: 151). Indeed, Spain's accession to the EU has outstripped the capacity of the *Cortes* to react (Cienfuegos, 1996: 83).

The limited role of the *Cortes* does not result exclusively from its institutional design. It is true that in institutional terms, Spain's parliament strongly favours the majority party (and, hence, the government) through devices such as the constructive motion of no-confidence or weakened control mechanisms (Heywood, 1995: 83–102). Weak control affects European policy as much as any other policy. An additional factor, though, is the predominant perception of European policy as forming part of Spain's foreign policy, on which the Constitution entrusts the government with the leading role. Against this background, the institutional position of Spanish *Cortes* tends towards seeking information and hoping to influence the government over policy-making. A third and decisive factor has been the strong pro-integrationist consensus (see Chapter 2). Rather than serving as an arena for debating EU affairs, the Spanish *Cortes* has generally acted to provide domestic support for the government's negotiating positions in Brussels.

General instruments for parliamentary involvement with EU affairs

Of the three traditional parliamentary powers – legislative, budgetary and executive oversight – EU membership most directly affects the first. The Spanish *Cortes*, in common with other national parliaments within the EU, lacks the power to reject or alter Community legislation. There is some margin for manoeuvre when implementing directives which outline broad objectives but allow national authorities to establish the means to achieve them. However, since most EU directives have a highly technical character, their implementation in Spain, as in other member states, has been predominantly an administrative task.

From a parliamentary perspective, therefore, the bulk of EU-related affairs falls within the orbit of information and oversight. The Spanish *Cortes* has a repertory of instruments for oversight and information in relation to EU matters: the formal authorization of international treaties; questions to the government; elaboration of programmes, plans and communications; reports; formal hearings; and the creation of specialist committees (Cienfuegos, 1996). However, as in most parliaments in EU member states, the tendency in Spain has been to set up specific bodies to deal with information and oversight functions on EU matters. The main parliament has adopted a subsidiary role, limiting its intervention to the most important and topical issues.

Parliament's most significant role concerns the ratification of international treaties. This is one of the few parliamentary powers not undermined by EU membership and gives the *Cortes* a degree of control over major EU constitutional decisions, such as reform and enlargement. The fact that ratification votes must be supported by an absolute majority provides extra strength to this potential instrument of control. Indeed, on a number of occasions the *Cortes* has threatened to veto enlargement; for instance, over the accession of Norway, or reform as in the case of the 1996 Intergovernmental Conference (IGC) should Spanish interests not be accommodated. However, rather than acting as a control on government, parliamentary ratification of EU treaties has become a useful device to strengthen the government's negotiating position *vis-à-vis* other EU partners. The conditions laid down by the *Cortes* to ensure ratification have in fact coincided with the Spanish executive's own concerns.

A second source of information, which also acts as a form of oversight, is the Prime Minister's address to parliament after every European summit. These addresses were initiated as an informal custom by Felipe González and have come to acquire the character of an unavoidable necessity, not least because the growing awareness amongst the public, the media and politicians of the importance of European Council decisions. Inevitably, such a procedure contributes to a certain presidentalisation of EU policy.

The parliamentary Joint Committee for EU Affairs

The principal specialist parliamentary body dealing with EU matters is the Joint Committee for EU Affairs (*Comisión Mixta del Congreso y el Senado para la UE*). Created in 1985 and modified in 1994, it has a different status to other standing committees of either chamber, since it was established by law rather than through the parliament's internal rules of procedure. Such a status gives the committee greater stability, but also means that the government's assent is essential for modifying its design. The unusual institutional relationship thus reinforces consensus and unity in the field of European policy, at the expense of parliamentary autonomy.

The joint committee submits a report on its activities to both chambers during each parliamentary session. These reports cover the following specific functions:

- *Oversight of the government.* The government is required by law to report to the Joint Committee for EU affairs, which also issues written questions and holds hearings. Government guidelines for European policy and a report on the activities of each presidency are included in the information that must be provided. In practical terms, oversight results more from government initiatives, since ministers and top officials have adopted the practice of asking for hearings, rather than awaiting an invitation from the committee. Moreover, hearings tend to have a general character and are relatively relaxed debates in which government officials control the sources of information.

- *Information on EU legislation.* Initially, the government was required to provide information only on those aspects of Community legislation which would explicitly affect parliament's own powers (mainly, fundamental rights and freedoms). Since this excluded the majority of Community rules, the joint committee was also permitted to look at projects for Regulations, Directives and Decisions which had been submitted for discussion to the European Council. Since 1994, the government has been required to submit a report on each of these areas and their likely impact on Spain. In order to enhance the committee's role it has been suggested that it should develop closer ties to European Commission committees and working groups, as well as draft reports on planned directives and regulations (Molina del Pozo, 1995: 157).

- *Information on the implementation of Community rules.* The rules in question were those relating to the implementation of the Community *acquis* that Spain had to adopt immediately after accession. However, since 1988 the focus has expanded to include European Council agreements, and the government can be asked to explain Council negotiations around a specific proposal. In contrast to other standing committees, though, the joint committee lacks legislative competence. Instead, policy-focused parliamentary standing committees (for instance, on agriculture or energy) deal with any legislation required for the implementation of EC directives. The result has been a certain fragmentation and also some disputes over who should have competence to deal with certain issues, but it has also led to the joint committee having a more political profile and a rather less technical role.

* *Creation of sub-committees (Ponencias)*. The sub-committees are entrusted with the study and follow-up of specific issues. *Ad hoc* sub-committees have reported on successive EU reforms, covering EMU, political union, enlargement and the 1996 IGC. Whereas the sub-committees on EMU and political union held relatively few hearings and presented their reports after the 1991 IGC was concluded, reform of the Maastricht Treaty was monitored closely during 1996 and 1997, leading to a much more substantial input, both in quantity and quality. The operation of the sub-committees underline two characteristic features of Spanish foreign policy: its consensual nature and the tight network of personal links among a small group of officials and politicians. To take one example, the report entitled *Consequences for Spain of the enlargement of the European Union and its institutional reforms* (1995) supported the government's line, and provided an explicit statement of Spain's national interest (Rodrigo, 1996: 26). The report explicitly rejected the idea of a 'hard core' around EMU (at that time, there were fears that Spain would not qualify), called for the gradual introduction of the principle of relative prosperity to the EU budget, and supported the operation of the CAP and structural funds (Comisión Mixta, 1995). The conclusions were strikingly similar to those of the Ministry of Foreign Affairs committee in preparation for the 1996 IGC (see Chapter 5). Following the 2000 general elections, three further sub-committees were set up to cover the 2000 IGC, to monitor preparations for the 2004 IGC on the future of the EU, and to monitor the process of EU enlargement.

The same kind of personal network that permeates and structures the relationship between the Spanish administration and Spanish officials in Brussels, described above, is also evident in the joint committee. Thus, former Foreign Affairs Ministers and Secretaries of State for the EU, Marcelino Oreja Aguirre and Pedro Solbes, have both chaired the committee, helping promote detailed knowledge of the Community arena as well as enhancing the consensual character of European policy. To sum up, the joint committee has a limited oversight or control capacity, and instead serves mainly as an arena for information and debate (Molina del Pozo, 1995; Cienfuegos, 1996, 1997). The main reason for this is the widespread agreement on European issues among almost all parliamentary groups (Closa, 1996).

Judicial politics: Spanish courts and European integration

Europeanization (domestic changes brought about by the integration process) has probably been most evident through substantive modifications in the law. Indeed, the transformation of Spanish law as a result of EU legislation has been described as a 'slow and quiet revolution' (Cazorla, 1997). Changes in the law affect the institutional machinery for elaborating and implementing policies, but EU membership also impinges upon domestic structures for legal adjudication. As is widely recognized, the success of the integration process has derived to a great extent from the willingness of national courts to apply European law.

In the Spanish case, European integration has also meant a slow change of judicial terms, concepts and categories and the incorporation of, for instance, Anglo-Saxon or German legal influences. In exploring the role of courts as actors with political significance, we need to draw a clear distinction between ordinary and constitutional courts. The Spanish political system is characterized by a specific constitutional jurisdiction, separated from normal courts (a model similar to the German one). Although European law and the ECJ case law have singled out ordinary courts as the main actors in the adjudication of their rulings, the Constitutional Court still has a role in adjudication.

The Constitutional Court and European integration

Spain's 1978 Constitution was drawn up with an eye to EU membership, and therefore contains a general clause (Article 93) enabling accession, albeit a very vague one. This general clause has become increasingly insufficient for three reasons. First, the bland wording does not reflect the pro-integrationist attitude of Spanish political parties and public opinion. Secondly, by contrast, nor does it set any eventual limit to the integration process, thereby indirectly empowering the Constitutional Court to interpret any such limit (as in the German case). Thirdly, the open character of Article 93 (and a prevailing climate of permissive consensus) has allowed for what has been called a 'constitutional mutation' – that is, a change in the spirit of the Constitution without any formal process of amendment (Muñoz Machado, 1993). Several commentators locate such a mutation in alleged changes in Spain's basic economic principles, deriving from EU membership (Story and Grugel, 1991).

In general, there has been a marked reluctance to modify Spain's Constitution to match the profound changes which took place in the EU during the 1990s. Even by 2002, the only constitutional reform amounted to a single word being added to enable EU citizens to vote in local and European Parliament elections. This resistance to constitutional reform derives mainly from the almost fetishistic character of the 1978 Constitution, the founding myth of the transition from divisive dictatorship into a successful and above all consensual democracy. Any change to the Constitution could be seen as altering that compromise, and thereby jeopardizing one of the key transition principles which, alongside EU membership, serves as a symbol of Spain's modern identity.

The role of the Spanish constitutional court thus has to be seen against this political background. Of course, constitutional courts have always been important actors in domestic EU politics, and have often appealed to their role as guardians of constitutional propriety in an attempt to assert the supremacy of constitutional law over community law. Indeed, no constitutional court has openly recognized the supremacy of EC law over constitutional law. After the Maastricht Treaty, constitutional courts engaged in what effectively amounted to a race to identify constitutional limits to the integration process, partly in a bid to establish their role as domestic watchdogs of European integration.

The Spanish constitutional court has not been particularly assertive in claiming its right to scrutinize EC law to check its conformity with fundamental constitutional values. But this does not mean that the court is out of step with its European equivalents. On the contrary, the Spanish constitutional court has made its opinion clear that European Community law lacks constitutional standing. The Court merely recognized the supremacy of Community law over domestic law at infra-constitutional level and EC law has been deemed infra-constitutional. Two consequences follow for judicial politics. First, the Constitutional Court does not see itself as a vehicle for the application of Community law (López Castillo, 1998): in a 1991 ruling, it explicitly stated that Community law has its own organs and the Spanish constitutional court is not one of them. Adjudication on EC law thus belongs to normal courts. This stance indirectly affects the quality of EC law: even though the Court has recognized the special character of Community law, infractions of EC law are not deemed to be unconstitutional (López Castillo, 1998: 199–212).

A second consequence is that Spanish authorities, including judges, are bound by the 1978 Constitution, which enjoys unconditional supremacy. This interpretation, of course, provides grounds for constitutional court activism. In a 1992 judgement following a government petition on the constitutionality of the Maastricht Treaty, the Court went further in its interpretation of the provisions than the government had sought (Díez Picazo, 1998: 265). It also found an opportunity to set limits to the integration process, prohibiting implicit or latent reforms of the Constitution. Thus, like its counterparts in other member states, the Constitutional Court has established itself as a guardian of the integration process in Spain.

Judicial adjudication of EC law

The success of European integration has been largely dependent upon the commitment of member states to respect the rule of law and the readiness of national courts to apply EU law. In this regard, the attitude of Spanish judges has been described as one of collaboration rather than conflict (Pérez Tremps, 1999). Adjudication can be assessed through an empirical analysis of court rulings in which EC law has been applied or through the use of pre-judicial questions. On the first of these, judicial pronouncements in Spain have increasingly appealed to EU law (Valle and Fajardo, 1999: 110; López and Cuesta, 1999: 395) and Spanish courts have progressively incorporated the principles of the primacy and direct applicability of EU law and directives.

Pre-judicial questions are the mechanism by which national courts interrogate the ECJ on the interpretation of EU law in its application to a specific case. Spanish use of pre-judicial questions is summarized in Table 3.3, which shows that they have not been extensively used. Some have suggested this low usage may reflect the attitude of the Constitutional Court (López Castillo, 1998: 212), but it is also interesting to note that use of pre-judicial questions seems to depend on location within the Spanish judicial hierarchy. Thus, the *Tribunal Supremo* (Supreme Court) has very rarely made use of the pre-judicial question, in contrast to the Autonomous Community High Courts. It should be noted that these latter are not autonomous judicial bodies,

Table 3.3 *Pre-judicial questions referred by Spain, compared with EU total*

	1986	1987	1988	1989	1990	1991	1992	1993
Spain (Supreme Court)	–	–	–	–	–	–	4	3
Spain (total)	–	1	1	2	6	4	5	7
EU total			256	239	142	186	162	204

	1994	1995	1996	1997	1998	1999	2000	2001
Spain (Supreme Court)	5	–	6	5	1	2	2	2
Spain (total)	13	10	6	9	55	4	5	4
EU total	203	251	256	239	264	255	224	237

Source: Data adapted from EU Commission, Annual Reports on the Application of Community Law in Member States.

as opposed to the regional organizations of single judicial power, but it does underline their level of awareness of EU legal frameworks (Roldán and Hinojosa, 1997: 575).

In regard to the impact of pre-judicial questions, some have provided grounds to strengthen ECJ case law (Díez Peralta, 2001): for instance, the Micheletti case (a pre-judicial question put by the Supreme Court of Cantabria) allowed the ECJ to establish that EU law must be respected by the nationality laws in member states. Spanish Courts have also progressively incorporated principles from the judicial traditions of other member stares via ECJ case law, such as the principle of legitimate confidence derived from Germany (Valle and Fajardo, 1999: 125).

Finally, mention should be made of the Court for the Defence of Competition (*Tribunal de Defensa de la Competencia*), an administrative court charged with scrutinizing and monitoring competition policy and which relies extensively on EU law as the basis for interpretation in its rulings (Roldán and Hinojosa, 1997: 559).

To sum up, then, Spain's membership of the European Union has given rise to a series of adaptations within the executive and legislative branches of government, as well as in the judiciary. Whilst these have been relatively modest, and usually made in response to events rather than in anticipation of them, they nonetheless reflect a process of 'Europeanization' which has been most obvious at the level of actual policy. In general terms, Spain's national policy style – characterized by a strong executive and with few opportunities for peak associations and interest groups to influence decision-making processes – has remained broadly unaffected by membership of the EU. However, as we shall see in the next chapter, the situation in regard to the national government's institutional relationship with the Autonomous Communities presents a more complex picture.

Chapter 4

Territorial Politics: The Autonomous Communities and Europe

For some, one of the most positive impacts of European integration is that it may lead to the eventual transformation of the territorial structure of nation-states within the EU. It is certainly the case that EU membership has added an extra resource to the opportunity structures of sub-state regions within member states. Specifically, two factors have enhanced the role of regions. First, the range of powers within the Union affects not just the powers of regions, but also their relationship with central governments. This occurs both during the so-called 'upstream stage' (when the national position is elaborated and EU legislation is drafted), and in the 'downstream stage' (when EU measures have to be implemented). Second, EU regional policy assigns an active role to regions, which has progressively grown. The 1988 reform of the structural funds (the Delors I package) introduced the partnership principle between three levels of government – regions, national states and the EU – for the development of regional policy. In addition, the Committee of the Regions and the principle of subsidiarity are often seen as extra resources for the empowerment of regions. Taken together, these developments point towards a deep change in the territorial structure of the EU, giving rise to what has been called a 'Europe of the Regions'.

However, such as assessment should be qualified. Despite the greater role for regions in general, socio-economic heterogeneity and the marked political, administrative and financial differences between European regions calls into question the existence of a general model throughout the EU in which regions play a leading political part. Moreover, the constant appeal to a 'Europe of the Regions' has been described as not so much an accurate account of actual developments but rather a dogmatic attempt to justify an increase in powers for sub-national entities (Borras *et al.*, 1994: 1). Instead, many scholars favour a 'multilevel governance' model, characterized by the sharing of authority and policy-making influence across sub-national, national and supra-national levels (Marks, 1993, 1997; Marks *et al.*, 1996; Hooghe, 1996; Scharpf, 1994, 1997; Morata, 2000: 184–5).

Against this background, it is logical to assume that European integration should have had a substantial impact on Spain's regional model and territorial politics. The asymmetric territorial structure which resulted from the 1978 Spanish Constitution does not easily fit the usual models of federalism and/or unitary state. The so-called State of the Autonomies is a hybrid that attempts to meet three different (and to some extent contradictory) demands: first, the continued unity of the Spanish nation, inherited from its history as a strongly centralized state. Second, the recognition of the right to self-government of those regions with a strong sense of national identity (the so-called 'historic nationalities' of the Basque Country, Catalonia and Galicia). Third, the option for decentralization for other regions which aspired to autonomous self-government. This model gave rise to the creation of 17 Autonomous Communities, with varying degrees of political competency according to individually negotiated statutes (Heywood, 2000).

Spain's Autonomous Communities (ACs) have varying degrees of power, with a few enjoying significant political autonomy and the remainder mainly administrative autonomy. In general, though, they are empowered to deal with a broad range of issues: economic and territorial planning, public works, housing, transport, tourism, environment, small trade and industry, agriculture and fisheries, social policy (health, consumer rights and social services), education, the media. They have also varying degrees of financial autonomy: in most cases, ACs have significant control over spending, but the central state retains effective control over financing, with intergovernmental transfers remaining the most important component of revenue. As with federal systems, conflicts between governmental levels are resolved by the Constitutional Court. Each AC has a regional parliament directly elected for a period of four years, and an executive accountable to the parliament. However, in contrast to federal systems, the Spanish Senate was not designed as a chamber for representation of the regions, although reform has been on the political agenda in Spain for several years.

This chapter analyses how regional administrations have adapted to EU membership, explores channels for AC participation in European decision-making, and assesses the impact of EU policies (notably, structural policies) on Spanish territorial politics.

Defining the role of Autonomous Communities within the EU

Two main factors shape the role of the Autonomous Communities within the EU. First, in contrast to Germany, Austria or Belgium, there is no explicit constitutional entitlement allowing for AC participation in foreign affairs in general and EU affairs in particular. At the same time, EU membership has had a negative impact on AC competencies in the areas of agriculture, fisheries, industrial policy, environment, regional planning, transport, energy policy, fiscal policy and culture, reducing the autonomy of regional governments either directly or else through the fact that central government has exclusive rights to decide on these issues within EU bodies (Colino, 2001). Second, therefore, Spanish membership of the EU has impinged on the domestic distribution of powers between levels of government, although this has not been exclusively against AC interests.

In practice, ACs have acquired a growing role both in international affairs in general and EU affairs in particular. In both cases, the ambiguities of the Spanish Constitution initially led to conflicts with the central government, which questioned the role of the ACs. However, whilst the Spanish Constitution grants the central government exclusive power over international affairs, this very general and unqualified attribution makes no reference to a whole series of activities (from trade to culture) that impact on international relations, and which fall within the remit of ACs. At first sight, therefore, two images of the Spanish state appear to be superimposed upon each other: an internal one which reflects the existence of a complex system of regional autonomy, and an external one which sees the Spanish state as a unitary actor in foreign policy terms (García, 1995: 25).

Of course, the reality of Spain's relations with the EU somewhat belies this initial impression. The individual Statutes of Autonomy go further than the Constitution in outlining the competencies of the regions in international matters, thereby generating an apparent mismatch between the external activities of ACs as authorized in their Statutes and the constitutional grounds for these. The Constitutional Court resolved this conflict pragmatically by authorizing AC activity in international affairs so long as it does not compromise the unity of Spanish foreign policy.

More important is the impact of EU policies on the distribution of competencies between central government and regions. On environmental policy, for instance, central government is the sole negotiator in the EU and the internal coordinator, yet implementation is an AC responsibility. Such an intermingling of levels of government on specific policies can produce in the case of more assertive regions, such as Catalonia, a change in the model of intergovernmental relations within the EU. What emerges is a form of 'territorial complexity' defined by the interaction of four levels of government (EU, national, regional or local): which of these levels is dominant at any given moment depends on the policy stage (such as formulation, regulation or implementation) and policy sector in question. The so-called 'emerging' policy areas (environment, immigration, telecommunications, gender equality) tend to exhibit the greatest levels of intergovernmental confluence (Brugué *et al.*, 1999).

Internal changes in regional institutions

As was the case with Spain's central administration, EU membership has led to changes in the organizational structures of the Autonomous Communities. At first, regional bodies dealt with EU issues on an *ad hoc* basis and the guidance of central government was allowed to substitute for effective action by the ACs (Cienfuegos, 2000: 138). However, three factors have contributed to the development of new mechanisms to support internal coordination: an increasing awareness of the impact of the EU on AC interests; the creation of formal instruments for AC participation in EU affairs; and the clarification of the role of ACs in external relations (Pérez Tremps, 1999: 354). Almost all ACs have adopted the so-called 'threefold' organizational model, which involves: (a) each department having a focus on EU affairs; (b) a body dedicated to formulating general policy and orientation; and (c) a coordination mechanism (Pérez Tremps *et al.*, 1998: 355).

All regional administrations participate to some degree in EU policies, if only through implementing Community policies (especially the CAP and environmental policies) and managing EU transfers to regional budgets. Almost all departments at regional level have therefore set up bodies to monitor their particular area of EU policy. Internal coordination mechanisms follow two basic forms, modelled on central government practices (see Chapter 3): ACs either have a single body (following the example of the State Secretariat for European Affairs, SEAE) or else they set up an interdepartmental committee (like the central government's delegated committee for EU affairs) (Cienfuegos, 2000: 139).

Specialist bodies on the model of the SEAE have become the favoured instrument for EU policy at regional level, despite the fact that, in most cases, they lack decision-making capacity. However, their coordination capacity allows for a unified approach to EU issues which cannot be organized through individual departments. The location of these bodies also indicates the growing importance of EU affairs for regional governments. Initially, most of them operated within departments of the economy, consistent with the important role of these departments in coordinating structural funds. Increasingly, however, they have been moved into the president's private office (the Basque Country, Navarra, Galicia and Castilla-La Mancha) or the department of the presidency (Asturias, Baleares, Cantabria, Catalonia, Extremadura, Valencia, La Rioja, Madrid and Murcia). By mid-2002, only Andalucía, Aragón and Castilla-León retained the former structure.

In order to help coordinate between departments, all of which have become increasingly involved in EU policies, most ACs have created *ad hoc* mechanisms modelled on the central government's Inter-ministerial Committee for EU Affairs. Composed of representatives from the various departments, the functions of these interdepartmental bodies include the gathering and coordination of information, monitoring and offering advice on EU issues, developing common positions, and implementing EU policies (Cienfuegos, 2000: 122)

Finally, many ACs have created bodies for promotion and research, or consultative bodies in which public and private actors may participate. These are often quasi-autonomous organs, even though regional governments act as the driving force behind them. Their main task is promotional, as in the case of the Catalan *Patronato Catalán Pro Europa*, the *Consejo Asesor de Asuntos Europeos* (Madrid) and the *Consorcio Centro Baleares-Europa* (Balearic Islands). Several regions have also created *ad hoc* committees, such as those dealing with the introduction of the euro in Madrid and Valencia (Colino, 2001).

The role of regional parliaments

The involvement of regions in EU affairs is now seen as a necessary element of democratization (see, for instance, the Laeken Declaration of December 2001 on the future of Europe). In the Spanish case, as in Germany, a seemingly paradoxical effect of this approach is that EU policies have contributed to a parallel development at regional government level as has occurred at national level: that is, a reinforcement of executives *vis-à-vis* legislatures. AC legislatures have very limited influence, and in parallel with the national pattern, executives monopolize EU policy at regional level. None of the Statutes of Autonomy refers to regional parliaments playing a role as actors in either the upstream phase or the downstream one – although the Aragón statute exceptionally refers to the right of the regional assembly to receive information from national government on international treaties (Arce, 1997: 82). Non-legislative parliamentary standing committees on EU affairs exist only in Asturias, Castilla-León, Catalonia, the Canary Islands, Madrid, Valencia and the Basque Country. There are limited opportunities, therefore, for regional parliaments to exercise oversight functions or even to collect information.

The low profile of regional parliaments is particularly surprising in relation to structural funds, which represent a significant share of regional budgets and require parliamentary approval. Regional parliaments are also rendered marginal in relation to regional development plans (see below), the main instrument for receiving EU funds. Regional development plans are usually approved by regional executives and only three regional parliaments (Andalucía, Castilla-León and Castilla-La Mancha) have approved them in all cases and three more (Aragón, Navarra and Valencia) have done so only occasionally. Moreover, only three regional parliaments (Aragón, Cantabria and Madrid) have passed laws on the processing of programmes and plans to be supported by structural funds, thereby seeking to exercise some control over regional executives (Ordóñez Solís, 1997: 298).

Direct participation by Autonomous Communities in EU affairs

Institutional participation may happen either directly (as result of AC involvement with EU institutions) or indirectly (for instance, through the mediation of the central government). In both cases, the ACs (following the example of the German *Länder*) have had their differences with central government and have called for new institutions for regional involvement in EU affairs.

Regional offices in Brussels

The constitutional position over the role of ACs in EU affairs, as we have seen, is ambiguous. However, some clarification came via a conflict with the central government over the rights of regions to set up representative offices in Brussels. After Spain's accession, the regional government of the Basque Country established an information office in Brussels, the legality of which was questioned by the central government on the grounds that it challenged the unity of Spain's position on foreign affairs. The case was brought to the Constitutional Court, which ruled in 1995 that ACs could engage in certain activities even outside the Spanish state, provided certain conditions were met: they must not create obligations to foreign powers, either for the region or the central state, and they must not impinge on Spain's foreign policy (Constitutional Court ruling 165/1995, 26 May).

The Constitutional Court's ruling helped empower the regions (García, 1995: 127). Since 1995, AC representative offices in Brussels have continued to be established and now cover all 17 regions. Unsurprisingly, perhaps, each has adopted its own particular format in regard to membership, status and activities. The majority of offices have been created through regional decrees as delegations of the autonomous government or as representative offices, which means they are integrated into the regional administration. In nearly all cases, they are under the control of the president's private office or the department of the presidency, except for Castilla-La Mancha, Aragón and Navarra, where they are part of the department of the economy. In no case, however, can these offices be seen as embassies of regional governments, a position clearly underlined by the Constitutional Court (Cienfuegos, 2000: 130).

Despite their organizational heterogeneity, all the regional offices in Brussels engage in similar activities, which can be broadly summarized under the general heading of lobbying (Pérez Tremps *et al.*, 1998: 321). The offices:

- Obtain and translate information. This is their most important activity and they act in response to requests from regional government departments.
- Promote regional interests and concerns.
- Support regional activities in Brussels (for instance, by attending meetings of the Committee of Regions).

- Support and advise EU institutions on regional matters. Occasionally, the Commission asks regional offices to establish consultative committees on particular issues.
- Express regional identity.

Most of the work of these regional offices is devoted to following up those EU issues and Commission programmes which have a potential regional impact, keeping in touch with the Commission and the REPER, preparing visits by regional authorities and providing consultancy services to the private sector (Molins and Morata, 1993: 125). The offices have an easy relationship with the REPER which has been essential for supporting Spanish negotiators. Specifically, they play a significant role in projects submitted by central authorities: in 1997, for instance, Spain submitted a total of 400 projects of which 90 came from regions and local authorities. Regional offices closely monitor the progress of these projects, a task which would be impossible for the REPER given the small size of its staff (Cienfuegos, 2000: 131). However, the regional offices lack any form of institutionalized cooperation and coordination mechanism, although there is intense activity through informal and *ad hoc* networks.

The Autonomous Communities and the Committee of Regions

The Committee of Regions (CR), established under the terms of the Maastricht Treaty, was in part a response to demands by the German *Länder* and, to a lesser extent, the Spanish ACs. Although the ACs have not called into question its creation, the Committee's workings are seen as unsatisfactory on two counts. First, the Committee combines representatives from two different levels, regional and local. This is believed to reduce the salience of regional authorities, and provides central states the opportunity to mobilize local demands against regional ones. Such a tactic is made easier by the fact that local and regional politicians often belong to different parties. The composition of Spanish membership of the CR was defined by the Senate as follows: all 21 members should hold a representative post, either within central, regional or local assemblies. Each AC nominates one member (17 in total) and the remaining four – chosen by the *Federación Española de Municipios y Provincias* (FEMP) – represent local authorities. The FEMP has criticized the imbalance between local and regional representatives and asked the Commission to appeal to the European Court of Justice on the grounds that it believes there should be equal representation for regions and local authorities. A second source of dissatisfaction with the CR is that it mixes representatives from those member states with devolved territorial structures (such as Germany, Belgium or Spain itself) with those from administrative regions which remain under central government control. During the debates on the Treaty of Amsterdam, representatives from the ACs asked the Spanish government to call for the CR's role to be enhanced and for a clear differentiation to be established between regional and local levels. However, Madrid rejected this proposal on the grounds that it would prejudice the sovereign right of each member state to decide on its domestic institutional organization. Moreover, the argument of the ACs was also undermined by practical considerations. Although AC representatives are nominally the regional presidents, in fact they are often substituted by top non-elected officials. Whilst this secures continuity within the CR, it does call into question its representative status (Mangas, 1994: 11).

Despite these perceived shortcomings, ACs have been keen to increase the profile of the Committee of Regions. To this end, they asked the Madrid government to put forward a number of proposals to the 1996 IGC. These included the demand that the CR should be allowed to take cases to the ECJ (in particular, to demand the application of the subsidiarity principle); that the CR should be made more democratically legitimate by ensuring its members were either elected or else accountable to an elected assembly; and that the consultation procedure should be widened. The central government was lukewarm on these proposals. Whilst it accepted that the administrative machinery of the Committee should be improved and that it should have the right to take cases to the ECJ, it rejected the idea of extending subsidiarity below state level. The CR's 1996 Report, for which the Catalan president, Jordi Pujol, acted as rapporteur, regretted that the principle of subsidiarity was limited to those powers shared by the European Union and the member states, without considering regions.

Interregional associations

One of the more novel and active areas of European involvement by Autonomous Communities concerns the establishment of interregional associations. These associations have gone further than first envisaged by the Commission-sponsored initiatives on trans-frontier cooperation. All Spanish ACs are members of the Association of

European Regions (ARE) where they play an active role. In addition, Spanish regions have been heavily involved in other regional associations:

- The *Four Motors of Europe*, created in 1988 by Catalonia, Baden-Wuerttemberg, Rhône-Alpes, and Lombardy, acts as a lobby organization. It came about as a result of the conviction that the political and institutional diversity of ARE members reduced their capacity to influence the EU. The Four Motors agreement covers matters such as foreign economic relations, economic cooperation, technology transfer, research and design, environment and culture policies.
- The *Trans-Pyrenees Euro-region*, created in 1989 by Catalonia, Languedoc-Roussillon and Midi-Pyrenees, with the aim of promoting the development of public infrastructures.
- The *High-technology Route*, created in 1990, is a network of eight Mediterranean regions (Valencia, Catalonia, Midi-Pyrenees, Languedoc-Roussillon, Provence-Alpes-Côte d'Azur, Liguria, Piedmont and Lombardy) established to act as an alternative to northern technological dominance.
- The *Arco Atlántico*, which unites peripheral regions on the Atlantic coast, including Asturias, Cantabria, Galicia and the Basque Country.

Indirect participation by Autonomous Communities in EU affairs: negotiating with the central government

Spain's Constitution, which asserts the primacy of the central government in foreign affairs, means that the most important route for Autonomous Community participation in EU affairs is usually an indirect one, via the central government There is an important distinction between the 'upstream phase' of negotiations with the EU, during which the central government is in sole control (even in those areas which may directly affect the powers of the ACs), and the 'downstream phase', when the ACs may be involved in implementation. The Constitutional Court has ruled that the fact of EU membership must not lead to any reassignment of internal powers from the ACs to the central state, and therefore compliance with EU legislation is the responsibility of the governmental level to which it applies.

This differentiation of responsibilities naturally requires coordination mechanisms between central and regional governments. The history of coordination between central and regional government has gone through various phases, and the early experience of regular conflict has given way to a more collaborative relationship (Pérez Tremps *et al.*, 1998: 262). The improvement in relations reflects both greater experience on the part of the ACs and also the adoption of more flexible attitudes by central governments, which were forced to rely on regional party support to retain office between 1993 and 2000 (Morata, 1998). Moreover, the constitutional requirement to collaborate has been reiterated in case law judgements by the Constitutional Court. Nonetheless, the second Partido Popular administration, elected in 2000 with an absolute majority, has been strongly resistant to AC demands for an institutional presence in EU institutions and fora.

The Spanish model of coordination is generally based on multilateral negotiations, organized through policy-focused conferences, plus bilateral agreements to take account of the specific interests of the Basque Country and Catalonia. In practice, though, collaboration between the central state and the ACs takes place mainly through informal channels (García, 1995: 128).

The Conference for EU Affairs (CARCE)

At the heart of the coordination mechanism between regional and central authorities is the Conference on EU Affairs (*Conferencia de Asuntos relativos a las Comunidades Europeas*, CARCE), established as the result of a long process of negotiation. During the 1980s, Socialist ministers for public administration, Félix Pons and Joaquín Almunia, put forward several proposals for some form of convention between the central government and the ACs. Regional parties rejected all of them until 1988, when they agreed to participate in the CARCE. An agreement in 1992 saw the CARCE gain institutional status, with amendments in 1994 and 1997. Later in 1997, legislation was passed to fix its structure and functions, based on the German model. The Minister for Public Administration chairs the CARCE, whose membership comprises the Secretaries of State for the EU and for Territorial Administration, plus a representative nominated by each regional president. The activities of the CARCE reflect three basic principles, first set out in 1989:

- Decision-making authority over foreign affairs rests with Parliament in respect of Treaties and Conventions, and with central government in regard to implementation.
- Explicit recognition that EU decisions should not imply a change in the distribution of powers between central and regional authorities. However, both the ACs and central government recognize and accept that EU membership would lead to some reduction in their respective powers.
- Respect for constitutional principles and the rule of law must be guaranteed.

The institutionalization of the CARCE formed part of a wider Autonomies Pact, signed in 1992 by the PSOE and the PP, and was designed to recognize the different levels of powers between regions: thus, the participation of each AC reflects the region's competency in the area under discussion.

The Autonomies Pact was endorsed by all the ACs except the Basque Country and Catalonia, where critics pointed to the lack of a hierarchical structure to cover sectoral issues, as well as the failure to guarantee that the views of the ACs would be taken into account. However, members of the PNV and CiU were offered the chance to shape the Conference as a pay-off for supporting the minority PP government elected in 1996. As a result, the CARCE was ranked above sectoral conference and the frequency of its meetings was increased to once a month. Furthermore, the central government guaranteed the ACs a presence in EU affairs, although no mechanism was proposed to arbitrate between the centre and the regions.

The functions of the CARCE involve acting as the venue for exchange of information and joint discussions between central government and the regions on the European integration process; coordinating the outcomes of the sectoral conferences and acting as the central hub of the conference system; and dealing directly with any residual issues that do not fall within the remit of the sectoral conferences (Pérez Tremps *et al.*, 1998: 287). The CARCE's working procedure is to seek to establish a common position, agreed by all the ACs. If this common position also coincides with that of the central government, it becomes the official Spanish position – as occurred during the 1996 IGC in regard to regional issues. Where there is no common agreement, central government merely notes the position of the ACs (Dastis, 1995: 340). Despite any shortcomings in this working procedure, there is widespread agreement that the CARCE has served to provide timely and useful information to the ACs on EU issues, which even go beyond its explicit powers (Cienfuegos, 1997b: 190).

To perform effectively, the system also requires horizontal coordination between ACs, and this is enabled through the CARCE's Coordination Committee. Although the heterogeneity of regional administrations militates against coordination, this mechanism appears to have functioned reasonably well (Cienfuegos, 2000: 135–6), although more informal channels remain an essential instrument of coordination.

Sectoral conferences

In addition to the CARCE, there are some further 17 conferences which seek to reflect key policy areas in the EU's Councils of Ministers. These conferences have no binding force, and have to take into account the central government's margin for manoeuvre in negotiations. The balance of opinion on sectoral conferences is that they have not been effective. One reason put forward is that their working methods are inadequate for achieving both horizontal coordination between ACs and vertical coordination with the central government (Cienfuegos, 1997b: 200). Although each sectoral conference meets at the beginning of each semester to analyse the programme of the incoming EU presidency, the majority have no fixed pattern of working and are highly dependent on their particular make-up, with the chair playing a critical role (Pérez Tremps *et al.*, 1998: 300). Their work is further complicated by the asymmetrical interests that each AC may have in different sectors (Cienfuegos, 1997b: 195).

Bilateral committees

The various bodies established to ensure participation by all the ACs in EU affairs have failed to satisfy the demands of nationalist parties in some regions. Accordingly, the more assertive regions, such as the Basque Country and Catalonia, have sought to develop bilateral relations with the central government in preference to operating through the CARCE. Indeed, in response to such initiatives and to pressure from the Basque Country, the 1992 agreement on the institutional status of the CARCE also allowed for the option of bilateral committees. Thus, in 1994 a Bilateral Commission for Cooperation on EU Matters between the Basque Country and the State was established (*Comisión Bilateral de Cooperación, Administración del Estado,*

Administración de la Comunidad Autónoma del País Vasco para Asuntos relacionados con las Comunidades Europeas) (Ortúzar *et al.*, 1995: 158).

A similar commission was set up in 1998 in Catalonia (*Comisión Bilateral de Cooperación entre la Administración del Estado y de la Comunidad Autónoma de Cataluña para cuestiones relacionadas con las Comunidades Europeas*). The importance of the committee is reflected in the high-level composition of its membership: representatives from the central government are the Minister of Public Administration, the Secretary of State for European Affairs, and the Secretary of State and Director General for Cooperation with the Regions; the Catalan government is represented by the Minister and the Secretary General of the Presidency, the Minister for Relations with Parliament, and the Director General of Foreign Affairs. A key task of the commission is to avoid conflict in the implementation of EU policies, and in contrast to the Basque Country's commission, it form part of broader strategy aimed at supporting unilateral initiatives, bargaining with central government, and promoting inter-regional cooperation (Muñoz and Morata, 1996).

Intergovernmental coordination in Brussels

The 1996 agreement between the minority Partido Popular (PP) government and the Convergència i Unió (CiU) and Partido Nacionalista Vasco (PNV) parties resulted in two further developments: the appointment of AC representatives within the REPER and also in Spanish delegations in EU Commission committees and working groups. The ACs' REPER representative formally comes under the Ministry of Public Administration (MAP), although s/he is nominated by the Minister of Foreign Affairs (MAE) following consultation with the CARCE and the Inter-ministerial Committee for EU Affairs. Regional parties, however, believe the REPER representative should be nominated by the regions themselves and be fully accountable to them.

The main function of the representative is to establish close relations with the AC offices in Brussels and channel information towards them. In addition, s/he may participate in COREPER meetings when matters with an impact on regions are under discussion. Indirectly, the AC representative has stimulated coordination between regional offices in Brussels, which have adopted the practice of meeting every two months. Some regional politicians want two AC representatives in the REPER, one for the 'historic' nationalities and the other for the remaining fourteen ACs (Colino, 2001).

A further result of the 1996 parliamentary agreements between the PP and the CiU was to offer the ACs representation on 55 EU committees, including some of the most important consultative and management committees for structural funds (Ordóñez Solís, 1997: 180–2).

The Senate's General Commission for the Autonomous Communities (Comisión General de las Autonomías)

This standing committee, which ranges widely over EU matters, exercises oversight of central and regional governments (Colino, 2001). Composed of 62 senators, half nominated by the AC parliaments, the committee receives information from central government on EU rules with regional implications, elaborates criteria for Spanish representation in international bodies which involve participation by the ACs (for instance, the Committee of the Regions) and monitors the receipt and distribution of EU structural funds. As is the case of the *Cortes* joint committee (see Chapter 3), reporting on EU issues has become its most visible activity. To this end, the committee establishes *ponencias* (effectively, sub-committees) and, by 2002, reports had been completed on the future role and functions of territorial entities in the EU, and on EU structural funds and the Spanish interterritorial compensation fund (FCI, *Fondo de Compensación Interterritorial*) (see further, below). The committee has been seen as performing an effective role from early in its activities (Cienfuegos, 1997b: 181).

Demands for direct presence in EU institutions

In 2000, the CARCE set up a working party to study AC participation in EU Council meetings. Socialist representatives from the regional government of Extremadura submitted a proposal to allow for regional representatives whenever the Council dealt with matters which fell within the remit of ACs or were of any interest to them. The proposal envisaged three forms of participation:

• If the issue under discussion concerned an area which fell exclusively within the powers of the regions, the AC representative within the Spanish delegation should automatically be allowed to participate.

- If the issue concerned an area of shared power between central government and the regions, AC participation would depend upon prior agreement with the head of the Spanish delegation.
- If the issue concerned an area reserved to the central state, the AC representative would not be allowed to participate in discussions.

Regional representation in this model would rotate on an annual basis between the 17 ACs. The reaction of nationalist parties was as expected, with both the CiU and the PNV demanding direct rather than shared presence on any body that dealt with powers reserved to the Catalan or Basque regions respectively. However, the Partido Popular government of Aznar ignored all their demands, insisting that competence over external policy belongs exclusively to the central government. The ACs, therefore, would be allowed to participate in formulating EU policy only at the domestic level.

The impact of EU regional policy and structural funds on Spanish territorial politics

Conventional wisdom argues that one salient effect of EU regional policy has been to empower sub-national territorial units in compound states (Marks, 1993; Bullman, 1997). Such a development has been particularly evident since the 1988 reform of the structural funds and the introduction of the partnership principle, which created a system of coordination and articulation between the various layers of government (so-called 'multilevel governance'). In the Spanish case, central government officials were against the proposed decentralization of regional programmes in the 1998 reforms, arguing that any modification to the role of intervening authorities should be made within the institutional and legal framework of the state in question (Fernández Martínez, 1999: 80).

Spanish regions, particularly Catalonia and the Basque Country, have been assiduous in their use of institutional instruments made available to them by regional policy. It should be stressed, though, that use of such instruments has developed gradually as part of an evolutionary process in which the ACs have acquired an ever-greater role in the various stages of EU regional policy. Clear steering by the European Commission, pressure from regional governments themselves, as well as rulings by Spain's Constitutional Court, have all been instrumental in reversing the initially negative attitude of the central government.

The growing involvement of the ACs in regional policy has developed in line with the successive versions of the structural-funds programme, covering the periods 1986–89, 1989–93, 1994–99, and 2000–03. Spain has submitted four Regional Development Plans (RDP), the first of which was drafted by the central government in Madrid. This 1986 Plan was deemed a complete failure for various reasons: it was highly politicized, overlooked issues of social concertation, and lacked an implementation strategy (Barroso and Rodero, 1996). In the subsequent plans, participation by the ACs increased significantly.

The 1989–93 Plan opened the way for regional involvement. This second RDP was based on drafts by regional authorities and a regional planning committee was established to coordinate its preparation. The committee, comprising representatives of central government and regional administrations, was located within the Ministry of the Economy. Both the 1994 and 2000 RDPs adopted a similar model, with each region drafting its own plan and discussing with central government representatives financial requirements over Objectives 1, 3 and 5a issues. Objective 4 issues have been handled by the central government, whilst Objective 2 issues are jointly managed. The RDPs are submitted through Community Support Frameworks (CSF).

Caution needs to be exercised in evaluating the impact of greater involvement by the regions. In 1989, the central government decided to submit three CSFs, one for each Community objective (1, 3 and 5a), instead of 17 separate ones covering each region. The government wanted to retain a broader operational margin over the territorial allocation of resources, in particular to allow infrastructure projects to be prioritized (see Chapter 8). Thus, it has been argued that structural funds have not always increased the financial autonomy of the ACs (Colino, 2001). Indeed, it has been suggested that the ACs had a limited impact on the formulation and implementation of programmes (Morata and Muñoz, 1996). The privileged role of central government has been justified on strategic grounds, since disagreements between the ACs and central authorities might be exploited by the Commission to impose its own criteria (Pérez Tremps *et al.*, 1998: 349). Spanish officials were worried that the Commission could use draft regulations on regional funds to influence Community priorities over how structural funds should be used; such a move would reduce Spain's discretion over the elaboration of its own regional policy (Fernández Martínez, 1999: 78).

Nor was AC involvement in the implementation stage wholly satisfactory. For each CSF, a monitoring committee was created, consisting of representatives from both regional and central governments. In practice, central government directly managed all three of them, but did allow regional authorities to manage a range of subsidiary projects. Data from the 1989–93 period suggest a link between the nationalist political orientation of regional governments and their capacity to manage European regional policy. Whilst Objective 1 ACs directly managed 33.8 per cent of regional funds (compared to 7 per cent by local governments and 58.8 per cent by central authorities), Objective 2 regions, which included Catalonia and the Basque Country, managed 50 per cent of regional funds (compared to 10 per cent by local governments and just 40 per cent by central authorities).

AC involvement was rather greater in the 1993 and 1999 plans. Coordination efforts were taken more seriously (Ordóñez Solís, 1997: 202) and the central government relaxed the tight procedures over other structural funds, such as the European Social Fund (ESF). Moreover, after 1990, structural funds for actions co-funded by the EU were directly transferred to ACs, local authorities and enterprises, instead of via the national budget. Finally, after further pressure from the ACs, the central government agreed in 1994 to regionalize the Cohesion Fund (see Chapter 8). The regions had contested the right of central government to act unilaterally on environmental issues (one of the two basic concerns of the Cohesion Fund), since regional authorities were responsible for implementing and managing environmental policy (Morata and Muñoz, 1996: 216). The significance of EU structural funds differs between the various ACs. Whereas they are of great importance for Objective 1 regions, Catalonia and the Basque Country, which are both Objective 2 regions, see them primarily as a means to ensure their involvement as full partners in the Community (Morata and Muñoz, 1996: 196).

The impact of EU regional policy should not be limited to an assessment of how regions have been empowered. EU regional policy has also has a significant impact on Spain's domestic regional policy, which has in turn promoted greater cohesion among the ACs. Prior to accession, Spanish regional policy was at best embryonic and limited to a number of discrete initiatives, reflecting the constraints imposed by the political priority of establishing the regions in the context of economic crisis. EU membership served as a key factor in the elaboration of a national regional policy (Zaragoza, 1990; Morata and Muñoz, 1996: 201), which focused initially on establishing an appropriate funding mechanism to help reduce the impact of industrial restructuring policy.

EU regional policy had a twin impact. First, the EU has provided a model to help design and shape national policy instruments. In particular, Spanish authorities were obliged to elaborate Regional Development Plans in order to receive structural funds. It is widely accepted that EU regional policy was an essential factor helping to modernize the less developed regions through the introduction of such techniques as innovative programming and evaluation (Morata, 2000: 187; Ordóñez Solís, 1997). Second, redistribution – rather than merely funding – has become a central focus of Spain's domestic regional policy, bringing Spain more into line with its European neighbours (Borras *et al.*, 1998). Specifically, the principle of additionality – introduced to stop national funds being substituted by EU support, and according to which EU funds had to be complemented by national contributions – further underlined the move towards redistribution.

Spain's financial mechanism for supporting regional policy is the *Fondo de Compensación Interterritorial* (interterritorial compensation fund, FCI), which is allocated by the central government. Following the 1987 reform of the structural funds, the FCI adopted EU objectives and instruments (typologies and maps of eligible areas) and deepened its redistributive profile. The FCI was reformed in 1990 to adopt FEDER guidelines: a map of eligible regions (those under 75% of EU average) and other criteria such as population, surface area and unemployment rate. Moreover, the principle of additionality led to a change in thinking among Spanish politicians, who now accepted the impossibility of eliminating social and economic inequalities using EU structural funds alone. These had to be supported by national policies to promote investment and employment with the aim of favouring real convergence. This shift indirectly led Spain's regional policy to adopt a second principle which underpins EU regional policy, that of concentration (Zaragoza, 1990), which means concentrating resources in those areas which most need them.

To summarize, the Europeanization of Spanish regional policy has encouraged the adoption of a more redistributive policy in place of the former approach towards regional promotion. A subtle distinction exists between these approaches, not just in regard to their objectives but also to the actors involved. The redistribution approach is directed by the central state, whereas the latter not only lacks a redistributive character but also relies on the ACs using their own resources (Barroso and Rodero, 1996: 266). Thus, EU regional policy has had the paradoxical effect of both empowering the Autonomous Communities and also strengthening the central government's regional policy. One conclusion to draw is that enhanced coordination between regional authorities can also act as a source of empowerment for central government (Barroso and Rodero, 1996: 269).

The impact of the EU on Spanish intergovernmental relations

The overall balance-sheet of the impact of EU membership on intergovernmental relations must take into account several dimensions. Some analysts believe the constitutional position of the ACs has been weakened by the transfer of competencies to the EU, even though they are directly involved in the implementation of Community policies (Morata, 1996: 153). On the other hand, Catalan and Basque nationalists support the strengthening of European institutions since they believe it erodes the powers of the nation-state and opens possibilities for cooperation with other European regions. Their calculation is that, in the long term, the process of political and economic union will lead to a reshaping of European space along the lines of coherent and competitive macro-regions (Morata, 1996: 153). In addition, the more complex and plural distribution of power within the EU between several levels of governance has modified nationalist discourse. Thus, whilst the EU has opened up new political opportunity structures, it has also led to a parallel decline in the maximalist objective of creating independent states (Marks and Llamazares, 1995).

As in the German case (Goetz, 1995), Spain's membership of the EU has reinforced existing tendencies in intergovernmental relations. Colino (2001) has identified five types of adaptive strategy adopted by both central and regional authorities in response to integration: participation, influence and inclusion; control, defence and prevention; self-affirmation, confrontation and competition; cooperation and alliances; and institutional innovation. Most of this chapter has focused on participation, influence and inclusion as well as cooperative strategies, but the EU can also act as arena for regional confrontation strategies, for instance through the adoption of independent and uncoordinated policies by regions. Such an approach has often been followed by the

Basque government, which has sought formal direct relations with the EU as well as diplomatic status and rights for Basque representatives in Brussels. The EU has been systematically used by Basque nationalists to enhance statehood symbols.

The level of participation (and ambition) of regions varies significantly between different domestic actors. In contrast to the assertiveness of the Basque Country and Catalonia, some regions welcome the role played by central government which helps prevent them losing out to the more politically active regions. In turn, central government has sought to follow strategies of control or prevention by maintaining the status quo against attempts by regions to change the rules of the game. Thus, central government has defended regional interests within the Community arena, but has sought to restrict their capacity to influence domestic regional policy.

On a number of occasions, the Spanish government has put a brake on regional ambitions. In 1991, for instance, Spain rejected a German proposal for the Maastricht Treaty to recognize explicitly the possible presence of representatives of sub-state entities as full members of the Council of the European Union (instead of just central government representatives). In the Amsterdam Treaty, Spain did not sign up to the annexed declaration that extends the application of the subsidiarity principle to territorial entities with legislative competence (signed by Austria and Germany), arguing that subsidiarity runs counter to the Spanish distribution of competencies between central and regional authorities. Both the assignation and responsibility for the implementation of policy-making are constitutionally defined in Spain and, therefore, the influence of the subsidiarity principle has been more rhetorical than real. Even though it has been argued that the ACs have been given greater influence as a result of the subsidiarity principle (García, 1995: 139), the evidence supports the view that their role is more heavily dependent on political bargaining.

Moreover, in spite of the rhetoric, regional authorities are not particularly keen on subsidiarity for two reasons. First, nationalist parties prefer the concept of asymmetric federalism and their agreements with central government as the basis of their competencies. Second, local authorities can invoke the subsidiarity principle against the regional administration. In fact, local authorities have often complained that they are marginalized by the ACs and subsidiarity offers a useful lever for this fourth level of government, particularly in those regions, such as Catalonia, where the major city is under the control of a different party than the regional government.

In 2001, the PP government played down the role of the ACs in the debate on the future of Europe, both as a substantive issue and as eventual players. Thus, during the drafting of the Laeken Declaration on the Future of the European Union, Aznar sought to avoid any reference to regions in relation to the distribution of powers. Although he was unable to rule out such references, he did succeed in tying these to national constitutional provisions. He also bargained hard to avoid regions with legislative powers being granted their own representatives at the European Convention which emerged from Laeken. Part of Aznar's concern was to avoid regions seeing exit as an attractive option if smaller states in the EU were given disproportionate weightings.

Finally, the central government has also been very cautious over any modification of the position of regions *vis-à-vis* the European Court of Justice (ECJ). Since 1997, ACs have been allowed to ask Spanish central authorities to appeal on their behalf to the ECJ. But the government has rejected any attempt by the ACs to acquire the right to act directly as plaintiffs in ECJ proceedings, arguing that cases brought by the ACs could involve a judgement on the domestic distribution of powers, which it regards as a purely national issue.

Chapter 5

Shaping the Union and Defending National Interests

Intergovernmentalist perspectives on the European Union tend to view it as an enlarged arena in which the national governments pursue their own interests, however these may be formulated in any given domestic setting (Moravcsik, 1993, 1998). This chapter discusses three arenas or dimensions that appear to support the intergovernmentalist interpretation: 'insider policies' which seek to place nationals in key positions in the Brussels administration and help shape policy from the inside; use of the EU Presidency to steer policies in a particular direction; and the pursuit of national interests through IGCs and enlargement negotiations. There is certainly evidence that domestic preferences have helped to shape all three arenas. However, the Spanish experience suggests a degree of tautology in the intergovernmentalist approach, in that policy outcomes tend to reflect national preferences precisely when intergovernmental bargaining instruments are strong. In the case of Spain, socialist (PSOE – Partido Socialista Obrero Español) governments generally endorsed a federalist discourse that matched their own priorities, whilst the conservatives (PP – Partido Popular) have adopted a more nationalist rhetoric. In both cases, though, Spanish governments have found themselves obliged by the EU's institutional influence to frame their national claims and policies within prevailing discourses, norms and policy styles.

Spain in Brussels: Trojan horse or Achilles' heel?

The idea of a 'Trojan horse' is designed to convey the idea of state representatives working in the EU administration and actively pursuing their own national goals. In the early 1990s, Kassim and Wright (1991) argued that national governments seek to protect their interests by working through the network of their national officials located within the Community system. To this end, member states engage in a constant effort to ensure the strategic placement of their own nationals, using mechanisms such as national quotas, national 'flags' (that is, certain posts being reserved for particular nationalities) and active policies of supporting and blocking career progress. This chapter seeks to assess the evidence for such activities on the part of Spain.

Spaniards in Brussels

The appointment of Spanish nationals to top posts in international organizations during the 1980s and 1990s has been noteworthy. For instance, Juan Antonio Samaranch was president of the International Olympic Committee (IOC) between 1980 and 2001, Javier Solana served as Secretary General of NATO from 1995 until 1999 and was subsequently appointed EU High Representative for Common Foreign and Security Policy (CFSP) and Secretary General of the West European Union (WEU), Federico Mayor Zaragoza was elected Director-General of UNESCO between 1987 and 1999, and Lluis María de Puig was President of the WEU Assembly from 1997 to 1999. In addition, former premier Felipe González acted as the international mediator in Serbia during 1997 for the Organisation for Security and Co-operation in Europe (OSCE). In all these cases, successful government lobbying was built upon domestic inter-party consensus in support of the appointments. The only significant recent failure to promote a Spanish national to a leading position occurred in 1995 when the WEU ruled out the candidature of Enrique Barón (former President of the European Parliament between 1989 and 1992) as Secretary General in favour of Portugal's José Cutileiro.

EU recruitment procedures differ from those usually found in other international organizations. The appointment of the most senior position in the EU, President of the Commission, reflects a combination of given circumstances at the time and the political profile of the candidate in question. No Spanish candidate has sought the position, although Spaniards have been mentioned on occasion as possible presidents, as was the case with Felipe González after he left government in 1996 and also Javier Solana, by then NATO Secretary General, after the resignation of the Santer Commission (1999). In both cases, the individuals in question were not interested in the position: González was not attracted by the job, and Solana's possible candidacy was proposed just when NATO attacked Yugoslavia.

At the lower levels of EU bureaucracy, the established mechanisms of national quotas and flags have been used (at least until the theoretical

reforms of the Prodi Commission). During the long accession negotiations prior to Spain's entry, frustration over the process prompted the
Spanish team to ensure that they established the number and rank of
positions to be initially occupied by Spanish officials (Viñas, 2001). As
part of the deal, Spain 'negotiated' two Commissioners, two Director
Generals, three Deputy Director Generals and a 'large' number of
directorships. Appointments to these positions, however, have been
made against a backdrop of party political competition, the lack of a
clearly defined staffing policy, and the lack of coordination between
political parties, the central administration and Spanish officials
working within the EU.

Party politics

One salient feature of Spain's approach to staffing in the EU has been
the consensual distribution of available posts, at least during the early
years of membership. Following the 1986 accession, Prime Minister
Felipe González agreed with the then conservative opposition leader
to distribute newly available posts according to party membership. In
fact, posts were initially to be distributed according to a broader
quota system that took into account parties, unions and professional
associations, but polarization around the two largest parties was
almost bound to result (Bernárdez, 1995: 121).

A study in the 1990s revealed that 66.3 per cent of all EU
Commissioners had experience of elected office at the national level
(Page, 1997: 119). In the Spanish case, the figure is 100 per cent – that
is, all Spanish Commissioners had previously been deputies in the
Cortes. Moreover, whilst 56.6 per cent of all Commissioners had held
ministerial office, 60 per cent of Spaniards had done so, rising to 80
per cent if subsequent career trajectories are also taken into account
(which indicates that the post of Commissioner does not automatically lead to exclusion from the national political arena). According to
the established pattern of EU quotas (pre-Prodi reform), Spain has
two Commissioners and at least two Director Generals. Such an allocation suggests an obvious distribution between the two largest
parties, but in recent years the original consensual arrangement has
been replaced by more fierce inter-party struggles between the PP and
the PSOE. Indeed, it has been argued that such sharp partisan conflict
has sometimes undermined the reputation of Spanish governments for
pushing their nationals hard in career matters (Hooghe, 1998).

One manifestation of such partisan conflict lies in government attempts to influence the opposition candidates for the post of EU commissioner. The first conservative commissioner, Abel Matutes, had not even been short-listed by the PP party leader – but González put his name forward regardless (Bernárdez, 1995: 121). During the 1999 renewal of the Commission, a similar incident was aggravated by the fact that it coincided with the European Parliament elections. The opposition PSOE designated Pedro Solbes, former Secretary of State for EU Affairs and Minister of the Economy, as their candidate, but the nomination appeared to be questioned by the Prime Minister, José María Aznar, who pointed out that it was the government which formally proposed commissioners. Whilst the PP government had no personal animosity towards Solbes, it wanted to promote its own candidate, Loyola de Palacio, the former Minister of Agriculture and well-known for her nationalistic rhetoric. Aznar justified the nomination of De Palacio on the grounds that Prodi had called for more women in the Commission, but in practice it helped to deflect attention during the Euro-elections from her possible association with a scandal over EU subsidies for lignum production whilst she had headed the Agriculture department. Once the election was over, the government ratified both Solbes and de Palacio as Spanish Commissioners.

Inter-party conflict intensified after the PP came to power in 1996. During the preceding 14 years of uninterrupted PSOE rule, a number of socialist figures had acquired an international reputation and standing. As a result, the PSOE government had few difficulties in finding experienced and suitable candidates when posts became available at the EU and international level. Once the PP took office, they initially suffered from a lack of experienced candidates. They were thus faced with two options: either staff high-level administrative offices with politically sympathetic newcomers, or endorse more experienced members of the PSOE.

These inter-party tensions were clearly illustrated during the 1999 renewal of top EU positions. Several posts were at stake, including Secretary General of the Council (enlarged following the Amsterdam Treaty to encompass the role of High Representative for CFSP, known in Spain as '*Mister Pesc*'). Lacking its own candidate, the PP government instead supported Carlos Westendorp, former Foreign Affairs Minister and EU Secretary of State during the PSOE administration and later chairman of the 1996 Reflection Group and High Representative for Bosnia-Herzegovina. In contrast to Javier Solana, who had held ministerial posts in all the PSOE governments from

1982 to 1995, the former diplomat Westendorp was not seen as a party animal. Solana, by contrast, was perceived as a potential political adversary, with a good chance of using his international experience as a platform for a subsequent bid to be Spanish prime minister. In the event, the Austrian Foreign Affairs Minister, Wolfgang Schüssel, nominated Solana, supported by the UK, Germany and France. The Spanish government reluctantly accepted the prevailing view, although it was widely noted that it did not campaign in favour of Solana, leading to criticism by the PSOE.

In the meantime, Spanish officials in Brussels had been promoting Pedro Solbes, at the time chair of the *Cortes* Joint Committee for the EU, for the post of President of the European Investment Bank (EIB). Solbes was also considered to be a potential political rival, so the PP instead put forward the name of Fernando Becker, president of a Spanish public investment institution and close to the party – but virtually unknown in Brussels circles. However, the Austrian Presidency formally proposed Solbes and other member states supported him. Most unusually, in neither the case of Solbes nor Solana did the Spanish government campaign in favour of its own nationals. Indeed, once Solana was designated Secretary General of the Council, the Spanish government actually withdrew its support for Solbes as a candidate for the EIB presidency on the grounds that it would create difficulties having two people of the same nationality in such senior positions. Nevertheless, the PP did tentatively suggest the former Minister of the Economy under the Unión de Centro Democrático (UCD), Luis Gamir, as next chair of the European Bank for Reconstruction and Development (EBRD). A successful nomination was finally achieved in 2002, when the PP was able to secure the appointment of its former MEP, José Manuel Fabra Vallés, as President of the European Court of Auditors.

In addition to routine struggles between parties, tensions *within* parties can also play a significant role in appointments. On two occasions, the designation of a DG has been affected by disputes within the two major parties. In the late 1980s, the leader of the socialist General Workers' Union (UGT) – which was in open conflict with the PSOE government at the time – was reportedly lobbying hard within the European Economic and Social Committee (EESC) to avoid the DG for Social Affairs being staffed by someone close to the González government (Bernárdez,1995: 244). Again in 1995, when the PP had the option of nominating a candidate for DG V (energy), Brussels-based party members, Abel Matutes and Marcelino Oreja Aguirre, proposed Ramón de Miguel, their former *chef de cabinet*. But the PP leadership was unhappy with the fact that he was not a member of the party, and instead proposed an alternative. However, the selection procedure indicated that the nominee should be a Commission official and Aznar therefore accepted de Miguel's candidature (Bernárdez, 1995: 24).

On the other hand, ideological and programmatic factors have been skilfully exploited for those positions in which governmental lobbying is less important. Two Spaniards have been President of the European Parliament (EP) – Enrique Barón (PSOE, 1989–91) and José María Gil-Robles (PP, 1997–99) – and Spanish MEPs have held several high positions in the EP's political groups. Whilst this may suggest a high level of integration of Spanish MEPs in the leading decision-making bodies of the EP (Magone, 1993: 24), it actually reflects the relative weight of the two largest Spanish parties, which have consistently been amongst the largest within their respective groups. A similar situation pertains in some other institutions, such as the Committee of Regions: in 2002, the PP lobbied hard within the EP for Eduardo Zaplana, president of the Valencian regional government, to be appointed chair (with the added benefit of keeping out a nationalist representative).

Personnel and staffing policy

In addition to party political divisions, Spain's approach to staffing Community institutions has been affected by the lack of a clearly elaborated personnel policy. This lack has had most impact in those areas where there is no national quota for posts, in particular at the lower levels of the EU administrative structure. Page (1997: 43) has compiled data which show that Spanish nationals are underrepresented as Commission employees (particularly in the lower categories B, C and D), with only the United Kingdom and Germany faring worse. Spain is not overrepresented amongst top officials (level A4 and above), nor in any single Commission body. Yet, in both quantitative terms and at the lower levels, Spanish officials did well in the first years of membership. By 1989, around 1000 Spaniards had been recruited by the Commission and formed the sixth largest group. The comparatively high remuneration and social benefits that the EU offered acted as a powerful magnet (Viñas, 2001), but Page suggests that this initial attractiveness might have been dissipated as pay levels failed to compensate sufficiently for the lack of appeal of Brussels life.

Spain has suffered from poor coordination between insiders at the Commission and the central government in Madrid, reflecting in part the absence of a specific institution or administrative organ entrusted with monitoring and planning Spanish career trajectories in Brussels. Spain's personnel policy appears more the result of *ad hoc* efforts. Although career trajectories reflect a combination of preferences, opportunities, competence and luck, Spanish officials have frequently complained that national authorities have not taken great interest in supporting them (Viñas, 2001). When Spain first joined the Community, the Prime Minister's Private Office (*Gabinete de la Presidencia del Gobierno*) promoted Spanish candidates to vacancies in the EU administration, and Manuel Marín – Spain's first Commissioner and Vice-President from 1986 until the resignation of the Santer Commission in 1999 – was in favour of formalizing this structure, but the Minister of Foreign Affairs objected (Bernárdez, 1995: 227). In 1995, following the example of other member states, a working group of diplomats and officials was established within the Foreign Affairs Ministry to promote Spanish candidates for EU office (Molina, 2001). In practice, though, such a move hardly reflected any explicit policy, and Spain lacks any elite institute (along the lines of the French École Nationale d'Administration, for example) able to provide high-level officials.

As a substitute for a clear staffing policy, Spanish governments have relied on 'parachuting', that is placing officials or other candidates from outside the EU administration directly into senior posts. Over 90 per cent of Spain's officials across all EU institutions have been appointed in this manner, a tradition which began immediately upon accession. Page (1997: 83) argues that parachuting is less a reflection of national administrative practices than of when a given country joined the EU. Spain was a relative latecomer and, after accession, SEAE and REPER officials had to rapidly fill the Spanish quota in EU institutions. In line with Page's findings, Spanish officials have tended to remain in Brussels and become long-serving officials in Community administration.

Spain has seen its EU staffing policy affected by coordination difficulties between central institutions, notably the Prime Minister's Private Office and the Foreign Affairs Ministry (MAE) (Molins and Morata, 1993). Poor coordination has also affected relations between the MAE and other departments, such as the Ministry of the Economy. The staffing of the newly created European Central Bank (ECB) provides a clear example. The lack of coordination between the

Bank of Spain and the Ministry of the Economy, compounded by a lack of incentives to relocate to Frankfurt, resulted in a significantly reduced Spanish representation. Although Spain did secure one of the six members of the Executive Council (Eugenio Domingo), it is under-represented in the ECB's lower levels. If a proportional criterion were applied, in line with capital contributions, Spain could expect to provide some 50 officials out of 570, but in practice just 27 were Spanish. Even more telling is the level at which they were appointed: of the 57 director generals, deputy director generals and divisional directors, just three were Spaniards. Even the President of the ECB, Willem Duisenberg, commented on this lack of Spanish presence, alongside that of the French and Portuguese. Spain appears to have missed an opportunity to promote its nationals with experience of working in the IMF or the World Bank.

In contrast to its record with established positions, Spanish governments have been more successful in securing the appointment of their own nationals to *ad hoc* bodies, which have helped shape some key EU issues. For instance, two Spaniards were appointed to the committee that drafted the EMU project (the Governor of the Bank of Spain, Mariano Rubio, and the former PSOE Minister of the Economy, Miguel Boyer), Felipe González managed to ensure that Carlos Westendorp was appointed chair of the Reporting Committee for the 1996 IGC, and some of the EU's one-off foreign affairs posts (such as Special Envoy to Bosnia-Herzegovina or Special Envoy for the Peace Process in the Middle East) have also been filled by Spaniards.

Promoting national interests?

Of course, presence in EU institutions, as discussed up to this point, does not necessarily equate to real influence – although it is likely that control over top positions helps exert some influence on those areas which are deemed sensitive issues for Spain. Moreover, it might also be assumed that Spain's top EU officials would promote a national viewpoint and/or substantive interests. Indeed, the practice of 'parachuting' has traditionally been seen as a mechanism which enhances the links between members of the Commission's bureaucracy and their national interests. Research has also sought to show the importance of the 'national flag' system (that is, certain posts being seen as 'belonging' to a particular nationality) as a mechanism for linking posts to the defence of national interests.

When we apply these arguments to the experience of Spanish

Table 5.1   *Spanish commissioners and their portfolios, 1986–2003*

Name	Party	Portfolio
Manuel Marín	PSOE	1986–89: Social Affairs, Education and Employment 1989–92: Development cooperation policy, CFP, ACP relations 1993–94: Development cooperation policy, foreign economic relations with the Mediterranean basin, Latin America, Asia and ACP, humanitarian help 1995–99: *Idem*
Abel Matutes	PP	1986–89: Credit, small and medium companies, finances 1989–93: Credit, small and medium companies, finances plus North–South relations 1993–94: Energy, EURATOM supply agency, transport
Marcelino Oreja Aguirre	PP	1994: Energy, EURATOM supply agency, transport 1995–99: Relations with the EP, relations with the member states (transparency, communication and information), culture and audio-visual sector, Publications office, Institutional Affairs and preparation of the 1996 IGC
Loyola de Palacio	PP	1999: Transport, Energy and relations with the EP
Pedro Solbes	PSOE	1999: Economic and monetary affairs

Source: Data compiled from EU Commission (http://europa.eu.int/comm).

commissioners, a mixed picture emerges. Certainly, Manuel Marín, who was Spain's chief negotiator during accession talks, has played a key role. But Spain has never secured those portfolios which are most obviously relevant to its concerns, such as Regions or Agriculture. As shown in Table 5.1, Spanish commissioners have held portfolios related to their foreign policy concerns in the Mediterranean and

Latin America. Both Matutes and Marín did use their position to help design initiatives such as the Renovated Mediterranean Policy, or develop new trade links with Mercosur and Mexico (Tovias, 1995: 103). As Viñas (2001) has observed, these policy areas had previously been underdeveloped. During the second Delors Commission (1989–1995), all Spain's commissioners held portfolios relevant to their external policy interests.

According to Barbé (1999), the election of the Santer Commission in 1995 reinforced the role of the Spanish members, but as Table 5.1 shows, one portfolio remained unchanged whilst the remit of the second was widened but mainly to compensate for the loss of energy and transport. In 1999, the Aznar government submitted a list of proposed portfolios, which included the most important ones, to Romano Prodi. Spain's attitude had become more assertive after Germany overruled Prodi by proposing two commissioners from the government coalition instead of the long-established distribution between government and opposition. Aznar targeted portfolios with economic weight and the government warned that it would not be fobbed off with a meaningless vice-presidency. This approach did result in the Spanish commissioners receiving enhanced portfolios: de Palacio was given Industry, Energy and Relations with the EP, as well as a vice-presidency, and Solbes was given responsibility for Economic and Monetary Affairs. The allocations maintained Spain's record of having a Commission vice-presidency since its accession in 1986.

At the level of Director Generals, where the national flag system has traditionally operated, a slightly different picture emerges (Table 5.2). Essentially, Spain has usually had two DGs and, for a long period, one of these covered regional policy, clearly of vital Spanish interest. For this reason, it has been suggested that the DG for Regional Policy is always a Spaniard (Grant, 1994: 95). When Commission President Romano Prodi initiated his re-shuffling of Commission portfolios in an effort to erode the practice of national flags, the long-standing Spanish Commissioner, Eneko Landáburu, relinquished Regional Policy and was given another important portfolio, Eastern Enlargement (before moving, in July 2003, to External Relations). Meanwhile, Spain's other 'established' DG, Energy, was expanded to encompass Transport as well, and passed to the hands of a French national. In its place, Spain was given Agriculture, under José Manuel Silva, whilst the DG he replaced, Pablo Benavides, was named EU representative. In addition, Francesc Granell directed (with DG rank) the task force dealing with Nordic enlargement, an important issue for Spain, and Santiago

Table 5.2 *Spanish DGs and their portfolios, 1986–2003*

Name	Provenance	DG	Deputy DGs
Eneko Landáburu (1986–99)	PSOE MP	Regional Policy	1986 Fernando Mansito (Agriculture)
Eduardo Peña Abizanda (1986 –91)	Diplomat	Transport	Vicente Pajarón (Telecommunications)
Segismundo Crespo (1992–93)		Employment, Work Relations and Social Affairs	Pedro Torres (Personnel)
Ramón de Miguel (1995–96)	Diplomat	Energy	
Pablo Benavides (1996–2000)	Diplomat	Energy	2002 Fernando de Esteban (Energy and Transport)
Eneko Landáburu (1999–2003)		Enlargement (1999–2003)	Fernando Valenzuela (CFSP)
Eneko Landáburu (2003–)		External Relations (2003–)	Vicente Pajarón (Information society)
José Manuel Silva Rodríguez (2000–)		Agriculture	

Source: Data compiled from EU Commission (http://europa.eu.int/comm) and *Anuarios El País*.

Gómez Reino directed (with A1 rank, Adjunct DG) the Humanitarian Office (ECHO) that had originally been created by Marín and in which several Spaniards worked.

To sum up, although Mediterranean or Latin America issues have usually been assigned to Spanish commissioners, Spain has been unable to 'colonize' the portfolios linked most closely to its key priorities (regions and agriculture). In practice, Spain's commissioners have usually defended the standpoint of their government in cases of conflict with the Commission. For example, Loyola de Palacio lobbied hard within the Commission to try to avoid Spain being taken to the ECJ court in July 2000 following legislation on golden shares and public aids. At DG level, Spain has fared better in terms of national interests, although in comparison with other member states, Spanish representatives in Brussels do not operate in a highly coordinated fashion. Hooghe (1998) has characterized Spanish officials in Brussels as demonstrating medium 'club-ness', which refers to those formal and informal networks within which members tend to act in concert and which reflect cultural cohesion, organizational and financial resources, or government personnel policy. From an insider's point of view, Viñas (2001) indicated that Spaniards tended to stick together, at least in the early stages of membership, although cultural clashes and a perceived need to demonstrate validity through competitive performance led also to accusations of arrogance and clannishness.

Managing the EU: Spanish presidencies

The Presidency of the EU Council rotates every six months, and the performance of a Member State in this role offers a perspective on both how it tackles issues of common concern, as well as how it seeks to incorporate its own interests onto the EU agenda. Spain has so far held the Presidency of the EU on three occasions: January–June 1989, July–December 1995, and January–June 2002.

The first Spanish Presidency (1989)

The PSOE government saw Spain's first presidency as a clear challenge, given continuing reservations amongst some European partners about Spanish capacities. In material terms, the organization of the presidency required significant modernization and adaptation of the Ministry of Foreign Affairs, as well as changes in other departments. To provide experience about EU affairs, the Spanish government organized special training courses for civil servants and also sent of group of diplomats to the European Institute for Public Administration in Maastricht. In addition, three diplomats were sent on a tour of EU capitals to acquire further knowledge (Kirchner, 1992: 89). Thus, the presidency represented a key staging-post on the road towards the modernization of democratic Spain (Barbé, 1996:14), providing the finishing touch to the normalization of Spanish relations with Europe (Fernández Ordoñez, 1989). Felipe González spoke of the presidency in terms of dignity and underlined Spain's commitment to accord it due prestige and significance (Kirchner, 1992: 105).

Spain's Foreign Affairs Minister, Francisco Fernández Ordóñez, described the aims of the Spanish presidency as institutional and realistic, and commentators have generally designated it a 'management presidency', since it did not launch new or major initiatives. Instead, Spain carried forward the agenda inherited from the earlier German presidency and followed closely the Commission's working programme (Solbes *et al.*, 1988). Spain's assumption of the presidency came when the major Community issues of the moment had already been settled: the completion of the internal market, the European Social Charter and defining the stages of monetary union. Spain's major area of interest was the treatment of environmental problems in Southern Europe. The Spanish presidency also proposed measures to enhance the role of citizens within the EU (which were subsequently developed further in the Maastricht Treaty), and promoted measures to eliminate borders, as well as to secure the right of residence, political participation and consular protection for all EU citizens.

The most important publicly acknowledged goal for the presidency concerned foreign relations and European political cooperation (EPC, later superseded by CFSP – Common Foreign and Security Policy), with a particular emphasis on developing further links between Europe and Latin America, focusing more attention on the Mediterranean basin (especially Morocco) and developing relationships with EFTA countries. Specifically, Spain sought recognition of the principle that participation in the internal market should require a commitment to cohesion efforts.

Spain's performance in the EU Presidency has been judged as better than expected, especially with regard to internal market matters and monetary cooperation (Kirchner, 1992: 100). The adoption of the Delors Report and the first stage of economic and monetary union (EMU) can be seen as the most significant achievement of the Madrid summit. The government underlined its political commitment to EMU by pegging the peseta to the EMS immediately before the Madrid summit, thereby stressing the importance of participation in the forthcoming union despite the domestic costs (see Chapter 7). However, the Spanish presidency did not follow the example of the Italian presidency at the Milan summit in 1984 by convening an intergovernmental Conference (IGC) in order to expose the isolation of Margaret Thatcher. González wanted to avoid a confrontation with the UK, whose opposition had already prevented the adoption of the Social Charter in Madrid, and whilst a simple majority would suffice to convene the IGC, its conclusions would require unanimous approval. The Spanish Prime Minister therefore emphasized the need to seek agreement on the possible and not necessarily the most desirable. In practice, the Spanish presidency failed to secure approval for its proposals on citizenship and made limited progress on EPC, consisting essentially of minor agreements on Latin America.

The second Spanish presidency, 1995

Despite elements of continuity, there were also substantial changes in the style of the second presidency. By 1995, Spain had consolidated its position and prestige within the Union, but the presidency came during a period of adverse domestic and external circumstances. Domestically, the presidency provoked bitter political disputes, with both the PP and IU arguing that Felipe González lacked legitimacy following a string of corruption cases (Heywood, 1997) which rendered him unsuitable to assume the role of President of the EU Council. For the PSOE government, on the other hand, the presidency represented something of a life-jacket, offering an element of international prestige to offset against internal weakness (Barbé, 1996: 18). Externally, the presidency took place during a period of growing 'Euro-scepticism' which dampened down the appeal of Spain's pro-integration rhetoric as well as reducing the ambitions of member states.

In comparison to 1989, the presidency had a more distinctively nationalistic profile, visible even in its symbols. Thus, the official logo of the presidency was a very small 'ñ', an idiosyncratic letter in the Spanish alphabet, against a yellow and red background, which mimicked the colours of the Spanish flag. The logo not only offered a contrast to the more avant-garde one used during the first Spanish presidency (designed by the Spanish abstract painter, Antoni Tapiés), but also acted as a reminder of the ongoing conflict between Spanish government and the Commission over a ban on computer keyboards without the letter 'ñ'. The Commission claimed this broke competition rules, which in turn provoked a strong campaign, widely backed by intellectuals and the media, against Brussels interference. The choice of presidency logo was presented in the Spanish media as the revenge of Spanish diplomacy.

As had been the case in 1989, the government sought to maintain continuity with the preceding French and German presidencies, and indeed sought inclusion in the bilateral coordination mechanisms they had established. The main items on the agenda of the second Spanish presidency were employment policy (following on from the Essen European Council), preparations for stage III of EMU, and developing the forthcoming EU agenda. In regard to foreign policy, the agenda included the perennial issue of Europe's relationship with the USA, as well as the more Spanish-centred concerns with Latin America and the Mediterranean. Felipe González toured EU capitals to try to secure commitment to the Madrid summit agenda, and reported in person on the Spanish presidency to the European Parliament. The Madrid Council confirmed the stages for the adoption of the single currency and the name 'euro'. According to Grasa (1997), the key achievements came in foreign affairs, notably the Madrid Declaration and the Transatlantic agenda with USA, the Interregional agreement with Mercosur and the Euro Mediterranean conference.

During this second presidency, Spanish priorities were more visible and the government had taken care to prepare them well in advance. Work on the Euro-Mediterranean dialogue started during the German presidency in the second half of 1994, when Spain and other southern member states sought a similar deal on financial aid for Mediterranean countries as had been offered to the Central and East European countries under the Phare programme. Under the French presidency during the first half of 1995, Germany had agreed to allocate to the Mediterranean 70 per cent of the total available for Eastern Europe. The agreement provided a material basis for the Euro-Mediterranean Conference (and, in addition, helped unblock fishing negotiations with Morocco). Whilst some have pointed out that the Spanish presidency was unable to achieve some of its objectives, such as reform of the CAP or fisheries policy (Barbé, 1999: 107), Spain was nonetheless able to develop greater linkages between Fisheries and Association agreements in order to obtain the optimum deal for its fishing sector (Jones, 2000).

The Spanish government's most effective defence of its own interests probably came through setting the EU's long-term agenda. For the Spanish government and the parliament alike, there was an essential political interdependence between key issues on the EU agenda: the IGC, enlargement negotiations, the potential impact of enlargement on EU policies and resources, the third stage of EMU, the renegotiation of the budget, and the future of the WEU. The reform of NATO, although outside the EU's direct sphere of influence, completed the list of Spanish concerns. Spain's strategy was to seek to secure maximum benefits by pushing for separate negotiations on each issue in turn. González justified this tactic by arguing that the dimensions of each challenge in its own right meant they should be linked (but not merged) and dealt with coherently. Thus, at the Madrid European Council in June 1995, Spain established a running order for the agenda that suited its own interests: separate negotiations on institutional reform, financial perspectives, and enlargement. Spanish officials were concerned that dealing with these issues jointly would lead to significant losses for Spain.

The third Spanish presidency, 2002

The third presidency was marked by a different set of circumstances. José María Aznar had won the 2000 general elections with a convincing majority, and – by virtue of the declining electoral fortunes of European right-wing parties – had became leader of the European People's Party (EPP). Aznar's discourse was more obviously centred on Spain's national interests and sought legitimation through national achievements. Three features characterized Aznar's European policy: a changing pattern of alliances, a shift towards Atlanticism and, above all, economic liberalization (Closa, 2001). A series of clashes with German Chancellor Gerhard Schröder (over structural funds, the distribution of Council votes, and the so-called statistical effect), was matched by a growing closeness to UK Prime Minister, Tony Blair. Like Blair, Aznar adopted an overtly pro-USA outlook and offered full support for the 1998 bombing of Iraq, endorsed the Strategic Defence Initiative, and backed the Afghanistan war and its anti-terrorist aftermath. The Spanish–US Bilateral Declaration of 2001 represented a shift towards support for US policies which would have been unthinkable during the post-Franco transition and subsequent PSOE governments. The events of 11 September 2001, meanwhile, allowed Aznar to adopt a much tougher anti-ETA stance in line with the so-called global war on terrorism. In regard to economic liberalization, the PP government prepared the ground at both the Lisbon (1999) and Tampere (1999) summits for further moves in this direction.

The programme of the 2002 Spanish presidency, called *More Europe*, listed six basic priorities. Unsurprisingly, the first focused on combating terrorism, an issue which had acquired greatly added significance following the World Trade Center attacks of September 11. Three other priorities – the introduction of the euro, EU enlargement, and the debate on the future of Europe – were issues on which the Aznar government was not seeking to push any particular agenda, although the question of enlargement involved negotiating the most difficult chapters on CAP and structural funds. The fifth priority concerned external relations, and Spain chose to follow the path set out in the 1998 Saint Malo Declaration (which stated that the EU should play a full role on the international stage) and called for the European Security and Defence Policy (ESDP) to become operational. The final priority, that of giving impetus to the Lisbon process on economic modernization, was the central theme of the Barcelona Council of 15–16 March 2002. The government worked closely with the EU Commission and Council over the planning of the Barcelona summit, at which the candidate countries were also invited to participate in those talks which covered liberalization. Aznar identified five areas in which he anticipated concrete advances: better connections between transport networks (inherited from the Belgian presidency), liberalization of the utilities markets, integration of financial markets, the creation of a more flexible labour market, and improvements in education and training.

In terms of outcomes, the Barcelona summit presented a rather mixed picture. On liberalization, there was a compromise between those most in favour of further measures (Aznar and Berlusconi, together with Blair) and the social democrats Jospin and Schröder. On the one hand, liberalization of the electricity and gas markets for non-household consumers was scheduled for 2004, with 10 per cent of electricity supply networks to be interconnected by 2005. On the other, Jospin secured an agreement that liberalization measures should recognize the duties of public services, the security of supply and the protection of the most vulnerable groups. In regard to financial markets, it was agreed that 2005 should be the target date for their full integration (2003 for capital markets), but on condition that there should be a parallel agreement on fiscal regimes, as demanded by Jospin. On transport, the member states agreed to aim for the implementation of the Single Sky proposal by 2004, and both the UK and Germany dropped their objections to the adoption of the Galileo Programme. Further agreements covered flexibility in labour markets, a commitment to invest 3 per cent of GDP in R&D, and a general commitment to 'minor control of the economy by the state'. Other issues dealt with at the summit included agreement on Solana's proposal to restructure the Council with a joint presidency (involving groups of five or six states holding the presidency for a period of two and a half years) and to elect the President of the Council.

Shaping the Union: reform and enlargement

Treaty amendments offer an opportunity to observe diplomacy at work within the EU as state representatives seek to defend their national interests. The nature of these negotiations, which take place through IGCs in which each partner has a veto right, promotes the kinds of rational calculations which underpin intergovernmentalist accounts of decision-making in the EU. Spain's participation in EU treaty reforms provides evidence of a 'logic of appropriateness' (March and Olsen, 1989: 21–38), according to which member states establish general principles and create commitments which oblige them to defend national interests within the EU's institutional patterns of behaviour, but it also illustrates a tough defence of national interest using the threat of veto. Spain has been involved in four rounds of treaty reform, which includes its role as observer during the negotiations on the Single European Act (SEA, 1987), as well as the Treaty on European Union (Maastricht, 1992), the Treaty of Amsterdam (signed in 1997 and implemented in 1999) and the Treaty of Nice (signed in 2001), and two rounds of enlargement (Nordic and Eastern).

Reform of the EU

Spanish governments have generally been in favour of institutional reforms which would move the EU towards a federal design. Under the PP, however, Spain's attitude has moved away from embedding national interests and preferences within a strongly pro-integrationist stance towards a more overt defence of national interests.

Negotiating the Maastricht Treaty: the 1991 IGC

For the Spanish government, its presence at the 1991 IGC represented an historic event: for the first time, Spain was in a position to help influence the shape and progress of the integration process. The González government launched three initiatives (Gil, 1992). First, it sought to display its commitment to a federal vision of the EU by proposing the concept of European citizenship, which was to became one of the core elements in the Maastricht Treaty (Closa, 1992) and also provided Spain with added legitimacy amongst its partners. Spain's two other proposals – on the principle of sufficiency of means and on economic and social cohesion – sought to underpin the federal tenor of the EU's policies on economic redistribution (see Chapter 8). In addition, Spain submitted proposals on CFSP that followed closely the Franco–German position.

Spain's position on institutional reform was linked to budgetary issues. First, González successfully argued that larger member states should continue to have two EU Commissioners. More important, though, Spanish negotiators were able to make any extension of the qualified-majority-voting procedure conditional upon the principle of 'adequacy of means' – that is, the existence of sufficient financial and human resources to carry out Community actions. Three options were outlined: first, those actions entirely financed by the Community should be adopted by qualified majority; second, those actions financed only partially by the Community should require unanimity because of their financial impact upon member states; and third, those actions that do not entail direct funding could be adopted by a qualified majority only when they did not affect the budgets of member states. Otherwise, they should be approved by unanimity. On voting, therefore, Spain's position was related to the financial impact of decisions. In contrast to other member states, Spain has not explicitly referred to the Luxembourg Compromise as an essential or integral part of its conception of EU membership and has not opposed as a matter of principle the extension of qualified majority voting. This should not be taken to mean that Spanish officials are not prepared to use their 'veto' in certain cases should other bargaining strategies fail (Torreblanca, 1998). In particular, Spain has threatened on several occasions to use its veto over issues related to Gibraltar (Elorza, 1997: 25).

Negotiating Amsterdam: the 1996 IGC

The Spanish government perceived the 1996 IGC very differently to the Maastricht treaty, since it was just one (and not the most important) of a series of stages on the road towards a comprehensive process of reform. Moreover, Spain ran the risk of weakening its structural position during this process. Therefore, in the words of Rodrigo (1996: 27), Spain's basic objective for the IGC was to maintain and protect the benefits it received from membership of the EU. Spain's approach to negotiation and the proposals submitted to the IGC were driven by a desire to prevent certain issues reaching the final draft treaty.

Spain's negotiating position was considerably helped by the fact that the Spanish permanent representative, Carlos Westendorp, chaired the Reflection Group which prepared the report on the IGC submitted to the Council as the basis for its proceedings. Westendorp's nomination for the role was not accidental, but rather the result of a clear strategy. Using the argument that the Report would be presented during the Spanish presidency, González managed to convince the European Council in June 1994 that the Reflection Group should have a Spanish chairman, even though it would be constituted under the French presidency. The appointment of Westendorp allowed for synergy between Spain's own preparations for the summit and those of the Reflection Group, and it is no coincidence that the Spanish paper (Ministerio de Asuntos Exteriores, 1996) repeats many of the points made in the latter's report.

The Spanish government was naturally well-informed about the views of other member states and possible negotiation options. Spain was in favour of a low-profile treaty, believing that the key issues in the EU agenda – enlargement, financial reform and EMU – should be tackled separately. In particular, Spain was anxious to head off the German proposal to 'constitutionalize' the Stability Pact, for fear of not being able to meet its targets. Spain also wanted to avoid employment levels being used as the fifth convergence criterion for EMU, as the EU's net contributors had suggested. Instead, Spain's priorities were to increase the EU's efficiency and institutional functioning, as well as its capacity for taking action in response to internal and external challenges.

Flexibility

The concept of flexibility had been re-launched in a 1994 document produced by the German CDU-CSU. However, Spain's view was that variable geometry or multi-speed Europe would inevitably degenerate into disintegration, and there was therefore strong opposition to any formula that might lead to a '*Europe à la Carte*'. In a speech to the College of Europe in Bruges, King Juan Carlos had also rejected the notion of an 'inner core' of EU member states, and Felipe González (1992: 21) proposed as an alternative that there should be a longer transitional period in order to accommodate all EU countries.

The issue of flexibility gave rise to a new pattern of alliances, essentially constructed around the centre–periphery axis, which united Spain, the UK, Greece and the Scandinavians. Over time, however, Spain came to accept the possibility of variable geometry provided it did not entail any permanent exclusions. Moreover, in Spain's view, flexibility should apply only to Pillars 2 and 3, dealing respectively with common foreign and security policy and with justice and home affairs, and on a case-by-case basis following endorsement by the Commission and the ECJ, together with a unanimous vote.

Institutional reform

One of Spain's top priorities was to increase its voting power within the European Council. The preferred option was a 'double-majority'

approach, whereby a majority of member states and of the population would have to be in favour before a decision could be taken,
which would give an increased weight to the vote of the five largest
states. Spain did not see such a move as setting up any necessary
opposition between large and small countries, since different
configurations of interests emerge between states of all sizes
according to the issue in question. A key concern was to prevent the
adoption of any voting arrangements that would undermine Spain's
position and force it into a structural minority alongside other
Mediterranean and cohesion countries. Since the IGC postponed
any resolution of the issue, Spain urged that the 1994 Ioannina
compromise on qualified majority voting be formally adopted as
part of the EU's constitution.

In addition, Spain's negotiators raised their specific concern
(referred to as the 'Spanish problem') about the link between reweighting Council votes and the number of Commissioners. Given the
prospect of an enlarged EU, with over 20 member states, the Spanish
position was that larger countries should have a permanent commissioner whilst smaller countries would have one on a rotational basis.
Spain further argued that if it gave up one of its two commissioners,
it should be compensated with a larger share of Council votes. Aznar
blocked progress at the IGC until he attained a satisfactory solution
for Spain, in the shape of an annexed Declaration in the Treaty of
Amsterdam recognizing this issue (Elorza, 1998b).

On reform of the voting procedure, Spain proposed a case-by-case
approach, but with conditions attached. These included respect for
the principle of adequacy of means, an embargo of transfers of powers
in areas where disparities in wealth could create implementation difficulties (such as social security), and a clear specification of the conditions and rules under which QMV would operate. On a number of
issues, Spain saw a vital need to retain the principle of unanimity
voting: regulations on the funding, functioning and objectives of
structural and cohesion funds; legislation on social security and social
protection; environmental protection measures; fiscal reform.

Spain's position on reform of the powers of the European
Parliament was also determined by specific concerns. For instance,
whilst the government accepted the need to widen the EP's powers, it
wanted to ensure that any improvement to the co-decision procedure
were not applied to the operation of the Cohesion Fund (art. 130 D).
Spanish officials feared that these funds might be at risk if the EP
could introduce amendments, since MEPs from those countries which

benefited represented a minority. On the other hand, the Spanish government believed that decisions on the implementation of the Regional Development Fund (FEDER) and the European Social Fund (ESF) (arts. 130E and 125) could fall under co-decision procedures, since these did not entail any particular risk for Spain.

Financial aspects

Spain was particularly concerned about any change to the EU's financial equilibrium, especially in relation to future enlargements. The Spanish government had moderated its earlier somewhat sceptical attitude towards enlargement, but remained opposed to any reform of common policies deriving from the necessity of incorporating new members. Instead, Spain argued that additional resources should finance enlargement, arguing strongly in defence of the *acquis communautaire* on social and economic cohesion. Spain again reiterated its 1991 proposal on the principle of adequacy of means (on which a draft article was submitted for the conference), believing that no EU decision should place unacceptable financial burdens on member state budgets.

Employment

When employment became a top EU priority, pushed by the French socialist leader Lionel Jospin, the Spanish government reacted very cautiously. Although this may seem odd coming from the country with the highest unemployment rate among EU members, two specific issues underpinned such a concern. First, the government thought employment initiatives might deflect funds from structural policies and, particularly, from the cohesion fund. Accordingly, during the 1996 IGC the Spanish government successfully lobbied to have funding for employment policies included in the budgetary chapter on 'internal policies' (research, education, communication, environment, and so forth), but kept separate from cohesion funding. Second, the Spanish government was reluctant to see the creation of an EU-wide policy on employment and favoured instead the coordination of national policies on the EMU model. Spain rejected an Austrian and Swedish proposal to establish binding objectives, with attached penalties for breaching them, for fear that it would establish a legally enforceable case for committing national funds to promoting employment. Instead, the Spanish position argued that the EU should provide a policy steer, but also allow Member States room for manoeuvre over implementation.

Second and third pillar issues

On the issue of the Common Foreign and Security Policy (CFSP), Spain supported a combination of qualified majority voting for policy-related measures together with unanimity for any decision which required common action – although strong support was again voiced for the development of a common defence policy.

The reinforcement of Justice and Home Affairs (Title VI of the TEU), according to Spain, should come about through communitization (that is, transfer from the intergovernmental method to the Community method). Spain also favoured the inclusion of the Schengen Agreement within the Treaty, but only through a formula which would maintain the Spanish right to veto issues related to Gibraltar (as, in effect, occurred through the unanimity requirement to join Schengen). In fact, it was on third-pillar issues that Spanish negotiators were most active, submitting a proposal to cover the creation of a single judicial space, the elimination of asylum rights for EU citizens, and the extension of Europol powers.

Spain's stance at the 1996 IGC is summarized in Table 5.3, which outlines the assessment provided by the Spanish Permanent Representative, Javier Elorza, at a hearing of the Joint Committee for EU affairs. Elorza identified the key issues facing Spain under four separate headings listed in the table.

The Spanish government's top three priorities for the IGC were focused on the first column of Table 5.3: an improved system of representation based on population size, a statute on ultra-peripheral regions (the French overseas departments, the archipelagos of the Azores and Madeira, and the Canary Islands), and the elimination of asylum rights for EU citizens. On the question of reweighting Council votes, Spain enforced recognition of its 'special' status under the terms of the Amsterdam Treaty's Declaration 50, which tied the giving up of one Spanish commissioner to a substantial extension of Spain's Council votes. The other two issues reflected more domestic concerns: a statue for ultra-peripheral regions had been demanded by the Canary Islands nationalist party as the price of support for the new PP government, and the fact that it had also been backed by the preceding PSOE government ensured cross-parliamentary support within Spain. The demand that asylum rights for EU citizens should be abolished provides an examples of how domestic issues can become 'Europeanized'. For the Spanish authorities, the abolition of asylum rights was seen as an additional means to prosecute suspected ETA terrorists who lodged asylum applications in other EU member

Table 5.3 Spanish stance on issues at the 1996 IGC

Positive issues where Spain wants to obtain some results.	Negative issues where Spain does not want any modification of the status quo	Issues where Spain follows mainstream positions	Very specific issues which are highly negative for Spain
1 Voting power, where veto could be used to prevent any undesirable outcome	1 Subsidiarity	1 CFSP	1 Independent Competition Agency
2 Justice and Home Affairs, including reinforcement of police co-operation, mutual recognition of judicial decisions and asylum.	2 Flexibility	2 EP powers	
3 The statute of ultra-peripheral regions	3 Plans to open the social protocol	3 Committee of the Regions	
4 The principle of adequacy of means	4 Environmental policy	4 Employment	
	5 Certain unanimity decisions: environment, fiscal issues, free movement in relation to Gibraltar, water policy	5 Consumer protection and public health	
	6 Quota hopping		
	7 British proposal to reduce ECJ powers		

Source: Data from Elorza, Hearing of the Joint Committee for EU Affairs (mimeo).

states. Although these applications were always denied, extradition procedures – which sometimes failed – slowed down the process of bringing suspects to trial. Most other member states saw the Spanish demand as excessive and in contravention of Human Rights conventions (Closa, 1998). Nonetheless, the Spanish government put a great deal of its negotiating capital at stake on this issue, thereby providing other member states with a potentially highly significant bargaining lever. Moreover, whilst there was broad party political consensus in Spain over the government's proposal, Spanish NGOs, intellectuals and the leading newspaper, *El País*, were all far more hostile.

Negotiating Nice: the 2000 IGC

In contrast to Amsterdam, Aznar approached the 2000 IGC having just secured an absolute majority in the Spanish general elections, and with his policy of establishing Spain as a 'medium-size' power having been bolstered by securing EMU membership. Thus, the government felt itself to be in a position of strength, reflected in its renewed emphasis on nationalist rhetoric. Essentially, Spain wanted the conference restricted to dealing with the institutional 'leftovers' of Amsterdam. On the two additional reform issues, Spain wanted the extension of qualified majority voting to be limited (accepting its application to freedom of movement and social issues, but opposing its use for fiscal matters, environmental policy, territorial issues and, above all, structural funds), and agreed to reinforced cooperation (having initially been hostile).

The government repeatedly emphasized its primary objective during the summit, which was to achieve major player status within the EU. And it warned that it was ready to block the final agreement if its key demands were not satisfied. Spain sought to link Commission and Council reforms: it was essential to guarantee the collegiality and independence of the Commission, with the ideal being a Commission reduced in size but with a rotation system to take into account the principle of geographical equilibrium. In parallel, Council votes should be reweighted in order to restore the geographical and population equilibria which had been modified by the 1995 enlargement and which faced further alteration with the upcoming eastern enlargement. As established in Declaration 50 of the Amsterdam Treaty, in return for giving up one of its Commissioners, Spain wanted as many Council votes as the 'Big Four', which would also provide similar blocking capability. However, by making so explicit his goals,

Aznar effectively painted himself into a corner and reduced his negotiating options. The Spanish premier held out to the very end of the Nice summit in order to achieve his goal of winning a larger share of votes: ultimately, Spain secured 27 votes in the Council – the same as Poland, but two fewer than the 'Big Four'. This remained insufficient to generate a similar blocking minority to that of the 'Big Four', which could stop any measure with the support of two of the other large states plus a small one.

On other issues, Aznar succeeded in maintaining the requirement for unanimity over the approval of financial projections for 2006, including cohesion funds. The government also persuaded other member states to exclude single market policies from reinforced cooperation, but did support its use for third-pillar issues. Nonetheless, the opposition in Spain criticized Aznar for what they saw as his narrow-minded defence of the number of votes, his failure to secure his aim of achieving similar strength to the 'Big Four' on the issue of a blocking minority, and his failure to avoid a reduction in the share of Spanish MEPs.

Enlargement

Since joining the EC in 1986, Spain has taken part in two further rounds of enlargement: the 1995 accession of Austria, Finland and Sweden, and the 2004 entry of the former communist states of Eastern Europe. In both cases, Spain has been perceived as being opposed to enlargement with a stubbornness bordering on intransigence. The Spanish position has derived from a strong commitment to maintaining EU orthodoxy and the Community *acquis*, together with a desire to defend Spain's own national interests. However, Spain's stance also offers a practical example of one of the tenets of 'club theory': members of a club use the applications of would-be members to negotiate a better deal for themselves.

The Nordic enlargement

The Spanish attitude towards the Nordic enlargement has been described as 'defensive Europeanism' (Barbé, 1999: 87) and was influenced by the weakness at the time of the PSOE government, which was forced to seek opposition support for its stance. Spain was concerned with five main issues – institutional reform, fisheries, agriculture, regional policy and the budget (Westendorp, 1995) – the first two of which were seen as being of critical importance. Fisheries issues are looked at in detail in Chapter 6, and the following section therefore concentrates on institutional matters.

Spain was particularly concerned about how Nordic enlargement would affect the number of votes it held in the Council. After the SEA when there were twelve member states, 23 votes out of 76 could block decisions adopted by qualified majority. This total allowed for the formation of a 'Southern front' (comprising Spain with 8 votes, plus Italy with 10 votes and either Greece or Portugal with 5 votes each), which was particularly visible on issues such as the budget, cohesion funds or agriculture (Westendorp, 1995). In the EU12, Spain's share of votes was virtually in direct proportion to its share of the overall population. The Spanish 'power index' (defined as a state's marginal contribution to create a winning coalition) was closer to its proportion of population or share of votes than that of any other member state. Widgrén (1994) had shown that, assuming the existence of a winning Mediterranean coalition on any given issue and provided that a counter-coalition was not formed, Spain's power index was the highest within the 12-member EU, but would not be in an EU with 15 members.

Enlargement would end the equilibrium between the three indices: power and vote indices would henceforth be inferior to the population share (as was already the case with the 'Big Four'). Initially supported by France and the UK, Spain proposed a mechanism to maintain the specific weight of the five most populous members, arguing that the increasing underrepresentation of larger states was becoming intolerable. But the question did not revolve solely around a confrontation between large and small: for Spain, the key lay in preserving the existing social, economic and political equilibrium. Different groups of interests were often organized without reference to size – for example, Mediterranean agriculture (Greece, Italy, Spain) which together accounted for 23 votes representing 100 million people but which would become a structural minority in an enlarged union. Thus, Spain proposed a compromise whereby the blocking minority could be either 26 votes, or else 23 provided that these 23 represented at least three member states and more than 100 million people. The Spanish government argued that without this condition, the new minority proposed by the Commission would be 27 votes out of 90, since all calculations were made in the expectation of Norway becoming a member. This would permit a group of countries representing just 44.7 million people to veto decisions, whereas two member states accounting for 100 million people would be denied the same right. In the event, the population qualification was dropped in the so-called 'Ioannina Compromise' of March 1994: according to its terms, whenever there were 23 to 25 votes against a proposal, the Council would delay taking a final decision. Studies showed that a qualified majority set at 68 votes maintained Spain in a similar position to the one it had enjoyed previously (Bilbao and López, 1994).

The Eastern enlargement

From the very beginning of the process, members and would-be members perceived Spain as being opposed to the fifth enlargement of the EU, and there was certainly some justification for such a perception. Spain openly adopted a 'club member' attitude: thus, before enlargement could proceed, certain internal issues (Agenda 2000 and institutional reform) had to be settled. In other words, Spain wanted to adapt the calendar to suit its own needs. Spain also used its 1995 Presidency to frame its relations with the former communist states, and González proposed that accession negotiations should start six months after the IGC was finished. Clumsy moves such as not inviting the Central and East European or the Baltic countries to the 1995 Madrid summit further reinforced the perception of Spain as being opposed to enlargement.

The need to downplay perceptions that it opposed enlargement obliged Spain to develop a dual policy of expressing commitments and declarations of support in principle, whilst at the same time seeking to extract maximum benefits from negotiations. Whilst there were real fears that the European Union would shift its primary focus northwards and eastwards, public opinion in Spain was even more supportive of enlargement than in those EU member states whose governments were most strongly committed to eastward expansion (Torreblanca, 1999). Thus, the Spanish government and political elites repeatedly expressed their support: indeed, in its 1995 Report on Reform and Enlargement, the Spanish parliament declared eastern enlargement to be a 'moral and political obligation' (see Chapter 3). After the 1997 Luxembourg summit, Aznar stated that Spain felt a special solidarity with the former communist countries and, after the Biarritz summit in 2000, he further declared that Europe would lack the necessary continental dimension without them. Parallels with Spain's own application (for instance, the political importance of accession for the applicant countries, their weak negotiating position, and the importance of agriculture to their economic interests) evoked Spanish sympathies, in particular when compared with the Nordic enlargement. On that occasion, the Spanish felt slighted by the speed at which negotiations were concluded compared to the Iberian experience (Barbé, 1999: 82, 89). In 2002, Foreign Affairs Minister Josep Piqué summarized the importance of enlargement as follows: first, as in the case of Spain, accession would help secure the transition to democracy; secondly, it would create the largest trading block in the world; thirdly, it would enhance the fight against terrorism (Piqué, 2002).

By using its own case as analogous, the Spanish government sought to send a political message to the applicant countries. Aware of the domestic political importance for the applicants, Spain was in favour of negotiations starting simultaneously with all of them (the 'regatta' model). This would not only avoid discrimination, but would also ensure that accession would be based on the extent to which applicants fulfilled EU criteria (de Miguel, 1999: 8). For this reason, the Spanish authorities wanted to see Bulgaria and Romania included as early as possible in the negotiations.

In addition to the rhetoric of enlargement negotiations, however, Spain had a number of concrete policy priorities. First, enlargement must be based on full compliance with the single market *acquis*. Spain was opposed to all forms of derogation and insisted that the adoption, implementation and enforcement of the *acquis* by candidate countries should be a *sine qua non* condition for enlargement. In particular, Spain feared exceptions for eastern candidates on environmental issues, since this would have a negative impact on competition. On the other hand, transport and the free movement of persons (issues of concern for other member states) did not worry Spanish officials.

Secondly, enlargement should not be used as an alibi for weakening the CAP or for its 'renationalization'. Long transitional periods would allow accession countries to adopt and develop the European agricultural model, as well as to harmonize price levels. Transitional periods were unavoidable because enlargement has to be made compatible with the maintenance of the existing budgetary and production equilibrium. In this always sensitive sector, enlargement was progressively perceived as being less of a threat, since studies showed that Spain had a favourable balance in agriculture trade (González Alemán, 1999: 106).

But one issue, that of structural funds, did poison Spain's negotiating stance and fuelled the perceptions of opposition to enlargement.

The Spanish government clumsily sought to link its fear of losing a substantial part of the structural funds to the issue of enlargement (see Chapter 8 for further discussion). It threatened to use its veto should its concerns on this issue not be dealt with and linked it directly to the German demand for a transitional period in the freedom of movement for workers. This generated considerable anger in the German government and ultimately led the Spanish to backtrack on its search for a specific solution within the context of the enlargement negotiations.

The acid test for Spain's enlargement policy came during its 2002 presidency. The EU wanted to complete the negotiations with the 10 candidate countries by the end of the year with a view to their full incorporation in 2004, and thus Spain had to preside over the negotiation of the most difficult chapters: agriculture, regional policy and structural funds, financial and budgetary provisions and institutional reform. In practice, for all Spain's concerns about enlargement, significant progress was made.

Chapter 6

Sources of Tension: The CAP and the CFP

Ever since Spain's accession in 1986, both the Common Agricultural Policy (CAP) and the Common Fisheries Policy (CFP) have been permanent sources of conflict between the Spanish authorities and the EU. The significance of these two policies is threefold. First, they show how a member state can negotiate from inside the EU to redress inequalities derived from harsh accession conditions. They illustrate the working of 'club theory' (that is, current members impose accession conditions designed to ensure that new members bear the full cost of adaptation), and also how hard it is for a newcomer to adapt to policies that are already fully developed. For Spain, adaptation proved a difficult and prolonged exercise, and all those involved agreed that the accession negotiations imposed tough conditions on both agriculture and fisheries. As a full member, therefore, Spain has consistently striven to reverse or improve those conditions.

Secondly, both the CAP and the CFP provide political openings for private individuals, institutions and lobbies. Because budget returns are used to subsidize the CAP, it naturally attracts subsidy-hunters. Fisheries policy is a highly regulative activity involving large numbers of people and organizations, including professional associations, local and regional governments, and so forth, which are territorially concentrated. Thus, despite the weakness of the Spanish lobby, Spanish public opinion was hostile to the EU agriculture and fisheries policies and they were subjected to intense scrutiny and discussion.

Thirdly, each policy illustrates a different model of Europeanization. The CAP is an example of 'reactive' Europeanization – the transformation of domestic mechanisms to adapt to a fully developed common European policy. The CFP represents the opposite situation, since the EU constructed the CFP precisely in order to curb the impact of Spanish fisheries. But since Spain joined the EU, Spanish concerns have dominated the development of this policy because it has the largest fishing fleet of any member state.

135

Spanish agriculture and the CAP

The CAP provides a range of aids and incentives that shield producers from the market, and it therefore attracts subsidy-hunters with a
vested interest in maintaining a system from which they derive enormous benefits. Moreover, agricultural production accounts for a
larger slice of GDP in Spain than in other member states, and because
industrialization and urbanization are relatively recent phenomena,
many Spaniards feel a particular empathy with the countryside and
farming. This helps to explain why the defence of agriculture as an
essential national interest readily mobilizes public opinion in Spain.

A profile of Spanish agriculture

Since 1950, Spain has evolved from a basic agricultural economy to a
modern, post-industrial one. This has involved fundamental changes
to the model of traditional agriculture based on a large workforce,
low wages and a largely undeveloped and undiversified food market
(Abad *et al.*, 1994, 70). The economic importance of agriculture has
declined, and it now employs a much smaller section of the population. Figure 6.1 illustrates this process: between 1950 and 1990, agriculture's contribution to GDP shrank to less than 5 per cent, and the
workforce shrank from just under half of all those employed to less
than 10 per cent.

The change was strikingly rapid. While similar developments have
taken place over several decades in most EU member states, it took
scarcely 25 years for agriculture to become a marginal sector within
the Spanish economy (García Delgado and García Grande, 1999).

But this change did not involve a structural transformation: most
authors (Barceló, 1993; Romero, 1993; Ramos, 2000) agree that
Spain has failed to modernize, specialize and, above all, restructure
her agriculture sector. It is still characterized by small units, an ageing
population, part-time working, demographic imbalance and low technology. Agrarian reform had been a pressing demand since the beginning of the twentieth century and was a major source of tension
before the Spanish Civil War. By 1992 Spain had barely even
embarked on the sort of structural adaptation which had been in
progress elsewhere in Europe since the 1960s (Barceló, 1993: 443;
Romero, 1993). The harsh physical environment and the diversity of
Spanish agricultural production provided additional obstacles to
modernization.

Figure 6.1 *The declining importance of the agricultural sector in the Spanish economy*

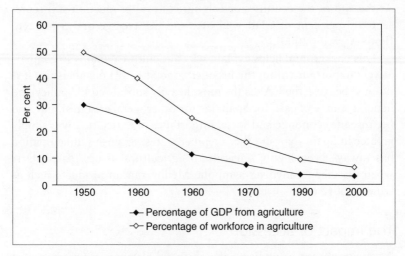

Sources: Data derived from Abad *et al.*, 1994: 74; UN Conference of European Statisticians (http://www.unece.org/).

In addition to structural weaknesses, an obsolete commercial policy burdened Spanish agriculture, and isolationism and autarky still informed agrarian policy even in the 1980s (Díaz Eimil, 1997: 70). An interventionist state controlled production and markets, whilst an official national authority had a legal monopoly on the purchase of wheat and a quasi-monopoly on other cereals. Other products, such as rice, could not be grown without government permission. The government also controlled the trade in foodstuffs, prohibiting imports except for corn. Although Spanish fruit and vegetables could well have competed with imported products, their national market was protected.

Thus, at the time of Spain's accession her agriculture was structurally and politically backward, yet more significant to her economy than the EU average. In 1986, agriculture represented 5.6 per cent of the Spanish economy (compared to an EU average of 3.4 per cent), and the proportion of the total population engaged in agriculture was 16.1 per cent (EU average 7 per cent). Spanish farm incomes were 79.82 per cent of the EU average – substantially higher than the overall Spanish average (in 1986, Spanish GDP per capita was 69 per cent of the EU average). In 1991, Spain accounted for 21 per cent of all EU land used for agriculture, whilst 12 per cent of the EU's rural population – and 17 per cent of its agricultural workforce – lived in Spain. At the end of the century Spanish agricultural production still represented 3 per cent of GDP, well over the EU average of 1.5 per cent (Foro Agrario, 2000).

This background helps explain why agriculture remains so comparatively important within the broader context of EU membership. It is not just because the CAP is the most heavily subsidized EU policy and hence a source of cash for Spain (as for other member states), but also because the economic and social importance of agriculture was simply greater in Spain than in other member states. Spanish public opinion has always been highly sensitive to agricultural issues, particularly when the dispute involves symbolic Mediterranean products such as wine or olive oil.

The impact of accession

Accession meant negotiating three central elements: convergence of prices and support payments; temporary exemptions from the implementation of EU rules; and exemptions to free circulation for very sensitive products. Table 6.1 summarizes the impact of accession on Spanish agricultural products along a number of parameters and conveys a broad picture of the sector. It is generally agreed that Spain had to accept tough membership conditions as regards agriculture. As regards legislative adaptation, there were a few specific problems relating to Spanish products (wheat, milk, wine) and some relating to potential health risks from meat products. In addition, the rules governing EU external relations with third countries created some problems in regard to products that competed with Spanish ones, for instance fruit and vegetables from Morocco and the Mediterranean.

In general terms, accession had a macroeconomic effect in that it affected agricultural prices (for both producers and consumers) and inflation. It also had some negative impact on certain sectors with extensive employment. Most obviously, accession accentuated the regionalization of Spanish agriculture. Some specialists have noted that the CAP deepened regional differentiation to such a degree that it is scarcely possible any more to speak of 'Spanish' agriculture (Sumpsi, 1994: 2; Camilleri, 1986: 721–6). Naturally, this regionalization process has been further enhanced by the diverse regional agricultural policies pursued by the *autonomías* (Lamela, 2000: 13).

Spanish agriculture is indeed diverse, ranging from the temperate to the tropical and including, of course, the typical Mediterranean products. The main areas are:

- *Cantabrian rim*. Predominantly livestock and dairy products.
- *Madrid and Catalonia*. Predominantly livestock, with some cultivation (wine, olive oil, fruit and vegetables).
- *Andalusia, Murcia, Canary Islands, Balearic Islands, Valencia*. Mainly fruit and vegetables (Andalusia produces 80 per cent of the Spanish olive crop)
- *Castile-León and La Rioja*. Wine and, in the former, cereals.
- *Castile-La Mancha*. Cereals and industrial crops.
- *Navarre and Extremadura*. Livestock and cultivation in roughly equal proportions. Cereals, fruit.

Accession had the biggest impact on northern Spain, whereas its effect in the centre of the Peninsula was more or less neutral. Areas producing the big export crops (fruit and vegetables) benefited most.

Membership affected the whole of Spanish trade, since all products which had been previously state-controlled had to open up to a liberalized market, both with other EU countries and with third countries enjoying special trade relationships with the EU. All trade and tariff barriers against EU member states had to go, but the way this was done served EU interests: Spain did not obtain free access to EU markets until 1996. More importantly, the French saw to it that trade in Spain's most competitive products (such as fruit and vegetables) was frozen until 1990, followed by a six-year transition period during which important safeguards continued to operate.

These unfavourable starting conditions in highly competitive areas created the impression that the fruit and vegetables sector was bearing the brunt of the costs of membership (in terms of market access). It also fuelled the popular perception that the EU was prejudiced against Mediterranean products in general and Spanish ones in particular. However, by 1993 Community tariffs had almost ceased to apply to Spanish fruit and vegetables and the Spanish government used the negotiations with other Mediterranean countries, the Andean Pact countries and Eastern Europe as a lever to negotiate a reduction in its intra-Community tariffs (Solbes, 1993: 25). As a result, the transition period for fruit and vegetables was effectively reduced to seven years, the same as for other crops.

In quantitative terms, only a few products were negatively affected

Table 6.1 *Global impact of accession by sectors*

Product	Special adaptation problems		Problems in adapting Spanish policy		Production trend	External trade	
	Internal market	External trade	Internal market	External trade		EU	Non-EU countries
Wheat	Use agreed varieties		A	B	+/−	+ Exports + Imports	= + Imports
Rice			D	B	+	+ Exports	=
Maize		Substitute imports	D	D	=	=	=
Barley			D	D	+	+ Exports	=
Milk	Improve fat content		D	B	−	+ Imports	=
Beef	Health Slaughterhouses		D	C	=	= or + Imports	= or − Imports
Lamb	Ditto		C	B	+	+ Exports	=
Pigmeat	Swine fever		B	B	= or +	= or + Exports	=
Poultry			D	B	=	=	+ Exports
Eggs			D	B	=	=	+ Exports
Olive oil			B	B	= or −	+ Exports	+ Exports
Seed oil			D	D	+	+ Exports	= or + Exports
Wine	Blending white/red		B	B	= or −	+ Exports	+ Exports
Citrus		Transit of Morocco products	D	D	+	+ Exports	=
Other fruit			B	B	+	+ Exports	=
Tomatoes		Ditto	E	D	+	+ Exports	+ Exports
Other veg.		Ditto	B	D	+	+ Exports	+ Exports
Sugar			D	D	−	+ Imports	=
Tobacco			B	B	+	+ Exports	− Imports
Cotton			D	D	=	= or +	=

Note: Where only one of 'Imports' or 'Exports' is specified, there is no significant change in the other.
A: No problems implementing legislation, but substantial changes in sector.
B: No problems implementing legislation, but hard to put into practice.
C: Difficult to implement.
D: No problems with implementation or putting into practice.
E: No problems with implementation for new products. Problems with modifications to existing products.

by accession (some varieties of wheat, milk, olive oil, wine and sugar), while EU imports of wheat, milk, beef and sugar penetrated the Spanish market. Meanwhile, the implementation of laws on intra-EU trade forced changes in some sectors, including wheat, pigmeat, olive oil, fruit, tobacco and vegetables.

Membership also changed the pattern of external trade in agricultural products as Spain adopted the EU's policies. Community preference meant that many non-EU imports had to be replaced by EU ones,

Table 6.1 cont.

Product prices	Consumer prices	Inflation	Employment	Investment	Mechanization of agriculture
+/=	+	+	=	=	=
+	+	+	+	+	+
−	=	=	=	=	=
+	+	+	+	=	=
= or −	+	+	−	+	F
+	+	+	=	F	F
=	=	=	+	+	F
=	+	+	=	=	=
=	+	+	=	=	=
=	+	+	=	=	=
+	+	+	= or −	+	F
+	+	+	+	+	F
+	+	+			
= or −	= or −	=	+	+	F
+	+	+	+	+	=
+	+	+	+		F
+	+	+	+	+	F
−	+	+	=	=	F
+	+	+	+	+	+
+	=	=	−	+	=

F: Obsolete plants closed, new plants opened using advanced technology.
+: Rising trend.
−: Falling trend.
=: No change.

Source: Adapted from Camilleri (1986).

with the result that the USA (for instance) complained about changed regulations for soya. But Spain also forced changes to EU trade patterns with competing third parties in two areas, the Mediterranean and the ACP (Africa, Caribbean and the Pacific) signatories of the Lomé Convention. Seeing that fruit and vegetables from Israel and Morocco enjoyed tariff advantages over Spanish ones, Spain also campaigned successfully for the tariffs to be equalized (Solbes, 1993: 27). In general, though, Spain was reluctant to implement the rules

Figure 6.2   *Spanish external trade in agriculture: percentage exports and imports*

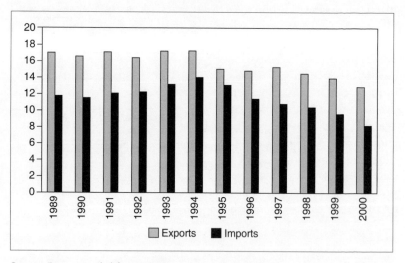

Source: Data compiled from Ministry of Agriculture, Fisheries and Food, *The Spanish Agrofood Sector and Rural Environment: Facts and Figures* (6th edn, Madrid: MAPYA, 2002).

governing external trade, especially as they had a direct impact on the transit of products from Morocco.

Overall, Spain's agricultural trade balance has benefited substantially from her accession: what was previously a chronic annual deficit became a series of surpluses or break-evens. The coverage rate (exports over imports) increased steadily from 1992 and has been positive since 1996, peaking at 120 per cent in 1997. Intra-community trade shows a much higher coverage rate (about 175 per cent in 1997), although this was during a period when the relative importance of agricultural products to Spanish trade was declining slowly but steadily (see Figure 6.2).

The effects of structural change have been mixed. On the one hand, it can be argued that modernization was stimulated by EU accession. Investment increased substantially, turning a sector which had previously provided funds for other economic activities into an active consumer – but this investment was directed at increasing production rather than at modernisation *per se*. Although accession did force the abolition of some obsolete agricultural processes and their replacement by more advanced technology, the real benefits of the CAP came from greater production rather than structural adaptation. The first three years of membership created expectations that Spanish agriculture would benefit from the CAP's support and guarantee mechanisms, but from 1988 onwards the industry was struck by the scourge of overproduction. The problem, as in other sectors, is that Spanish products are uncompetitive: Spain's agricultural productivity is 50 per cent of the EU average (Ramos, 2000: 89). This is particularly evident in the processed food market, and most of all in high valued-added products where the trade balance has deteriorated sharply since accession. Among the possible explanations (Sumpsi, 1994: 14) are the ending of protectionism, the elimination of tax relief, and the dismantling of organizations for the promotion of exports. Additionally, the industry depends on raw materials (agricultural products) which are priced much higher in Spain than on the global market. In this sub-sector, accession has been described as unidirectional Europeanization: Europe got into Spain (mainly in the form of multinationals eager to take over Spanish industries so as to exploit the Spanish market), but Spain failed to get into Europe (Sumpsi, 1994: 14). There is widespread agreement on the main reasons for this deficit, which continues to impede modernization: an ageing population, technological backwardness, serious problems of soil erosion, small farm units and rural depopulation (Sumpsi, 1994; Foro Agrario, 2000; Ramos, 2000: 84).

The most profound changes can be related to the central instrument of the CAP: the mechanisms for price support and market regulation (Sumpsi, 1994: 2). Spain was given seven years to bring her prices, which were mostly lower than European ones, into line with the rest of the EU. If Spanish prices were higher, they could be maintained until EU prices rose to the same level. This presented Spain with a twofold problem. First, she had to fight for a national quota in those products that already had a common market organization (CMO). Secondly, she had to try to create a CMO for products (mainly Mediterranean-type) that did not have one. These two issues provided an agenda for the permanent renegotiation of accession conditions.

Permanent re-negotiation

A chronic source of conflict between Spain and the EU is the former's status as a latecomer. The main guidelines of the CAP were laid down well before Spain's accession; the allocation of funds to products and

Figure 6.3   *Composition of Spanish agricultural products compared to EU total (1997)*

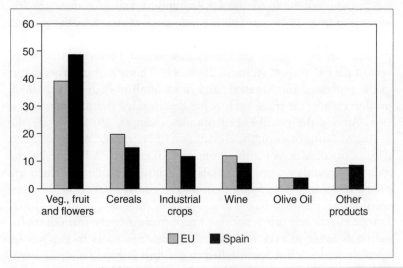

Source: Data compiled from Ministry of Agriculture, Fisheries and Food, *The Spanish Agrofood Sector and Rural Environment: Facts and Figures* (6th edn, Madrid: MAPYA, 2002).

the national quota system were already well-established, and many influential bodies had an interest in maintaining the status quo. Owing to the prevalence of Mediterranean products, the profile of Spain's agricultural product range (see Figure 6.3) does not exactly match that of the EU as a whole (although cereals and milk became less important in the 1980s owing to the EU's surplus control policy). Farmers, politicians and public opinion agreed in their perception of accession conditions for agriculture as unfair. Officials considered that some CMOs simply discriminated against Spanish Mediterranean products. The stage was set for ongoing bargaining to redress this perceived injustice: the so-called 'permanent re-negotiation' (Foro Agrario, 2000).

The Spanish negotiators set out to reduce the discrepancy between the levels of protection for northern and southern European agriculture. They obtained some improvements over Spain's original accession conditions (Foro Agrario, 2000: 222): for instance, the convergence between Spanish and EU prices in competitive Spanish products (fruit, vegetables, olive oil) was speeded up and the special

Figure 6.4 *Distribution of FEOGA Guarantee transfers, by sector, 1999*

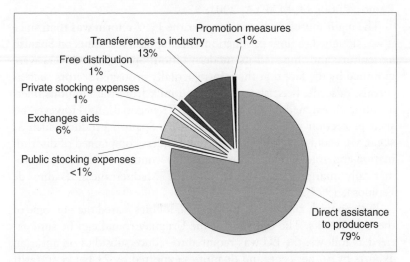

Source: Data compiled from Ministry of Agriculture, Fisheries and Food, *The Spanish Agrofood Sector and Rural Environment: Facts and Figures* (6th edn, Madrid: MAPYA, 2002).

measures adopted by the EU for 'sensitive' products were reduced. These negotiations were conducted against a background of change characterized by the 1992 MacSharry reform, the Uruguay Round (ending in 1993) which included some negotiations on agriculture products that pressured the EU towards internal liberalization, and the 1994 Marrakech agreement.

The MacSharry reform (1992) marked a departure from traditional protectionist policies: subsidies were reduced and quotas for subsidized products imposed (Kay, 1998). Generally speaking, Spanish agriculture responded well to this reform (Foro Agrario, 2000), which helped to maintain some products that would otherwise have disappeared. The switch towards income support implicit in the 1992 reform also, on the whole, favoured Spanish farmers. As Figure 6.4 shows, the lion's share of FEOGA Guarantee transfers to Spain went in direct payments to farmers. Between 1986 and 1997, Spain passed from being the tenth largest to the fourth largest beneficiary of CAP funds (Ramos, 2000: 83), with the very significant result that Spanish agriculture is now highly subsidized. It has been estimated that, despite enormous regional disparities, 25 per cent of agricultural income came from subsidies during this period (Foro Agrario, 2000; Ramos, 2000: 83; MAPYA, 2001: 92).

The main source of discontent over the 1992 reform was that, since it was designed to limit production, this imposed restraints on Spanish agriculture and impeded its modernization. Spanish producers were mollified by the fact that the reform actually protected sectors such as cereals, oilseeds, beef, sheep, meat and milk from the ominous liberalization threatened by the ongoing GATT negotiations. However, no such protection was afforded to sensitive Spanish products such as sugar, wine and olive oil. Officials and farmers complained of discrimination and argued that EU preference for 'continental' products automatically marginalized those from the Mediterranean (Lamo de Espinosa, 1999).

Both Spanish authorities and Spanish lobbies feared the outcome of the GATT talks. The outcome of the Uruguay round can be summarized as follows: the EU was required to reduce subsidies on agrarian exports by 36 per cent, and quantities exported by 21 per cent; tariff barriers on third-country imports had to be reduced; and the EU was required to progressively grant access to its internal market (up to a market share of 5 per cent). Spain believed the agreement chiefly served US interests (Lamo de Espinosa, 1999). Just as the EU export policy was being dismantled, the USA's was being strengthened through the 1996 Farm Bill. The international market was targeted by a highly assertive US policy implicitly aimed at expelling the Europeans and taking over as food exporter in both old and emerging markets. Both the GATT negotiations and the CAP reforms stimulated agricultural fundamentalism among Spanish farmers, who want their industry to be granted special treatment, sheltering it from the market economy which is seen as the root of all evil (Moyano, 1997: 792).

Against this background, Spanish policy has been defined by two more or less incompatible objectives. First, Spain has striven to get Mediterranean products included in the general CAP scheme by renegotiating the CMOs (on wine and oil, for example). Secondly, Spain wanted Mediterranean products to be excluded from the 1999 CMO talks because they would be adversely affected by measures applied to highly globalized products and markets such as cereals (Lamo de Espinosa, 1999: 195). Partnership agreements with Morocco, Tunis and Algeria have improved access for agricultural products, but concessions made to new member states are damaging both to Spain's home market and to her competitiveness in EU markets. Moreover, northern agricultural products stand to gain from the opening of southern Mediterranean markets (Lamo de Espinosa, 1999: 163). Two sectors, wine and oil, illustrate these tensions.

The negotiation of the common market organization for wine

The original CMO aimed to maintain producers' incomes by eliminating market surpluses, encouraging distillation, and reducing supply by taking some areas out of production. The Commission suggested a reduction from 37 million hectolitres to 29.3 million by the simple expedient of grubbing up vines. This proposal found favour with all non-producing countries, but was rejected by Spain with the backing of Italy, Greece and Portugal. The Spanish government had the unanimous support of all political parties, parliamentary groups, the agricultural unions and the *autonomías*. The Spanish Minister for Agriculture, Luis Atienza, argued that the proposed reform entailed a twofold discrimination. First, wine surpluses were being penalized more harshly than other surpluses (milk and meat), on a state-by-state rather than community-wide basis. This meant that member states with wine surpluses would have to pay for them, which contravened the principle of financial solidarity. Secondly, the reform permitted the addition of sugar to low-grade wines, and that benefited regions where the climate was actually unsuitable for vines (Atienza, 1994).

The Commission decided to delay the reform, and when it was finally approved it took account of the Spanish arguments: the new CMO prohibited the planting of new vineyards and encouraged voluntary distillation. Spanish growers complained that the prohibition put European wines at a disadvantage *vis-à-vis* American, Australian and Chilean wines on the global market. The truth was that Spanish wines were uncompetitive; Spain accounted for 30 per cent of European wine-producing areas but only 10 per cent of the added value. The challenge was to gear production towards higher quality wines, a project which has enjoyed some success in more recent years.

The olive oil CMO

The CMO for olive oil and vegetable fats remained substantially unchanged until the 1998 reform. Its central feature was guaranteed income support for producers via subsidies and intervention pricing. Spain took some time to integrate into this framework. Intervention prices increased year by year until, by 1993, they were level with those paid to Italian growers. The cultivation of olives increased: whereas from the 1970s up to 1986 the tendency had been to grub up olive trees, the reverse was the case thereafter. New areas were made highly productive through irrigation in order to attract maximum subsidies from Brussels.

The Commission's reform proposals were predicated on the idea of 'aid for every tree'. This meant that subsidies would go directly to farmers, the amounts would be kept constant and the mills would have no incentive to inflate output figures. Spain strongly opposed this reform, for a number of reasons. The Commission's criterion was the least favourable one possible for Spain, which accounted for 24 per cent of the total land devoted to olive trees and 31 per cent of olive oil production, but only 21 per cent of the total number of trees. Moreover, not all trees were equal: the reform would benefit Italy, whose trees were more numerous but less productive. Spain wanted the subsidies to be tied to actual production, with the imposition of national quotas. On this issue, the three main agricultural lobbies (ASAJA, COAG, UPA) backed the government, each for its own reasons. The ASAJA feared the scheme would turn farmers into mere harvesters of subsidies. The other two bodies had no objection to this, but argued that the scheme would favour larger units. Ultimately, the Commission yielded to the Spanish arguments and shifted to a production-based system. Spain received the largest quota, 42.7 per cent, whereas Italy got 30.5 per cent, Greece 23.6 per cent, Portugal 2.88 per cent and France 0.18 per cent. The only drawback was that Spain's quota (760,000 metric tonnes) was smaller than her average annual production (832,000 metric tonnes).

Agenda 2000 and the reform of the CAP

The Agenda 2000 negotiations (see Chapter 8) were influenced by the calls of net contributors for a reduction in their financial burden, and by the calls for liberalization at the WTO negotiations, which had a knock-on effect on agriculture as the largest item in the EU budget. Within the WTO framework, Spain broadly endorsed the French arguments, campaigning for the retention of the CAP while criticizing US protectionism.

Spain adopted the same attitude towards the CAP reforms required by Agenda 2000. She argued that CAP reform should be independent of both the forthcoming EU enlargement and WTO reform; the former was unlikely to begin, or the latter to end, before 2003 at the earliest. If there is no urgency for CAP reform, this should not be used as a way to cut down the bill for enlargement. From Spain's point of view, the objectives of the CAP are, and should remain, economic and social cohesion, community preference, and financial solidarity as enshrined in Article 39 of the Treaty of Rome.

Spain was opposed to the co-financing of direct subsidies, seeing this as a renationalization of the CAP in open contradiction to the 1992 reform, which stipulated that intervention prices would be reduced and subsidies paid directly to farmers. Spanish representatives and politicians took this to mean that the CAP would be renationalized to the benefit of richer countries who could afford to pay their farmers more, leading to a multi-speed Europe (Lamela, 2000: 25). They also pointed out that the CAP was a highly sensitive issue in Spain: the vast gap in productivity between Spanish and European agriculture makes support for the former essential, and difficult to reduce in the medium term without a high social and political cost (Ramos, 2000: 83).

Spanish anxieties also focused on specific items and products. In general, the government considered that the Commission's proposals discriminated against Mediterranean agriculture, which would be subjected to swingeing price reductions without compensatory subsidies. Spain also feared that pre-accession aid to Eastern Europe could translate into increased production of items already in surplus (milk, meat and cereals). Despite these fears, the outcome of the European Council meeting in Berlin which completed Agenda 2000 was very satisfactory for Spanish agriculture. The Council endorsed the agreement previously reached by the agriculture ministers: the EU was to maintain its level of expenditure on agriculture, thus conceding Spain's chief demand. Further important concessions were made:

- *Cereals*: Spain was granted an extra 10 per cent of total production plus increased subsidies. For the most sensitive products (that is, maize), Spain's existing level of production was used as a basis for calculation.
- *Milk*: Spain's quota was raised by 500,000 tonnes, and the number of subsidized cows was increased by 20 per cent.
- *Wine*: Reform of the wine CMO was put on Agenda 2000 at Spain's insistence. The EU abandoned its original plan to set aside vineyards, supporting instead quality wine production and creating a new wine marketing organization with substantially increased subsidies.

- *Beef*: Spain's production quota was increased.
- *Sugar*: Spain fended off changes to the CMO despite international pressure from big drinks manufacturers for an adjustment to sugar prices bringing them down to global levels.

Producers' organizations and regions have reacted in a variety of ways to these agreements. COAG and UPA were in favour, thinking that they corrected the discrimination against Spanish agriculture contained in the 1985 accession treaty. Of course, some sectors lost out, including sunflowers, where the loss was estimated at €100 million owing to a 33 per cent cut in subsidies.

Fisheries policy

Despite a clear divergence between Spanish and EU figures on Spain's fisheries sector, fishing remains significant in social and economic terms for Spain. A large fleet, extensive employment in fisheries and related sectors, and the size of its catches, all explain Spanish interest in, as well as impact upon, the Common Fisheries Policies (CFP). Additionally, fisheries policy has a political resonance that derives from its territorial concentration, with a major impact in coastal regions such as Galicia, the Canary Islands, Andalusia and the Basque Country. In Galicia, fishing represents the second most important sector of the economy, and the region has its own Department for Fisheries and a fully developed administrative organization (Closa, 2000). Fishing generates a web of economic activity in particular areas, and the socio-economic profile of workers in the sector makes it difficult to restructure. Moreover, rather than set up unions against employers, the fisheries sector is marked by an associational style which sees all those involved cluster together in a close network of organizations and organisms. Given this overall structure, it can be seen that not only is the policy-making process in regard to fisheries complex, but it also has a political impact which exceeds its real economic significance.

Spanish accession and the design of 'Blue Europe'

Before Spain's accession, the EU's fisheries policy had reflected its first enlargement, and the centrepiece was the adoption of the Exclusive Economic Zone (EEZ) in 1976. This established a 200-mile limit around the coastline of any state within which all exploitable resources are monopolized by that state. The EEZ was a blow to the Spanish fishing industry. Fishing vessels from the Cantabrian coast (from the Basque Country to Galicia) had been fishing in Community waters (particularly the Sole area) since the end of the Second World War thanks to their adoption of mechanized propulsion. This was used to justify a claim for historic fishing rights, and indeed the 1964 London Convention granted Spanish vessels the right to fish between 6 and 12 miles from the shore.

Hence the EEZ generated a paradoxical situation whereby Spanish ships could fish between 6 and 12 miles from the coast, but not between 12 and 200 miles. The Spanish fishermen took legal action and French courts recognized their right to access and fish – between 6 and 12 miles from the coast. In order to resolve this seemingly absurd situation, the EU sought to establish a single external agreement with Spain (instead of a series of bilateral agreements) whilst acknowledging the demands of certain other member states. The outcome was the 1978 Framework Agreement that became effective in 1980. It anticipated several measures that would subsequently be integrated into the Spanish accession treaty and were then extended to all member states in the form of the CFP: fishing licences, defined fishing zones, and national quotas for each species of fish. The Spanish government had to renegotiate the licences and quotas annually.

This agreement did not appear to favour Spanish interests. In order to secure the agreement, the Spanish government had to renounce its previous rights (access to the 6–12-mile zone) and accept the new zones, and Irish pressure compelled Spain permanently to renounce fishing rights in the Irish Box (Xunta de Galicia, 1993). There were two reasons why Spain accepted such stringent conditions. First, there was plainly no alternative. Secondly, the government assumed that the agreement could be renegotiated once Spain was in the EU.

Spain's application for membership led to a number of changes in the Community's internal policies in order to redefine the rules of the game and prevent the newcomer from reaping too many benefits. Arguably, the greatest changes were to the fisheries policy: in the early 1980s, it was virtually non-existent; by 1986 it was fully developed. The following figures help explain the Community's apprehension: upon entry, Spain would account for 50 per cent of the total Community catch; one-third of all fishermen would be Spaniards, and three-quarters of the Community fishing fleet would be flying the

Spanish flag (though a good many of them would be fishing inshore – that is, within Spanish territorial waters).

The EU reacted defensively to this challenge, and in 1983 it approved a number of Regulations which constituted the skeleton of 'Blue Europe' or the Common Fisheries Policy (CFP). This seeks to manage and conserve fish stocks by stipulating total admissible catches (TACs), national fishing quotas, and fishing zones, plus a system of checks and penalties. The EU also set up a special regime for the Shetland Box and established a 12-mile exclusion zone for foreign vessels. This was the Community's response to its worries over the Spanish fleet, which the Commission thought too large for the available resources. The Commission was concerned about quality as well as quantity: the Spanish fleet was both more specialized and more competitive. The fear was that the restructuring of the Spanish fleet would soak up all available funds, and the EU would also have to buy out the many bilateral fishing agreements Spain had with non-EU countries, which depended on access to the Spanish market. Spain had traditionally used this market access as an important incentive in these bilateral negotiations. The application of the common trading policy limited this option, but in fact Spain become very attractive to EU producers: Spanish fish imports from the EU rose from 4,000 metric tonnes in 1976 to 18,000 in 1981.

Spain entered the EU with a fisheries policy all to herself, but a number of restrictions prevented her immediate entry into the CFP. To begin with, she had to accept a very long transition period (17 years) before she came fully under the EU regime for access to fishing grounds. In 1985 the EU passed a regulation limiting numbers of fishing vessels (a special model was devised for Spain), fishing grounds and catches. Only vessels listed in the Accession Act are permitted to fish in EU waters, and they are subject to a licensing system that applies only to Spain. The Spanish authorities originally named 300 vessels, but the EU granted only 150 licences. This unilaterally imposed limit was one more mechanism to prevent the Spanish fleet exceeding its annual quota, since it was suspected that the Spanish authorities might not impose adequate controls or monitoring. Each vessel was granted access to a predetermined fishing zone, and, more important from the Spanish fishermen's point of view, the rich Irish Box was forbidden to them.

These accession conditions have been criticized. But, while the transition period was unusually long, harsh and some would even argue irrational, it was clearly the best that could be got. Spain's position was weak; in the words of one of the leading negotiators, she had nothing to negotiate with – she could not even threaten to cut fish imports from the EU (Bassols, 1995: 174), because the chronic shortage of fish on the Spanish market indicated that the threat would be an empty one. Not only was the solution the best attainable, it was also good in practical terms, despite all the opinions to the contrary: Spain was given fewer resources than her fishing fleet warranted, but many more than were available to her in her own waters (Franquesa, 1997: 173). Further, the earlier phasing-out policy (progressive reduction of quotas and licences) was eliminated – and all this at a time when the international trend was towards excluding foreign vessels from EEZs.

Once inside the EU, Spanish owners were able to exploit loopholes in EC law, retaliating against the EU's refusal to grant her resources commensurate with the real figures. Following the traditional practice of joint fishing undertakings, Spanish owners availed themselves of freedom of movement and freedom of establishment regulations to create fishing ventures in other member states, particularly the UK. The vessels concerned flew the British flag and used British licences and quotas; this was perfectly warrantable behaviour, protected by EC law, but the British saw it as quota-hopping. The British government retaliated through the Merchant Shipping Act, which required some of the capital and some crew members to be British, and catches to be landed at British ports. However, this Act flew in the fact of EC law, and the ECJ, in a preliminary ruling, provided the grounds on which the House of Lords was effectively obliged to reject it. The British government has nonetheless continued to complain of Spanish quota-hopping and has attempted to restrict Community freedoms as far as fisheries policy is concerned. It tried to get this issue included in the Amsterdam Treaty, and on several occasions has threatened to pull out of the CFP.

Bargaining over enlargement

Norway's application gave a chance to redress the situation: Spain now became one of the self-interested parties using club rules to burden the applicant with most of the costs of accession. Norway had trouble in balancing supply and demand. On the one hand, she relied heavily on her rich coastal waters, an asset which she would have liked to protect from EU vessels. She wanted exemption from existing EU regulations governing access to fishing grounds and resource management, ownership of fishing vessels and access to markets.

Hence the Norwegian authorities appealed to the social and national value of her long-established fishing industry. On the other hand, Norway wanted to be a full member of the CFP. This demand, and the apparent willingness of other member states to grant it, enraged the Spanish government. Here was a newcomer leapfrogging straight into the CFP, whilst Spain's transition period was not due to expire until 2002. Spain's approach to the negotiations hardened, with a threat to veto Norway's accession if Spanish demands were not met.

In 1994 Spain presented the Council of Ministers with a memorandum containing three main demands (Carderera, 1995: 3822; Westendorp, 1995: 3766):

• Defence of the EU *acquis*: Accession should not become an excuse for the renationalization of fishing policy. Transition periods should be used to facilitate adaptation to the EU situation, but the EU should not negotiate exemptions from, or permanent modifications to, the *acquis*.
• Increased capacity for the Spanish fleet. Spain wanted access to Norwegian waters, from which her vessels had been expelled in 1981. Spain would not accept Norwegian membership if this meant Spain was excluded from the cod fisheries.
• Spain must be fully incorporated into the CFP, that is, the transition period must be shortened.

This final demand was actually Spain's main objective in these negotiations. Indeed, Spain's negotiators stressed throughout that it would be illogical to allow new members straight into the CFP while Spain and Portugal remained subject to the transition period.

The Council, acting as a mini IGC in March 1994, agreed to incorporate the Spanish and Portuguese fleets. When some member states showed reluctance to ratify this compromise, the Spanish government, supported by all parliamentary groups, threatened to stop the enlargement by refusing to allow the *Cortes* to ratify the treaty. The Spanish Congress approved a proposal ordering the government to delay introducing the ratification instrument until the Council had adopted the legal instruments for allowing Spain full access to the General Fishing Regime.

Spanish pressure and arguments attained substantial results: Spain was granted full access to the CFO from 1996, a full seven years before the end of the original transition period. Its quota from EU waters was increased, the list of vessels was abolished and with it the system of double control. More significantly, Spain obtained access to the Irish Box, in the teeth of opposition from Britain and Ireland whose fishermen attempted to block the agreement. Spain was granted an extra cod quota from Norwegian waters (47.5 per cent of the total EU quota), equal to her pre-1981 catch. (Previously Spain had had a small quota from EEA compensation.) The EU also agreed to negotiate an extra 8,000 metric tonnes with third countries, 500 tonnes being with the North Atlantic Fishing Organization (NAFO). Finally, EU fishing companies, including Spanish ones, were allowed to invest freely in Norway from 1998. Norway's demands (relating to access, resource management and ownership of vessels) were accommodated through transition periods.

EU and Spanish fishing in third-country and international waters

Fishing agreements with third countries, and fishing in international waters, are an important part of Spain's fisheries policy, and one striking statistic serves to illustrate this: two-thirds of Spanish catches come from non-EU waters. Overall, then, Spain's fishing sector comprises a powerful fleet supplying a large market, with consumers willing to pay high prices for fish. Unlike the rest of the CFP, the external fishing agreements policy seems tailor-made for Spanish purposes.

Currently the EU has three types of agreement, each relating to a given geographical area. First, agreements with other European countries (the 'Northern' agreements) are based on reciprocal rights and opportunities. Secondly, the 'Southern' agreements with African and Indian Ocean countries are based on financial compensation to the non-EU countries, plus dues paid by private vessel owners. Finally, Argentina has a second-generation agreement based on joint ventures to exploit her EEZ. Table 6.2 gives the main figures for these agreements.

Spain placed a high priority on upholding these agreements. She is the only EU country that fishes worldwide, though most of this activity began well before she joined the EU. Before 1986 she had a large number of bilateral agreements (17 including those with Portugal and the EU itself), which served to make up for the inadequacy of Spanish fish stocks and the impact of the ever-increasing number of EEZs. EU membership brought all these agreements within the remit of the EU *acquis* and this meant full 'communitarization', via a twofold process whereby Spain assumed the *acquis* and the EU assumed the financial

Table 6.2 *Fishing agreements concluded with third countries and currently in force (data reflect the average of the period 1993–97)*

	Costs (€ million)			Vessels			Product value (€ million)			Added value (€ million)			Jobs[4] (direct and indirect)		
	EU part	Share (%)	Private actors share (%)	EU	Spain	Share (%)	EU	Spain	Share (%)	EU	Spain	Share (%)	EU	Spain	Share (%)
Northern countries Estonia, Faroes, Greenland, Iceland, Latvia, Lithuania, Norway, Poland[1] Russia	n.a.	n.a.	n.a.	1,832	232[2]	1.25	131	4.87	3.9	176	8.22	4.7	6,356	430	6.76
African and Indian Ocean countries Angola, Cape Verde, Comoros, Equatorial Guinea, Gabon, Gambia, Guinea, Guinea Bissau, Ivory Coast, Madagascar Morocco, Mauritania, Mauritius, São Tomé and Principe, Senegal, Seychelles	156	83.8	17.2	777	725	93.3	485	399	82	767	650	84.7	34,282	26,936	78.58
Latin America countries Argentina				29	25		n.a.	n.a.	n.a.	–	–	–	–	–	–
Total	1,053[3]			2,638	773	29.3	943	658.2	69.8				40,638	27,366	67.34

Source: Data compiled from IFREMER (1999) and CES (1999).
[1] Owing to assumption of existing agreements concluded by Finland and Sweden; [2] Spain from 1994 to 1997; [3] Costs for the whole period 1993–97; [4] Includes Argentina agreement.

burden of Spain's agreements. Spain's assumption of the *acquis* forced a modification of the system of joint ventures with third countries undertaken by private individuals. Previously, Spanish owners had been granted free access to third-country waters in exchange for unrestricted access to the Spanish market. But such access was incompatible with the EU's common external policy; the only way to resolve the situation was for the agreements to be assumed by the EU itself – that is, they had to be 'communitarized'. This was done in three ways: some of Spain's agreements were terminated (those with other EU countries); some were integrated with existing EU agreements; and in some cases the EU made bilateral agreements with countries with which it had had no previous relationship, such as Angola, Mauritania, Morocco and Mozambique. The overall outcome remains somewhat anomalous. The EU has far more bargaining clout than Spain alone, but this also enhances third parties' thirst for compensation, making agreements more and more costly.

The agreements with countries in the southern hemisphere, and with Morocco, are the most important from Spain's point of view. The Spanish fleet in northern waters also fishes in EU waters, so failure to obtain agreements there does not have the same direct social and economic impact. The dependence of the Spanish fleet on southern waters is very obvious, however: it is far larger than all the other EU fleets put together, representing some 93.3 per cent total a number of EU vessels (see Table 6.2). Spain takes over 80 per cent of total catches under the Southern agreements; the employment and added value they generate is concentrated in Spain. In terms of basic and added value, Spain's production under these agreements is higher than that in all the other member states put together. The gains are highly concentrated in a few Spanish regions. Third-country waters are fished by 91 per cent of the Canary Islands fleet, 75 per cent of Andalusia's, 55 per cent of Galicia's and 48 per cent of the Basque Country's. Twenty per cent of all those employed in the Spanish fishing industry work in third-country waters (CES, 1999: 19). Together, the Southern and Argentinian agreements represent about 20 per cent of the value of fisheries production in Spain. This helps explain why it was so urgent for Spain to ensure that the EU negotiated agreements with those countries.

Thus the role of the EU has become one of bank-rolling Spanish fisheries. Spain's own estimates show how positive the balance is. Total costs in 1999 were €283.2 million, which represented 30 per cent of the fishing budget and less than 0.31 per cent of the total EU budget. The total value of catches was €2 billion, and fishing provided direct employment for 20,000 people (CES, 1999: 19). Even the most cautious statisticians agree that the balance is positive. For each €1 paid by the EU for the southern and Greenland zones, the average return was €3.1.

The importance that Spain attaches to these agreements did not pass unnoticed by third parties. Aware of the EU's apparently bottomless coffers, they bargained for a constant increase in returns. Thus the number and quality of available EU compensation packages for third parties grew enormously, and this in turn increased the ambitions of negotiators and hardened their attitudes. The cost of the agreements with the Southern Zone and with Argentina rose by 60 per cent during the period under review. Access rights have been generally reduced: Morocco for example has been admitting fewer and fewer vessels. In a series of negotiations, non-EU countries attempted to reduce the numbers of Spanish fishermen and Spanish boats and increase those of their own nationals accordingly. Additionally, owing to the large size of the Spanish fleet, the EU's inability to secure sufficient fishing rights encouraged owners to supplement financial compensation in some of the Southern agreements (and all the tuna agreements) with private payments.

To date, the agreements with Morocco are the most significant and can serve as a typical example. In the 1990s, Morocco absorbed about 40 per cent of the EU budget for third-country agreements and accounted for about 54 per cent of the total value of catches under all the Southern agreements. Of the 477 EU vessels fishing in Moroccan waters, 404 were Spanish, and the industry directly employed 4,000 people. The Moroccan fisheries had enormous economic and social importance in Objective 1 regions (Andalusia, the Canaries and Galicia), though the impact was confined to certain small areas. Jones (2000: 155–76) gives an excellent account of the history and significance of these agreements. In 1988 the EU negotiated an agreement superseding the original one with Spain, which saved Spain from direct Moroccan pressure as she benefited from the EU's stronger bargaining position in negotiations. In 1992 the agreement was renewed with similar fishing rights, but a 50 per cent increase in payments to Morocco. If this was the carrot, the stick was the Association agreement between the EU and Morocco: it was made conditional upon Morocco's granting fishing rights.

Thus Morocco's cooperation depended largely on its desire for an association agreement, but for that very reason the EU had only one bargaining counter. By 1994 Morocco was exerting pressure on Spanish boats by withdrawing 200 fishing licences, which led to a fraught renegotiation of the agreement in 1995. Domestic pressures forced the Spanish government to adopt a tough stance, which it tried to sell to the Commission and the EU as a whole; but Morocco remained equally intransigent, and finally carried the day – reduced fishing rights and more money.

Morocco had already issued a warning that this was the last time it intended to renew, and attempts at renegotiation collapsed in March 2001. This meant the end of EU fishing activity in Moroccan waters. The impact on affected areas in Spain was dramatic and called for urgent restructuring. As Jones (2000) has shown, the Spanish government clamoured for a tougher negotiating stance by the EU, but Spain is now permanently caught between huge domestic pressure to produce a favourable agreement, pressure from the agricultural lobbies not to use trade concessions as a bargaining chip, and pressure from Brussels to adopt a more flexible attitude.

Chapter 7

Economic Integration: The Single Market, Competition and EMU

Conventional wisdom sees the deep and radical transformation of Spain's economy as one of the most decisive effects of her EU membership. It has been described as a struggle between the so-called *castizo* (traditionally Spanish) model of the economy and the requirements of the 'open' model adopted by the EU (Fuentes Quintana, 1995). The *castizo* model has four main features: a domestic market closed off by tariff protection; no encouragement of price competition and no exchange rate guarantee; continual state intervention to regulate economic activity (market decisions, financial arrangements); and an inefficient public sector. The replacement of the *castizo* by the open model was gradual: firstly, at structural level (rules and regulations), and then by means of a slower but more profound change in economic attitudes.

Spain joined the EU 'at just the right moment' (Clavera, 1996; Tovias, 1995: 104), when the conditions of global economic expansion and falling oil prices came together. Not all observers agree that Spain's strong economic performance between 1986 and 1992 was due solely to her EU accession (Tovias, 1995: 98), but at the time the prevailing belief was that accession would in itself resolve all the major problems of the Spanish economy (Fuentes Quintana, 1995: 133). The subsequent slowdown in the global economy starkly revealed the difficulties Spain was having in adapting her economy to the EU open model.

There is no doubt that EU membership served to catalyse existing reactions with the international economic environment (as we shall see in the next chapter, it also boosted modernization by injecting substantial structural funds). Spain gained in self-confidence, and her economy became more liberalized, capitalized and competitive (Elorza, 1997: 29). The macroeconomic impact of membership can be considered under two headings. First, there was a direct economic impact: patterns of production and consumption changed owing to the introduction of that pivotal EU institution, the single market. Secondly, there was an impact on policies: the EU has stimulated competition, transmitted its prevailing economic paradigms and, above all, provided the institutional framework and the external legitimization for national macroeconomic policy.

Market liberalization: the impact of EU rules and the changing role of the state

Since the late nineteenth century Spain had adhered to a protectionist economic regime (Velarde, 1995: 385): political nationalism had been matched by economic nationalism. Spanish capitalism was protected by tariffs, closed markets, monopolies and other restrictions. What liberalization there had been was largely due to external pressures or incentives (Alonso and Donoso, 1999: 216); the one exception was the 1959 Stabilization Plan, but even that followed an International Monetary Fund mission to investigate the difficulties of the Spanish economy. EU accession changed the prevailing model for good, introducing liberalization and competition (Fuentes Quintana, 1995: 110). Adaptation to the more liberal EU model took three main forms (Molina, 2001b): the elimination of trade barriers, the removal of chronic state intervention, and enhanced competitiveness. Altogether, accession to the EU implied a tougher economic regime and a regulatory framework favouring competition, plus a significant penetration by foreign capital.

Liberalization was a political objective for both the two largest parties, the socialist Partido Socialista Obrero Español (PSOE) and the conservative Partido Popular (PP). Some authors (see Fernández Ordóñez, 1999) have argued that there were no significant differences between their liberalization programmes. Whilst it is true that their intentions were broadly similar, the general economic climate was much harsher when the socialists were in power, and this made liberalization more difficult – a fact that was reflected in the measures adopted. The first liberalization measures were contained in the 'Decreto Boyer' (1985), relating to domestic rents and commercial opening hours. Up to 1985 the only measures that had actually been passed were those required by EU membership, plus a few in the banking sector. From 1992 onwards, however, the Convergence Programme provided a powerful incentive to liberalization

(Fernández Ordóñez 1999: 671–3), although in both the 1992 and the 1994 updates of the Programme the main focus was on labour markets. The PP government after 1996 was more zealous in its pursuit of liberalization, but as late as 2000 an upsurge in inflation was put down to insufficient liberalization in several key sectors: gas (which operated as a *de facto* monopoly), oil and electricity (where a small number of companies had carved up the market), land, commercial opening hours and local phone calls. Thus, in July 2000, the PP government – recently reelected with an absolute majority – adopted a package of new liberalizing measures aimed at curbing creeping inflationary pressures.

Liberalization did not mean solely or even primarily that private enterprise had to adapt to tougher competition. Apart from the elimination of tariffs, EU regulations affected the structure of Spanish industry in terms of both ownership and competition. State ownership played a key role in mining, heavy industry (such as steel and shipbuilding), utilities, communications and transport. In the early 1980s, state-owned companies accounted for nearly 10 per cent of both value added and total employee remuneration, and generated almost 15 per cent of gross fixed capital formation (Boix, 1999: 28). The extent and role of state ownership were progressively redefined. First, publicly owned industries now had less access to funding, since EU regulations placed a limit on injections of public money. Secondly, the Spanish government had a reputation for intervening heavily in the economy, a tendency which has been underlined on various occasions. Several privatizations (for instance, that of the automobile manufacturer SEAT) were preceded by capital injections that breached competition rules and led to fierce arguments between the Commission and the Spanish government (Chari, 1999). In some cases, such as Iberia, these blatant injections were repeated several times. Some Spanish officials argued that state aid to industry had always favoured the Community's richer countries, pointing out that the Big Four absorbed 82 per cent of state aid between 1990 and 1992, and 85 per cent between 1992 and 1994 (*El País*, 1 August 1999). It has been argued that four of the most industrialized countries (Germany, Italy, Belgium and Luxembourg) provided the largest amounts of state aid, whereas the amounts were much lower in the four cohesion countries with the lowest per capita income (González-Páramo and Melguizo, 1999: 601).

According to EU Commission figures, aid expenditure decreased very slightly between 1990 and 2000. In the period 1995–99, Spanish state aid as a percentage of GDP stood at 1.7 per cent (just below the EU average of 1.8 per cent), with only Denmark, the Netherlands, Sweden and the UK spending less. Spain was similarly positioned in regard to state aid per capita and as a percentage of employed workers. However, when measuring state aid as a share of total government expenditure, Spain stood somewhat above the EU average. Between 1999 and 2000, there were reductions of 25 per cent in aid to agriculture and of 10 per cent to manufacturing, with sharp falls for specific industries such as the railways (40 per cent) and coal (26 per cent). By contrast, the steel industry has continued to receive significant aid, and certain sectors and industries have been granted *ad hoc* payments: for instance, a billion pesetas to electricity companies as compensation for the transition to increased competition; additional funding for RTVE; and fiscal support for the Basque Country. In general terms, though, patterns of state aid in Spain are increasingly moving into line with the EU mainstream and converging towards the lower end of the spectrum.

Moreover, state ownership in Spain has declined in line with a general drive towards privatization in Western Europe. This has not been so prominent as in other EU member states, because (contrary to certain assumptions), the Spanish public sector was smaller in quantity (and lower in quality) than those of other EU member states (Fernández Ordóñez, 1999: 667; González-Páramo and Melguizo, 1999: 596). In the early 1980s, privatization was limited to the car industry in an attempt to revive flagging companiea (González-Páramo and Melguizo, 1999: 596). Oil, communications and banking were added at the end of the decade, the latter mainly due to new EU regulations.

Both PSOE and PP governments pursued privatization, and some commentators argue that they both followed the same privatization policy, despite differences in presentation and rhetoric (Fernández Ordóñez, 1999: 667). The facts do not support this assertion. Between 1982 and 1993, sales of public assets generated 0.9 per cent of Spanish GDP; privatization accelerated after 1993, with sales rising to 1.4 per cent of GDP between 1993 and 1996 (Boix, 1999: 28). It has been calculated that the sale of public assets raised 2 billion pesetas between 1988 and 1996 (under PSOE governments), whereas under the PP government's Plan for Modernization of the Public Sector the figure reached 4.1 billion pesetas (González-Páramo and Melguizo, 1999: 596). The PP was far more committed to privatization, both in principle and in practice, than the PSOE.

What both parties did share was a desire to retain the national character of the industries. Deregulation and privatization of former monopolies such as Iberia and Telefónica went hand in hand with retaining control over the privatized companies through a 'golden share' (by which the government continued to own a controlling share which would enable it legally to control fundamental decisions), and by encouraging Spanish investors to buy in and form a national 'hard core' of shareholders (Molina, 2001b).

The effect of market liberalization on trade patterns

Globally, market liberalization has turned out to be highly positive, bringing about a marked growth in the 'openness' of the Spanish economy (Figure 7.1). Increasing internationalization and, in particular, the growth of exports helped reduce what has been seen as the traditional curbs on economic growth: the absence of an external dimension combined with a chronic trade deficit. The improvement

Figure 7.1 *Openness of the Spanish economy, 1961–2003: exports and imports of goods and services (percentage of GDP at market prices)*

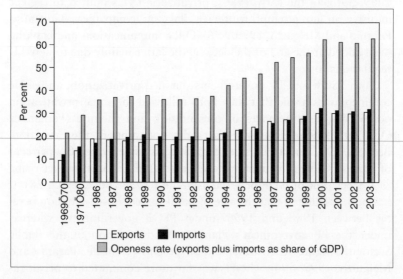

Source: Data compiled from European Economy (2002).

was, of course, only relative: since it joined the EU, Spain's trade in merchandise as a percentage of GDP has remained one of the lowest in the EU, and indeed in the OECD.

Liberalization has also shifted the quality and geographical orientation of Spanish trade. Membership has meant that EU states have become the main trading partners of Spanish companies (Alonso and Donoso, 1999), other partners being squeezed out by the Common External Tariff and Community restrictions on trade with nonmembers. In particular, the USA has lost importance as a trading partner. Apart from the geographical transformation of Spanish trade, the removal of tariffs and export aids has dramatically worsened the trade balance. According to some estimates, Spain has had a negative balance of around 3 per cent of GDP with EU member states every year since 1960 (Fuentes Quintana, 1995: 129). Since 1986, trade has grown, but imports from EU member states to Spain have increased faster owing to the removal of Spanish protectionist measures; global imports rose from 16.8 per cent of domestic demand in 1986 to 33.1 per cent in 1996 (Martín, 1997: 85, 97). The substantial economic growth that followed entry increased domestic consumption and so sucked in imports. In this sense, membership initially caused a significant displacement of Spanish products (mainly consumer goods) from the domestic market as demand grew for high-quality European goods.

Growth in exports, on the other hand, has actually been slower since the EU granted preferential treatment to Spanish products in the early 1970s (a 60 per cent reduction in the normal EU external tariff). And it is in exports that the EU's growing domination of Spanish trade has overshadowed that with all other parts of the world (Alonso and Donoso, 1999: 222). As a result, Spain's trade deficit is now the largest in the OECD and her trade balance with EU member states has worsened significantly. Since 1986, the only major EU trading partner with which Spain has had a consistent trade surplus has been Portugal. The special treatment accorded to Spanish agricultural exports did something to ameliorate the trade balance but did not ease the deficit.

Spain's import:export ratio *vis-à-vis* EU member states fell from 91 per cent in 1986 to 70 per cent in 1989, and the former ratio was not reached again until 1996 (Hernando, 1997: 148). As regards intra-community trade as a proportion of total trade, some authors have argued that Spain stands well above the EU average (Martín, 1997: 184–7; Hernando, 1997: 154). However, as shown in Figure 7.2,

Figure 7.2 *Spanish trade with the EU: exports and imports of goods and services (percentage of GDP at market prices)*

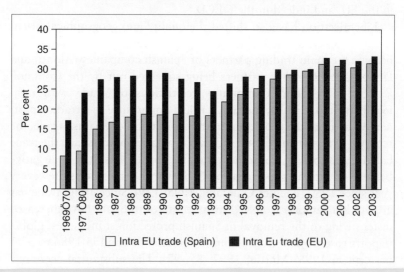

□ Intra EU trade (Spain)   ■ Intra Eu trade (EU)

Source: Data compiled from European Economy (2002).

Spanish intra-EU trade as a percentage of GDP is in fact converging with the EU average – from well behind. Taken together, however, these data clearly indicate that trade plays a smaller role in the Spanish economy than in most EU member states. On the whole, Spain's trade balance with other EU member states tends to worsen when the economy is buoyant and improve during a recession (Fuentes Quintana, 1995: 129). As Tovias (1995: 94) graphically remarks, the EU had entered Spain, not vice versa. Others have remarked that that the main beneficiaries of Spain's integration into the SEA have been foreign companies (Holman, 1996: 151).

However, this trade imbalance is hardly new for the Spanish economy; indeed, some authors speak in terms of a structural trade deficit (Bernardos and Aznar, 1996; Hernando, 1997). Spain's current account is in chronic deficit, with a negative trade balance for every year between 1964 and 1998 (Alonso and Donoso, 1999: 209), even though it has decreased as a proportion of GDP. Lack of energy resources contributed to this level of deficit, as did the overvaluation of the peseta, but the chief culprits were low productivity, lack of adaptation to a new international environment and general uncompetitiveness (Martín, 1997: 140, 203). These shortcomings were particularly acute in the industrial sector, where there was a lack of both high-quality and high-tech products. Liberalization caused a general contraction of Spanish industry, and the contribution of the manufacturing sector to GDP sank below the EU average (*ibid*.: 1999: 22).

It is widely agreed that external trade is one of the weakest points in the Spanish economy (Holman, 1996: 133; Alonso and Donoso, 1999: 231). In reality, however, structural imbalance is symptomatic of a deeper problem, that of uncompetitiveness (Fuentes Quintana, 1995: 94) and attempts to tackle this issue became a leitmotif in the policies of both the PSOE and the PP.

Competitiveness strategies and party preferences

Improving competitiveness became the chief economic objective of successive Spanish governments. In the global reports on competitiveness published by the World Economic Forum, Spain has consistently featured as one of the least competitive countries in the OECD. Between 1996 and 1999, Spain's ranking varied from 26th (1999 and 1997) to 25th (1998) and 32nd (1996). Only Portugal, Italy and Greece were deemed less competitive and all the other member states were placed higher – including some, such as Belgium and Austria, that began behind Spain but subsequently overtook her. The challenge, then, was to increase competitiveness, restructure the production base and position Spain in the world economy so as to gain maximum competitive advantage (Salmon, 1995: 68). All Spanish governments shared this aim, although the PSOE and the PP have differed over the best means of achieving it, not only because of ideological preferences but also because of political constraints on their actions and the prevailing economic paradigm.

In the first years of membership it became apparent that a drive for competitiveness at any price might entrap Spain in a system of productivity based on low wages, low-technology products and low costs (Maravall, 1987). Spanish productivity has been calculated at 75 per cent of the EU average, largely attributable to lower capitalization in the Spanish economy (Martín, 1997: 47). The PSOE government's strategy to reduce unemployment and catch up with Europe was therefore based on transforming the supply situation in the Spanish economy through massive public spending on human and physical capital. To this end, the government embarked on a systematic policy of public capital formation (Boix, 1999: 30).

The areas in which the PSOE's strategy of capitalization was chiefly implemented were industry and infrastructure. Industrial policy (at least up to 1986) was based on the assumption that if private enterprise could not adjust to the new conditions, government would have to take the lead in developing and adapting all branches of industry (Saro, 2000). The PSOE's industrial policy was one of highly selective privatization, consolidation of firms in order to generate economies of scale, and delayed introduction of competitive markets in some instances (Boix, 1999: 24). As part of this grand design, the public sector was to bear the burden of capital restructuring and the modernization of productive capital (Alberola, 2000; Boix, 1999: 28). Capital was injected into telecommunications, transport and oil and gas (Boix, 1999: 28). A 'reconversion' (that is, restructuring) strategy was designed to establish an industrial base capable of standing up to international competition. But, in practice, it amounted to

> shielding traditional industries from the full impact of the industrial crisis, diverting attention from more politically difficult structural change and delaying the process of international specialisation that was taking shape in the world economy. (Salmon 1995: 84)

Moreover, this industrial policy failed to tackle key issues related to the business environment, including the flexibility of factor markets (*ibid.*).

It was not until 1993 that the PSOE really began to view liberalization as a neutral tool for improving competitiveness. Previously, from 1986 onwards, the socialist government had striven mightily to consolidate national (private or public) groups in banking, energy and defence. This meant that competition increased only in sectors such as cable TV and mobile phones in which technological breakthroughs altered the production and distribution of goods and broke up national monopolies (Boix, 1999: 29). Service industries were more or less sheltered from deregulation and competitive pressures – which enabled them to pass wage rises and increasing costs directly on to the consumer, thus fuelling inflation (Alberola, 2000; Fuentes Quintana, 1995: 110). In sectors where there were no technological changes (that is, where the existing natural monopolies or fully competitive markets remained unchanged), the Spanish government pushed for consolidation in order to support economies of scale (Boix, 1999: 30).

Inflation, fuelled by a strong growth in domestic demand, represented another threat to competitiveness, at least until the change in policy mix around 1994. Spanish prices rose faster than those in other member states between 1986 and 1996. Further difficulties included the overvaluation of the peseta, caused first by the policy of keeping interest rates high in order to attract capital and so improve the trade balance, and secondly by the increased confidence generated by Spain's membership of the EMS (Martín, 1997: 92). Competitiveness was not restored until the government resorted to the time-honoured strategy of devaluing the peseta in 1992. But inflation, combined with a restrictive monetary policy and an expansive fiscal policy, still remained a problem (Bernardos and Aznar, 1996: 39; Martínez Serrano, 1999: 702).

The currency crisis severely limited the effectiveness of traditional recipes for competitiveness. In the early 1990s the PSOE government was determined that Spain should plan her own strategies for liberalization and deregulation (Fernández Ordóñez, 1999: 663), which meant redefining 'industrial policy' so as to improve competitiveness at the European level. The change of paradigm was encapsulated in changed attitudes to the role of public authorities: henceforward they were to energize the economy by creating macroeconomic stability, stimulating employment, investing in infrastructures and information technology, and supporting small businesses (Saro, 2001). It was now widely accepted that international competition had historically been the main engine of modernization (Martínez Serrano, 1999: 686), and so Spanish politicians were predisposed to accept liberalization as an instrument for boosting competitiveness. Spain gave up dragging its feet over the EU's demands, and the necessary liberalization of telecommunications and air transport was completed well ahead of schedule. In the new climate, liberalization was not viewed as a necessary evil consequent on EU membership, but as something good in itself (Fernández Ordóñez, 1999).

The PP government strengthened the liberalization process when it assumed office in 1996. Some socialists commented that the PP was merely implementing the programme devised by the *Tribunal de Defensa de la Competencia* (Competitiveness Tribunal) at the behest of the outgoing socialist government (Fernández Ordóñez, 1999: 675). But the PP leaders, unlike their opposite numbers in the PSOE, were able to speak with one voice on matters of economic policy, particularly privatization (Feito, 1997). They called for a redefinition of the role of public enterprise, together with extensive deregulation and privatization.

Privatization was seen not as a handy means of raising cash but as a vital step on the road to improved economic efficiency. But there was also a profound change in their concept of the role of the state: its function was restricted to guaranteeing the rights of its citizens, leaving the production of necessary goods and services to those best fitted to provide them (Rato, 1995/6: 30). Immediately after gaining office, the government approved its first plan for liberalization and economic restructuring (*Plan de Fomento del Empleo y Modernización de la Economía*). The plan involved changes to the tax system and the deregulation of such areas as land and housing, telecommunications, utilities, and registration of second-hand vehicles. In 1997 the government introduced its second liberalization programme (*Plan de Liberalización y Reactivación Económica*), which covered the same sectors plus transport, roads and harbours, competitiveness measures and the deregulation of professional corporations.

The PP Minister of the Economy, Rodrigo Rato, was convinced that inflation was fuelled by insufficient deregulation, a growing public deficit and poor competition in certain sectors and markets (Rato, 1995/6: 26). Spain's improved macroeconomic performance since 1997 has only strengthened this belief, and has contributed to a changed attitude towards the EU: from seeking simply to emulate the policies of other EU governments, Spain progressed to a thoroughgoing Europeanization of its macroeconomic programme. Initially hostile to the then dominant social-democratic approach, the PP advanced towards a kind of liberalization that was very much in line with the prevailing trend in EU thinking.

The same initial defensiveness towards EU policies characterized the PP's attitude to employment. The PP administration assumed that employment could be fostered only through a global macroeconomic policy; even more important, it is not government but society that creates employment, chiefly through the agency of small and medium-sized companies. The PP approach was to maintain macroeconomic stability and enhance the flexibility of markets through further liberalization and deregulation. In cooperation with the British Labour government, they created a group at ministerial level to study the reform of capital and goods markets.

The result was an ambitious programme for a New Economy that was jointly submitted by the Spanish and British governments to the March 2000 European summit at Lisbon. According to both José María Aznar and Tony Blair, governments should avoid *dirigiste* policies or any attempt to interfere in the workings of the market, as well as refraining from intervening in business decisions or imposing excessive regulation. Rather, the new role of government should be to foster the right conditions for private enterprise to create jobs. Such a view also had institutional repercussions, with national coordination being seen as more effective than harmonization, and intergovernmental coordination as better than the EU's traditional supra-national approach in the sphere of economic policy, which should remain in the hands of national leaders operating through the European Council structure (Aznar and Blair, 2000).

The target was full employment by around 2010. The USA provided the model, but the aim was to emulate US efficiency and competitiveness while preserving the European model of the welfare state. The main tool was to be the development and application of new technologies (in Spain itself this was paralleled by the creation of a new *ad hoc* ministry and national programme of R&D), focused on the concept of the 'knowledge economy'. The plan, which was built around a clearly liberal macroeconomic framework, had three central pillars:

- Progress towards the 'knowledge economy' through the implementation of specifically tailored and targeted R&D policies, structural economic reform, and completion of the single market.
- Rapid modernization of the European social model, to be achieved through a combination of investment in human capital, employment policies, and measures aimed at preventing social exclusion.
- Stable economic growth of around 3 per cent a year, supported by economic reform involving increased market deregulation over the medium term. It was argued that the development of new technologies had been hampered by excessive regulation and by the fragmented structure of national markets.

Like the programme for economic and monetary union (EMU), the implementation of the plan was divided into three stages. The first was aimed at eliminating barriers to electronic trade, bringing in a European charter for small companies, increasing the flexibility of the labour market and adopting new guidelines for macroeconomic policy; the Commission was to be given greater powers to guide and monitor these changes. In the second stage, Aznar proposed full liberalization of the electricity, energy and air transport markets plus full integration of capital markets, together with rigid limits on government funding and encouragement of public access to the Internet. This stage was to follow a preset timetable with clearly defined objectives, following the model of EMU. Finally, the third stage would involve a complete overhaul of the European social model, though no concrete measures were proposed for this (*El País*, 19 March 2000). Some key elements of the Spanish proposal were subsequently incorporated into European Council proposals.

Thus EU membership has altered the conventional structure of the Spanish economy through a combination of induction, learning and imitation. From being traditionally considered a country in the interventionist and statist mould typical of Southern Europe, Spain has reoriented itself towards liberalization on a more Anglo-Saxon model and even taken the lead in some aspects. Initially, EU rules had the paradoxical effect of forcing the Spanish economy into a 'liberalizing' straitjacket – effectively, an imposed Europeanization. Neither governing party had any option about this, but their subsequent performance was shaped both by party preferences and by the international economic environment.

Macroeconomic fiscal and monetary policy

The early part of this chapter identified market liberalization as the main impact of EU membership on the Spanish economy. However, membership served equally to provide a framework for macroeconomic (particularly fiscal and monetary) policy. In this domain the EU provided not just an anchor, or assurance of commitment, but also a scapegoat, particularly when it came to implementing unpopular policies. Accession to the EU reinforced the government's commitment to a policy paradigm in which competitiveness was the fundamental objective, to be achieved through low inflation, macroeconomic balance and structural reforms in the domestic market (Boix, 1999: 13).

Spanish policies before EMU

Building the welfare state

One of the most important results of Spain's accession to the EU was the transmission to Spain of the prevailing economic paradigm centred on market liberalization and restrictive fiscal policy. But this paradigm fitted uneasily with Spanish political priorities. During the transition period Spanish macroeconomic policy gave priority to the construction of a fully fledged welfare state with social services comparable to those in other EU member states (Martín, 1999: 101; Alberola, 2001; Boix, 1999). The political requirements of transition (which included various pacts involving unions and left-wing parties) encouraged expansion in the public sector and increased social expenditure. Until the mid-1980s, macroeconomic policy remained subordinated to the political goal of consolidating democracy. Between 1975 and 1985, public expenditure doubled as a share of GDP; nonetheless, at the time of accession, social expenditure was below the EU average and Spanish infrastructure was significantly underdeveloped (González Páramo and Melguizo, 1999: 585).

The increase in public expenditure was initiated by the Unión de Centro Democrático (UCD) governments of Adolfo Suárez and consolidated by PSOE governments after 1982. The latter endeavoured to build up the welfare state, slim down unprofitable nationalized industries (shipbuilding, steel) and invest in more potentially profitable activities. To compensate for the introduction of a stable macroeconomic framework, the PSOE's economic and social policies had a distinct redistributive bias (Boix, 1999: 30); increased public expenditure was targeted at the social services (health and pensions), education and infrastructure. This has been seen as a convergence with the prevailing European pattern (Martín, 1999: 104), but there have been critics of the PSOE's apparent prioritizing of austerity and adjustment (Holman, 1996: 147). Galera (1996: 115) claimed that this transformation of the 'Spanish economic constitution' favoured the market economy to the detriment of the 'social component', but the balance of opinion is against him: in practice, successive Spanish governments had no choice but to develop the social policies characteristic of a welfare state (Boix, 1999; Alberola, 2000; Martín, 1997; Martínez Serrano, 1999: 701). But this development has been spasmodic, and not until after 1988 was there significant growth (González-Páramo and Melguizo, 1999: 593; Barea, 1995b), largely the result of a general strike in December 1988 and the electoral losses suffered by the socialists in 1989.

Monetary policy: the significance of the European Monetary System (EMS)

The domestic background to macroeconomic policy was dominated by two sets of circumstances: the general uncompetitiveness of the Spanish economy (indicated by increasing trade deficits with EU member states) and the development of the welfare state (which meant an increasing public deficit). Thus, macroeconomic policy had somehow to reconcile the contradictory requirements of the existing paradigm (a restrictive monetary policy) with domestic political necessities (an expansive fiscal policy). In this paradigm the control of inflation was a central mechanism for adjustment, but since political circumstances precluded a restrictive fiscal policy, monetary policy was left alone to sustain the deflationary macroeconomic strategy of the PSOE government (Boix, 1999:33; Alberola, 2000). EMS membership became the cornerstone of this strategy.

The most powerful reason for joining the EMS was 'borrower credibility': domestic and external investors had to be persuaded of the government's commitment to its macroeconomic objectives, particularly the control of inflation. EMS membership provided a clearly defined objective: to match the inflation rate in other EU member states. This would ensure external credibility whilst internally it served to legitimate a tighter fiscal policy. But EMS membership was also a political priority linked to the forthcoming economic and monetary union (EMU): in the words of a top Spanish official, Spain's position in EMU would depend on when and how she decided to join the EMS exchange mechanism (Solbes *et al.*, 1988: 52). The socialist government had few qualms about sacrificing national sovereignty in this particular area of macroeconomic management (Boix, 1999: 18).

Making EMS membership into a political priority meant accepting an overvalued peseta exchange rate with the ecu and the German Deutschmark (DM), which would have a severe impact on the key indicators of the Spanish economy (Gómez Castañeda, 1994; Myro, 1999: 244). The Spanish peseta was allowed to float within an EMS band of ±6 per cent. Although EMS membership served to control inflation (see Figure 7.3), it had a negative impact on Spanish competitiveness. The overvalued peseta was coupled with high interest rates, which were necessary to correct excessive external deficits and attract foreign investment (Martín, 1997: 151). High interest rates were also the price of heavy government borrowing to fill the financial hole created by its welfare programme, and in turn depressed levels of productive investment.

Spain's attractiveness as a destination for long-term capital was based on expectations about the profitability of fixed investments, relatively low labour costs, an expanding domestic market and EU membership (Alberola, 1998: 51; Salmon, 1995: 78). Interest-rate differentials and exchange-rate variations attracted short-term capital, which meant that capital flows were intrinsically unstable. On the one hand, foreign investment increased total investment in Spain and enabled the Spanish economy in the late 1980s to sustain growth above the OECD average by offsetting the balance of payments deficit (Salmon, 1995: 79). It has been calculated that the flow of foreign investment reached 3 per cent of GDP (Story and Grugel 1991), and according to some estimates, Spain attracted around 12 per cent of investment in the EU from third countries and around 15 per cent of intra-EU investment (Myro, 1999: 254). But on the other hand, when the monetary crisis broke out in 1992, foreign capital fled from Spain, causing a sudden decapitalization of the Spanish economy. Abandoning Spain was quite easy since capital controls had been lifted by February 1992, ahead of schedule.

The 1992 crisis highlighted two weaknesses in the Spanish economy. First, it exposed its lack of competitiveness. Secondly, it brutally exposed the overvaluation of the peseta. Unable to sustain exchange rates by manipulating interest rates, the government had to accept four successive devaluations of the peseta between 1992 and 1995: by 5 per cent on 17 September 1992, 6 per cent on 22 November 1992, 8 per cent on 13 May 1993 and 7 per cent on 5 March 1995. The exchange rate with the German DM fell from 79.117 to 85.07. Initially, Spain had asked for a devaluation of 5 per cent followed by a 5 per cent revaluation of the DM. The German authorities rejected this, and the French authorities in turn rejected a 10 per cent devaluation of the peseta because it might expose the French franc to speculative attacks. Thus, while Spain paid dearly for its commitment to the EMS, it seems clear that this was a deliberate political choice (Alberola, 2000; Barbé, 1999: 93; Salmon, 1995: 70), a willing sacrifice in exchange for the prospective benefits of EMU membership. Holding out against speculative attacks on the peseta was a feasible strategy given the enormous reserves held by the Bank of Spain (Tovias, 1995: 96).

The monetary crisis also highlighted the limitations of a macroeconomic policy driven primarily by monetary instruments. Most commentators agree that the main defect of Spain's policy was that it was an untenable policy mix: a restrictive monetary policy which was not supported by strict budgetary and wage controls (Gómez Castañeda, 1994; Clavera, 1996: 51; Gamir, 1998: 202). As far as the budget was concerned, transition requirements and the drive to construct a welfare state militated against any attempt to reduce public expenditure. Critics have pointed out that early 1990s budgets gave up the attempt to eliminate the public deficit: the increase in

GDP was directed towards funding increased levels of social protection (Barea 1995a: 148). This was largely due to the electoral setback suffered by the PSOE in 1989, which persuaded the government to increase social redistribution so as to avoid losing more popular support (Boix, 1999: 31). But even cutbacks in public expenditure were a limited option: the Socialists could not reduce spending on infrastructure because this would have reduced EU pay-outs, since the principle of additionality required EU funding to be supplemented by national governments.

The government proved incapable of reforming the labour market. Some critics have argued that this should have been done immediately following accession, which would have enhanced competitiveness and made it effectively unnecessary to use the exchange rate as the central mechanism for curbing inflation (Bernardos and Aznar, 1996: 39). The need for reform was pressing: wage costs began to outstrip productivity from 1986 (Velarde, 1995: 395). The PSOE government proved unable to negotiate successfully with the unions to secure moderate wage claims and measures to control inflation. At first, the government attempted to keep wage inflation down by inviting the unions to collaborate in attaining macroeconomic objectives through the use of pacts (Heywood, 1999). But dissatisfaction with the redistribution of the benefits of economic growth, coupled with high wage demands, led to confrontation which culminated in the December 1988 general strike. In spring 1991, the government proposed a *Pacto de Competitividad* (Competitiveness Agreement) the main objectives of which were to secure economic growth along with price stability, limit wage rises and introduce structural reforms by improving the flexibility of the labour market and reducing public expenditure. To leftist critics this proposal was a typical austerity programme, based on fiscal and monetary restrictions designed for the benefit of large corporations (Montes, 1994: 174). Negotiations with both unions and employers failed, and the government had to impose its wages policy unilaterally. The effects of this failure to come to an agreement with the unions were profound: without an effective wage control policy the socialist government was deprived of an essential instrument for controlling inflation (Myro, 1999: 254). The only alternatives were a restrictive monetary policy or cuts in public expenditure (Boix, 1999: 15). Paradoxically, the Socialist government's management of macroeconomic policy after accession to the EU placed ever less reliance on agreement with the unions.

Spanish macroeconomic policy within EMU

The political and economic debate over EMU

The drive towards EMU provided a new framework within which action on fiscal policy could be firmly grounded without abandoning attempts to control inflation. It added muscle to the government's pronouncements on budgetary discipline and wage bargaining. The appeal of the European ideal was still a powerful argument in macro-economic policy, but while opposition was lower than in other member states, EMU accession was far from being unanimously supported. Criticisms were directed not so much against the net costs of being in EMU as against the costs of actually joining it. That was the case argued by two former Ministers of the Economy, Juan Antonio García Díez (UCD) and Miguel Boyer (PSOE). Keynesian critics from within academe also cast doubt on Spain's capacity to fulfil the convergence criteria set out in the Maastricht Treaty (Torrero, 1998), whilst criticism of the excessive social costs involved was even more pronounced. Thus, it was argued that any hasty application of policies required in order to fulfil the criteria for nominal convergence might limit economic growth and endanger real convergence. Neo-liberal stabilization policies and the severe curb on wage increases were also criticized by left-wing analysts and politicians (Holman, 1996; Montes, 1994).

Not surprisingly, given that convergence proved exceedingly difficult despite the sacrifices made, politicians in both the final PSOE and the first PP administrations considered whether it would be expedient to slow down the rate at which it was being pursued. However, the majority view was that the convergence criteria should be met as soon as possible. As with EU accession, a combination of political and economic reasons were used in favour of EMU membership, although on this occasion the economic considerations prevailed over political ones.

The central argument against EMU was that it would mean loss of control over both the exchange rate and monetary policy, as well as leaving a smaller margin for manoeuvre over fiscal policy. This would make it more difficult to manage the economy in circumstances which were specific to Spain, such as changes to national supply or demand. However, this argument was easy to downplay because such circumstances were not expected to be frequent. Moreover, the role of the exchange rate as a stabilization tool was questionable, as it could equally be used as a substitute for sound macroeconomic discipline

(Alberola, 1998). In short, the alternative solutions to EMU were deemed less attractive, whereas the benefits of EMU were seen as being substantial: it would improve macroeconomic stability and reduce structural imbalances (Alberola, 1998). Moreover, the Bank of Spain pointed out that the costs of remaining outside were potentially very high. The basic consensus on EMU pivoted on the link between nominal and real convergence. Nominal convergence meant restructuring the economy to increase growth and employment (Fuentes Quintana, 1995: 83; Gamir, 1998: 195). The Bank of Spain threw its weight behind this view by recommending that the convergence criteria should be met by forcing through structural reforms (Banco de Espana, 1997: 59). Additional arguments were that the Spanish economy would benefit from increased openness, from being anchored within one of the three great world economic blocks and from reduced transaction costs. Politically, EMU membership would increase Spain's influence: it would be a huge political mistake for her to miss the opportunity of getting in on EMU's ground floor (Lázaro, 1997: 43, 62; Banco de España, 1997; Gamir, 1998).

While there was no widespread opposition to the convergence criteria, there were some attempts to adapt the agenda to suit specific Spanish needs. Spain had particular difficulty in achieving nominal convergence, owing to a tendency to above-average inflation, lower competitiveness (offset by manipulating the exchange rate) and high wage demands. These fears of being unable to match the convergence criteria were expressed by the Spanish government in 1994 during the northern enlargement negotiations. Spain wanted a legally binding agreement to ignore the economic circumstances of new members when assessing convergence criteria, but Germany and France opposed this.

When the PP took office in 1996 there were calls to stop the convergence clock. Some well-known party members, such as Pedro Schwartz, were opposed to EMU membership, but they were not among the leadership. Instead, the new minister of the Economy, Rodrigo Rato, hastened to reaffirm that the PP's – and Spain's – main political challenge was to be part of EMU from the very beginning (Rato, 1995/6: 23). The challenge was made stark when some bankers and politicians from northern member states voiced their doubts over the capacity of Spain and other Mediterranean member states to fulfil the convergence criteria and therefore whether they were acceptable as EMU members. This in fact acted as a stimulus to Spain, since it made it look as if the only alternative was marginalization within

Europe. In any case, the PP was convinced that the economic foundations of convergence were good in themselves. As Rato (1995/6: 26) remarked, one of the main causes of the welfare shortfall was the imbalance created by Spain's public deficit, and therefore its correction was a priority objective.

The significance of EMU for the Spanish economy

The significance of EMU for the Spanish economy and macroeconomic management was far-reaching. It imposed tight requirements for transforming the traditional model of Spanish public spending: henceforward the public authorities would have to conform to externally set criteria. Once in EMU, the only significant macro-economic policy that would remain under government control was taxation, meaning that the former concentration on monetary policy would be curbed. This Europeanization of policy meant not only the adoption of central management instruments, but also a radical transformation of public attitudes, since hitherto a permanent public deficit had been considered normal.

The main instruments for the Europeanization of macroeconomic policy have been the successive convergence plans (Table 7.1) that have focused on the twin objectives of reducing inflation and containing the public deficit. Commitment to these objectives gave the government some much-needed credibility, as had been the case earlier with EMS membership (Gallastegui, 1992). How far the exacting requirements have been met, however, has depended on the parties' preferences and capabilities. The PSOE government designed the first plan in 1992 and updated it in 1994 because of the worsening of economic conditions in the intervening period. Some critics complained that this plan took no account of Spanish economic reality: in both 1992 and 1994 the convergence programmes had been behind schedule and quite unrealistic (Heywood, 1993; Fuentes Quintana, 1995: 69). It was apparent from the outset that the government would be unable to confine the public deficit to 3 per cent of GDP, or the national debt to 60 per cent of GDP. The elimination of the public deficit was supposed to be achieved through increased taxation (Barea, 1995a: 151), but critics pointed out that this would not begin to bite until 1996–97 – that is, after the elections (Gamir, 1998: 201). Ultimately, the failure of the 1992 programme was due to an unrealistic budget and a failure to control public spending (González-Páramo and Melguizo, 1999: 590; Barea, 1995b).

The conservative PP government developed a third Convergence

Table 7.1   Spanish convergence programmes, 1992–97

Plan	Markets	Public sector	Social Expenditure
1992	• Liberalize and deregulate • Limit price fixing, monopolies and restrictions on professional activity • Work towards flexible labour market. Create private employment agencies	*Fiscal and budgetary policy* • Maintain fiscal pressure • Improve management • Agreement on financing of *autonomías* *Administration* • Reduce number of public bodies *Public-sector ownership* • No sell-offs • Introduce free-enterprise management • Freeze on public investment	*Health* • Switch from an administrative to a management model for services; identify costs. • Expenditure not to go over targets • Reorganize
1994	• Continue working for flexible labour market • Modernize vocational training and research • Reduce monopolistic practices in local and professional services	*Fiscal and budgetary policy* • Discretionary measures to cut structural deficit and contain current expenditure • Users to contribute to cost of services • Revise administrative structures and funding; improve budget flexibility and set management targets *Administration* • Independence for Bank of Spain • Statutory regime for public functions • Reduce size of central administration *Public-sector ownership* • Reduce state share • Restructuring policies, with transfers conditional on downsizing plans	• Reduce expenditure on drugs • New instruments for co-operation with ACs • Maintain value of pensions • Reorganize unemployment benefit, with workers to pay some contributions

1997		
• Plan for the liberalization and stimulation of economic activity (land, telecommunications, energy transport, roads and harbours) • Stimulate competition • Improve flexibility of labour market through agreements with unions and employers	*Fiscal and budgetary policy* • Ensure implementation of budget, with new mechanism for correcting deviations • Legislative projects: economic discipline law, budget law, fiscal, administrative and social order law, law on rights and duties of taxpayers • Reduce share of resources absorbed by public sector • New system for funding of CAs: responsibility for taxation shared with central government • Internal Stability Pact: procedures for reducing CA deficits • Reduce public expenditure to two points below GDP • Costs of non-essential public services to be borne by users • Private funding of public infractructure *Administration* • Statute for users of public services • Freeze on public-sector recruitment • New statute of public servants *Public-sector ownership* • Nationalized industries to be restructured and eventually sold off; government funding reduced	• Rationalize management; reduce expenditure on healthcare and drugs • Agree consolidation and rationalization of social security system (Toledo agreement) • Health policy: rationalize management

Source: based on C. Conde Martínez, 'El proceso de convergencia y la europeización de las administraciones nacionales (Estudio comparado de los casos francés y español)', *Revista de Derecho Comunitario Europeo* 2:4 (1998): 696.

Figure 7.3   *Criteria for nominal convergence in Spain compared to the
EU average: inflation and interest rates*

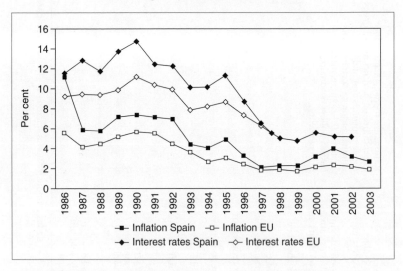

Source: Data from European Commission, *European Economy* (http://europa.eu.int/
comm/economy_finance/publications/europeaneconomy_en.htm)

Programme in 1997, after the 1994 plan had been wound up.
Following Spain's accession to EMU on 3 May 1998, the Spanish
government submitted its Stability Plan to the EU. Figures 7.3 and 7.4
outline the performance of the Spanish economy through the successive Plans and the Stability Programme.

Spanish inflation has always been above the EU average, even in
the 1970s. Since membership of EMU makes it impossible to control
inflation by manipulating interest rates, the only option (apart from
enhancing liberalization and competitiveness) is to reduce the public
deficit. The growth in the public deficit is a relatively new factor in
Spanish public accounting. Until 1977, the balance of payments had
been favourable: in 1980, the public deficit was 2.6 per cent and the
national debt only 18.4 per cent. Between 1975 and 1982, public
spending was increased to fund welfare benefits and subsidies to
public and private companies (Martínez Serrano, 1999: 701), but in
1982 Spain still had the lowest level of public deficit in the EU with
the exception of Luxembourg. Three periods can be distinguished in
budgetary policy following accession to the EU (González-Páramo
and Melguizo, 1999). The deficit reached a peak in 1986, owing to

Figure 7.4   *Criteria for nominal convergence in Spain compared to EU average: public deficit and public debt*

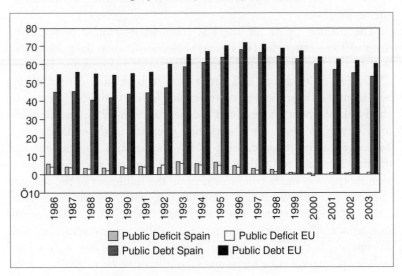

Source: Data from European Commission, *European Economy* (http://europa.eu.int/comm/economy_finance/publications/europeaneconomy_en.htm)

the political requirements of transition and the PSOE's commitment to the development of a welfare state, but decreased slightly in the two following years. From 1989 there was an expansion owing to the general strike and the electoral losses discussed earlier; huge increases in pensions and public investment put a stop to previous budgetary consolidation (González-Páramo and Melguizo, 1999: 590; Martínez Serrano, 1999: 698; Fuentes Quintana, 1995: 82). This period lasted until 1996 and it had a threefold negative impact: it unbalanced the policy mix by putting the entire onus of fighting inflation on to monetary policy; it undermined the opportunity to restructure the public finances; and it hit Spain's external trade balance (González-Páramo and Melguizo, 1999: 590).

The public deficit remained within more or less acceptable limits until 1993, when there was a spectacular jump partly owing to a fall in tax revenue. The socialist government found it difficult to manage taxation for a number of reasons. It was committed to curbing the public deficit (to 5.9 per cent of GDP in 1995 and 4.4 per cent in 1996), but this required great social sacrifices at a time of minority government, when party support was faltering: the tight budget forecast in the 1994

Programme was criticized by Catalan nationalists who wanted more spending. The deficit was further fuelled by the burden of interest on the national debt.

The turning point for the PSOE's macroeconomic policy came around 1994 (after the 1993 general election), when the government was finally forced to take the targets seriously (Alonso and Donoso, 1999: 238). The change of attitude derived both from earlier lessons and from the constraints of convergence. In line with EMU demands, the Bank of Spain was granted independence in 1994, and immediately began to work for a sustained decrease in the inflation rate. Moreover, apart from entering EMU, the Spanish government had another incentive to fulfil its own programmes: the payment of cohesion money was made conditional upon the fulfilment of the relevant convergence programmes. During the negotiation of the Maastricht Treaty, the Spanish government itself had not objected to this condition, since it reinforced its domestic calls for convergence with Europe, exploiting the traditional belief in the legitimacy of European policies. Convergence programmes now have to be fulfilled year on year, with no room for manoeuvre, and the funding of new projects can be suspended if the European Council decides that any member state is running an excessive deficit. In order to head off any deviations, the Commission reviews the accounts on a half-yearly basis (European Commission, 1996). In 1996, when the PP won office in Spain, the new government ordered an internal audit which revealed that Spain's deficit during 1995 had been 6.6 per cent, well above the 5.8 per cent target. The Commission detected the deviation much later, and agreed not to interrupt funding so long as there was no further deviation in 1996.

The last stage in fiscal and budgetary policy began in 1996, under the PP government, and it follows Stability Pact orthodoxy so slavishly that some have referred to a new budgetary model (González-Páramo and Melguizo, 1999). The guidelines called for a strict budgetary policy based on reform of the public sector and the reduction of public deficit by curbing public expenditure (Rato, 1995/6: 27). The new government introduced legal and institutional changes leading to tougher discipline, and the figures for public deficit, national debt and inflation all improved significantly. The change may be attributed in part to the change in government policy, but it also coincided with Spain's economic recovery, beginning in 1996, which delivered GDP growth of about 4 per cent. Among government measures were cuts in public investment and a public-sector wage freeze. The income generated from the privatization of large public corporations (such as Telefónica and Endesa) was fed into the public accounts. A reduced deficit plus lower interest rates facilitated a parallel reduction in the national public debt, which in turn had a decisive effect on inflation. Thus, Spain's EMU membership was achieved through a happy coincidence of tougher fiscal policy and general economic improvement. The Stability Plan forecast a continuation of this trend, with the public deficit expected to disappear by 2003, and the national debt to go below 60 per cent of GDP by 2002.

The most important consequence of Spain's accession to EMU has been the transformation of its macroeconomic policy, economy, and economic doctrine. As regards policy, the combination of economic growth with economic openness and macroeconomic equilibrium means a radical change in the previous economic norms (Myro, 1999: 269). As regards doctrine, Aznar's government has become a defender of macroeconomic orthodoxy. The attempt to 'Europeanize' domestic liberalization measures, described above, went hand in hand with a relaxed attitude to employment. Spain joined German calls to resist any increase in public expenditure (as suggested by the French Premier, Lionel Jospin). But Aznar was alone in rejecting any EU control on employment policy or the coordination of national targets. Spain only accepted the conclusions after being granted an opt-out clause whereby she would not be bound by the deadlines.

Chapter 8

Slicing up the European Cake: EU Budgets and Structural Funds

Historically speaking, the development of redistributive policies in the EU budget has resulted from the need to compensate member states (Ansell *et al.*, 1997; Smyrl, 1997; Pollack, 1995), rather than from any deliberate design based on constitutional principles of solidarity. Thus, the European Social Fund (ESF) was negotiated as a pay-off for the Italian *Mezzogiorno*, and later the regional fund (FEDER) was activated to channel European funds towards the United Kingdom. At the time of Spain's accession some of the budgetary expenditure had already been firmly allocated. Spain's aim was to get more of it, and she used a twofold strategy based first on rigorous intergovernmental negotiations and secondly on the development of a fully fledged discourse of solidarity. This chapter examines both strategies, and also evaluates the impact of structural funds in achieving the target of cohesion.

The negotiation of EU budgets

Successive Spanish governments have striven for a fully comprehensive redistribution policy, legitimized by a well-worked-out pro-integrationist discourse. Redistribution was a priority from the time of Spain's accession, when several member states favoured the idea of budgetary neutrality (that is, expenditure should be equal to contributions) during the transition period. For the Spanish government a positive balance was essential from the very beginning of membership, not least in order to sell the EU concept at home. Negotiations for the first budget in 1985 were, as one delegate remarked, dramatic: the Spanish representatives actually walked out. The Commission pointed out that if the budget was not increased to provide compensation for Spain, it would become a net contributor with a deficit of €697 million (Elorza, 1997: 18)

Commitment to the Single Market provided a solid base for argument by Spanish negotiators. It was generally accepted that the single market would be likely to polarize industry between growth areas and areas of stagnation. Therefore the Community would require adequate regional and structural adjustment and development funds to redress inequalities in the distribution of market costs and benefits (Smith and Wanke, 1993: 365–9). Moreover, the Spanish authorities viewed EU transfers as a contribution to offset the huge trade deficit that had been exacerbated by the SEA (see Chapter 7).

The link between market and financial transfers provided the background for the principle of economic and social cohesion that emerged in tandem with the single market (Landáburu, 1998: 29) and was seen as compensation for liberalization (Axt, 1992). The appeal to social and economic cohesion prompted the 1988 agreement to reform the EU's structural funds, which were doubled from €7 billion to €14 billion in 1992. Spain benefited hugely from this increase (see Figure 8.1). Moreover, the Spanish government had a considerable influence on the design of the budget: a new category of expenditure ('non-compulsory privileged expenditure') was created, which was

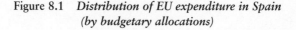

Figure 8.1 *Distribution of EU expenditure in Spain (by budgetary allocations)*

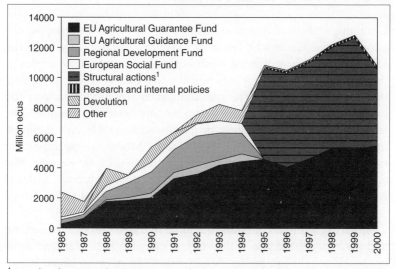

[1] Introduced in 1994, these incorporate cohesion, regional development and social funds.

Source: Data from *Annual Report* from the Court of Auditors.

protected from any amendment or reduction by the EP. On the revenue side, Spain, without overturning the Commission's approach, was able to introduce a fourth source of income: a share of GDP to finance new expenditure. Spanish negotiators had long stressed the unfairness of VAT, which bore directly on the consumer and therefore weighed more heavily on the poorer countries in which private consumption represented a larger share of GDP.

The Single European Act (SEA) picked up a rather vague principle of territorial redistribution and rehashed it as the principle of economic and social cohesion. Originally an Irish proposal, it was linked to the Single Market. In fact, the wording of the principle (Art. 130b of the SEA) has more to say about the social and economic impact of Community policies than about the redistribution fund that was subsequently created. Hence Spain continued to complain that the principle of economic and social cohesion had not been fully implemented, meaning that all Community enactments should consider this principle and therefore include compensatory measures. From 1989, with the prospect of economic and monetary union looming ever larger, the Spanish government developed a new link between EMU and cohesion.

Economic and social cohesion

Economic and social cohesion was Spain's top priority during negotiations for the Maastricht Treaty of European Union (TEU), since the Spanish government wanted it established as one of the principles of the Union. The reason for this urgency was mainly down to the fact that the time was ripe. The prevailing integrationist rhetoric at the beginning of the 1990s gave Spain an opportunity to exploit the fervent federalism underlying proposals such as EU citizenship in order to argue for serious redistribution. Moreover, the economic mood at the time was not as austere as it would later become. But concrete domestic interests also influenced Spain's stance: internal government studies had indicated that under the existing system of payments, Spain might become a net contributor from 1993.

Spain argued that cohesion should be reflected on both the income and the expenditure side of the budget (Elorza, 1992: 172), and three proposals sought to develop this argument. First, Spain called for an increase in the share of Community funding allocated to structural programmes in less-developed member states, because such programmes were seen as being disadvantaged by the existing system. Secondly, as regards income, Spain demanded the establishment of a new and progressive resource: given that progressiveness was a fiscal principle in all member states, it should also become an EU principle. The proposal was, of course, inspired by self-interest – the fact, as already mentioned, that Spain was in danger of becoming a net contributor. Given Spaniards' propensity for high consumption, the main source underpinning the existing fiscal system – share of VAT revenue – made Spain's contribution disproportionate to her real wealth. Spain therefore proposed that a new resource should be based on the relative wealth of each member state. But, more importantly, Spanish officials were concerned by the trend in distribution of structural funds, believing that a growing share of funds was being channelled towards the major EU member states.

Thus genuine arguments in favour of solidarity, as well as a calculation of what she would get out of it, lay behind Spain's third and most important proposal: that there be a specific cohesion fund. The original proposal was for an 'Interstate Compensation Fund', modelled on the territorial funds operating in compound states such as Spain itself. But the term 'compensation' was unpalatable to several member states, and the more neutral one of 'Cohesion Fund' was finally accepted. The cohesion fund would support EMU by helping finance environmental, transport and communications networks, and would have a greater flexibility in its application than traditional structural funds. Unlike other EU structural funds, the focus would be on inter-state, rather than regional, cohesion, since EMU itself would be working at state level. Qualifying conditions would be a per capita income below 90 per cent of the EU average and the setting up of a convergence programme to meet EMU criteria. These eligibility criteria would ensure that Spain would remain a net beneficiary from the Fund for between 15 and (in the most optimistic view) 20 years.

The design of the cohesion fund was thus tailored to suit Spain's particular needs. The avoidance of FEDER's regional focus was not accidental. This, together with the 90 per cent threshold, made it possible to exclude the Italian regions, as Germany had wanted. Moreover, the state-level focus suited Spanish domestic needs very nicely. In Spain, 40 per cent of the population lived in regions that had a per capita income over 75 per cent of the EU average and therefore did not qualify for Objective 1 funding under the existing structural funds (Elorza, 1997: 22). The new cohesion fund would alleviate the paradoxical situation whereby the most developed Spanish regions could not receive regional funds under Objective 1, although almost all of them had below-EU-average income.

Some member states wanted to separate what they regarded as a budgetary issue from the discussions on political union, but the Spanish government aimed to create a legal instrument at Treaty level. As González (1988) put it, cohesion did not just mean paying compensation to less-favoured EU members: it meant promoting a harmonious development of the EU, using a three-pronged strategy. First, member states' economic policies must converge; secondly, different areas of EU activity must be balanced; and thirdly, and most importantly, cohesion should be an integral part of every EU policy.

Economic and social cohesion was recognized as one of the European Union's essential objectives (Art. B of the TEU), and listed as one of the most important tasks of the European Community (Arts 2 and 3 of the Treaty establishing the European Community). The Cohesion Fund was created by the TEU (Art. G-130d), and the conditions proposed by the Spanish government were included in the Protocol on Social and Economic Cohesion.

Having established the legal principle, the next thing was to get the money. The TEU named 1 January 1994 as the starting date, but several member states argued that this should be conditional upon ratification of the Maastricht Treaty. The issue at stake was whether or not the cohesion fund should be included in the revised forecasts for 1993–99. Spain resolutely opposed any delay, and underlined her determination by making the start of enlargement negotiations with EFTA applicant countries conditional on the solution of outstanding budgetary questions. This is why the issue featured prominently at the Edinburgh summit in December 1992.

Spain's main objective was to ensure that the money was provided in one of two ways, both of which were hard for other member states to accept. The first was to increase the overall EU budget and channel the extra revenue into the cohesion fund. In fact, the Commission had proposed increasing the budget to 1.37 per cent of combined EU GDP by 1997, arguing that the structural funds had contributed to raising the wealth of less prosperous member states. The wealthier ones argued that this improvement had derived from the completion of the internal market and that there was no legitimate reason to increase the EU budget just when national purse-strings were having to be tightened to comply with EMU criteria. Consequently, the final figure was 1.24 per cent of EU GDP up to 1997 (and 1.27 per cent up to 1999).

Table 8.1 *Distribution of cohesion fund among recipient states, 1996–99*

Total €Millions		Spain		Greece and Portugal		Ireland	
	Ceilings	52%	58%	16%	20%	7%	10%
1,500	1993	780	870	240	300	105	150
1,750	1994	910	1,015	280	350	122	175
2,000	1995	1,040	1,160	320	400	140	200
2,250	1996	1,170	1,305	360	450	157	225
2,500	1997	1,300	1,450	400	500	175	250
2,550	1998	1,326	1,479	408	510	178	255
2,600	1999	1,352	1,508	416	520	282	260
15,150	Total 1993/99	7,878	8,787	2,424	3,030	1,160	1,515

Source: Data from Commission of the EC, *Annual Report of the Cohesion Fund 1996*, COM (96) 442 final.

Spain also tabled a second proposal for reducing other expenses in order to accommodate the cohesion fund. Predictably, all member states were hostile to any arrangement that might diminish their benefits from the budget, and there was little support for this Spanish proposal.

Nonetheless, Spain was well-satisfied with the final outcome. The Commission proposed an annual contribution of €10 billion up to 1997 and a further €5.1 billion between 1997 and 1999, and the European Council accepted these figures. Payments were subject to a minimum guaranteed allocation, going up to a stipulated maximum depending on the quality of the projects submitted. Between 1993 and 1999, Spain was to receive between 52 per cent and 58 per cent of the cohesion fund, Greece and Portugal between 16 per cent and 20 per cent each, and Ireland between 7 per cent and 10 per cent (see Table 8.1). Additionally, changes to the formula used to calculate EU contributions from the third source of revenue (VAT) saved Spain between €1.2 and €1.5 billion. The arrangement also included a sweetener for the main paymaster: Germany was permitted to include its Eastern *Länder* in the list of Objective 1 regions, and Objective 1 resources were increased to 154 per cent of the 1992 figure.

Figure 8.2   *Composition of EU own resources, 1985–2006*

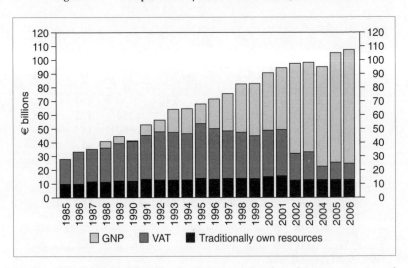

Source: *Unity, Solidarity, Diversity for Europe, its People and its Territory*, Second report on economic and social cohesion (adopted by the European Commission on 31 January 2001).

Agenda 2000: defending the status quo

Spain's ample returns from the structural funds in the 1980s and early 1990s were due to a fortunate concatenation of circumstances. However, the dramatic changes to Europe's political geography in the 1990s, and the restrictive macroeconomic policies required by EMU, meant that the new budgetary agreement, Agenda 2000, had a very different background. To begin with, both the quantity and the nature of the budget were affected by the prospective enlargement eastwards. If existing solidarity mechanisms remained unchanged, this eastern enlargement was going to be prohibitively expensive. At the same time, all member states were applying restrictive budgetary policies as required by prospective entry into EMU, and the combination of these two circumstances produced an underlying pattern that seems likely to shape all future budgetary negotiations from now on. Figure 8.2 shows the remorseless increase in member states' direct contributions to the EU budget since 1993.

Thus net contributors could advance some solid and well-reasoned arguments against the demands of net recipients. In view of the prevalent restrictive mood, Spain's position during the Agenda 2000 negotiations was rather weak: all proposals envisaged reductions that would directly affect her EU income. Ideas on both income and expenditure were equally problematic. The pro-integrationist rhetoric that had served Spain so well in the past suddenly lost its appeal, and her negotiators developed a nationalistic discourse rooted in the defence of national interests and strident demands for a continuing large slice of the European cake.

Spain had manoeuvred herself into a very comfortable budgetary position in which the cohesion fund was not her single or even her main source of income. Hence any attempt to cut back or modify the current status quo would go against Spanish interests. Therefore Spain rejected each successive budgetary proposal in 1998, threatening to use its veto, an attitude that has been dubbed 'Spanish maximalism' (Barbé, 1999: 141). In practice, Spain's negotiating position could be seen as a defence of *acquis*.

On the income side, the Commission – yielding to the clamour from net contributors – proposed an increase to no more than 1.27 per cent of EU GDP over the period from 2000 to 2006. That was reckoned sufficient both to fund existing EU policies and commitments, and to pay for eastern enlargement since the Commission forecast an average annual growth of around 2.5 per cent during the same period. The Commission calculated that this would produce an increase of €20 billion over the 1999 budget. Some limitations on expenditure could be anticipated, since the first group of candidate countries would not accede until half-way through the budgetary period and they would have transitional periods after that.

Economy Minister Rodrigo Rato outlined the Spanish position in a letter to the European Council of Finance Ministers (Ecofin) in October 1998 (Bastarreche *et al.*, 1999), with much talk of solidarity and existing legal (and political) commitments. Solidarity, he argued, should be the guiding principle not only of EU expenditure but of contributions as well. As with national taxation, those who had more should also pay more. The Protocol of the Treaty on Social and Economic Cohesion required each country's relative prosperity to be taken into account in the Own Resources System (the basis on which the EU is financed).

First, Spain challenged the Commission's suggested ceiling for the budget increases: according to Spanish calculations it was too low, since the CAP combined with cohesion expenditure consequent on the new accessions would require well over 1.27 per cent (Elorza, 1999:

18). Spain accused the net contributors of trying to push the burden of eastern enlargement on to the beneficiaries of the CAP and the cohesion fund. Secondly, Spain presented three proposals linking contributions to wealth:

- GDP and VAT contributions should be calculated according to the relative wealth (measured against the EU average) of each member state. With such a system Spain would pay between 64.9 per cent and 76.9 per cent of its current contribution.
- The above proposal would apply only to a part (to be negotiated) of the GDP and/or VAT contributions.
- Spain proposed categorizing member states according to their per capita income (less than 90 per cent of EU average, between 90 per cent and 100 per cent, between 100 per cent and 110 per cent, more than 110 per cent). These categories would determine their respective contributions.

These proposals were perceived more as bargaining counters, to counterbalance proposed restrictions, than as genuine and serious attempts to reach an agreement. More in line with the prevailing mood, though, Spain opposed the continuation of the British rebate. On the expenditure side the dispute revolved around distribution and, specifically, the re-casting of the regional fund and the future of cohesion payments. The Commission proposed setting the structural funds at 0.46 per cent of EU GDP (€275 billion).

The guidelines for structural expenditure contained in Agenda 2000 were advanced by three draft regulations submitted by the Commission in 1998. The Commission proposed a number of substantive changes, mainly affecting FEDER, in what was termed a 'concentration' (Landáburu, 1998). First came thematic concentration: the number of regional objectives should be cut from seven to three, of which two would be specifically regional and the third based on human resources. Objective 1 would be retained, but the ceiling of 75 per cent of per capita GDP as the criterion for eligibility would be *strictly* applied. Spain was not averse to a 'concentration' that would be highly advantageous to her own regions, but some of her negotiators wondered if the word 'strictly' might be used to exclude regions such as the Canary Islands and Aragón (Elorza, 1999: 18). The Commission, however, proposed a transition period for regions that went over the 75 per cent ceiling. In parallel, there would be a concentration of economic resources. Objective 1 regions would become the main recipients of regional funds, since the Commission proposed that two-thirds of the structural funds should be directed towards them. Secondly, there would be geographical concentration through a reduction of the share of population covered by Objectives 1 and 2 from 51 per cent of the EU to 35–40 per cent. All remaining regions would be grouped under a new Objective 2 (social and economic recovery of areas with structural deficits). Thirdly, the Commission designated a new Objective 3 that addressed the adaptation and modernization of educational, training and employment systems.

According to Spanish estimates (two internal memoranda prepared by the Ministries of the Economy and Employment), if the Commission's proposed criteria were accepted Spain would lose funds allocated to regions within Objectives 2 and 3, whereas no significant changes were likely to the funding of Objective 1 regions. The Ministry of Employment's memorandum argued that financial assistance for ongoing training would be confined to Objective 3. The Ministry calculated that this would lose Spain 1.37 billion pesetas annually (some €8.2 million). Between 1994 and 1997, she had received a total of €5.25 billion (*El País*, 21 November 1998).

The budgetary battle revolved around the cohesion fund because it provided such huge benefits for just one member state – Spain. This brought about the first serious confrontation between Spain and Germany, her main EU partner up to the late 1990s. Because of the restrictive budgetary policies required by EMU and the necessity of concentrating expenditure on its eastern *Länder*, Germany was eagerly seeking all possible ways to reduce its contributory burden. German negotiators targeted both the income and the expenditure sides. In July 1997 the German Economics Minister, Theo Waigel, proposed a reduction of the maximum for national contributions from 0.6 per cent to 0.4 per cent of GDP. Germany was supported by the Netherlands, Austria and Sweden, all of whom asked for rebates from the EU budget to adjust the balance between their contributions and their share of Community expenditure. The new German social-democratic government also called for a reduction in the German contribution: Gerhard Schröder insisted that eastern enlargement must wait on a settlement of the budgetary and institutional problems of the EU. In April 1998, Germany, seconded by the same three countries, demanded a pay-back mechanism akin to the British rebate. At the Cardiff summit in June 1998, Germany ensured that the communiqué mentioned the wish of some countries to create mechanisms for correcting the budgetary imbalance.

German pressure forced the Commission to submit new proposals. Its draft proposal for the Own Resources System (October 1998) followed the German line: the burdens on the main contributors should be reduced by paying automatic compensation to member states whose negative balance was more than 0.3 per cent of GDP. But, since the Commission had already proposed the elimination of the British rebate, a proposal to extend the rebate system to other states was scarcely credible.

Spain argued just the opposite case: there could be no legal justification for any such correction mechanisms, and concepts such as 'excessive contribution', 'equilibrium' and 'net balance' could not be used to establish the costs and benefits of EU membership, which went far beyond mere budgetary results. Spanish negotiators were fond of saying that the benefits from structural funds were not restricted to Spanish companies, since much of the increased demand from within Spain had gone towards Spanish imports from other member states (Fernández Martínez, 1997: 141). Spain made great play of the fact that German companies had benefited substantially from Spanish infrastructure projects.

Although the proposals for national budget rebates were not successful, they did create a suitable climate for addressing the real objective: a reduction in expenditure, with the scaling back of structural (mainly cohesion) funds as the centrepiece. But it was hard to find convincing arguments against cohesion. The Commission's 1998 draft regulation, recalling the first report on cohesion, emphasized the necessity and pertinence of a system that had genuinely achieved its objective. The Commission also endorsed the political arguments in favour of cohesion: it was democratic, because it benefited EU citizens directly and solved concrete problems, and it acted as a counterweight to market globalization, with the dual aim of 'humanizing' the integration process and bolstering the European model of society (Landáburu, 1998: 39).

Germany countered by invoking the close connection between cohesion and EMU. The German opinion was that the cohesion fund had one specific aim: to assist less-developed member states on their way towards nominal convergence prior to entering monetary union. Once a member state had qualified for EMU, there was no reason why it should receive further cohesion payments.

Spain and the Commission took a different view. In its draft regulation, the Commission proposed keeping the fund in its existing form: this meant that would-be EMU members would have to fulfil the Stability Pact criteria and comply with national stability programmes. Cohesion fund payments, instead of being linked to deficits as a fixed percentage of GDP, would be conditional on the beneficiary member state's fulfilling the targets in its own Stability Programme. If the beneficiary's public deficit went above the Stability Pact objective of 3 per cent, or the trend became unfavourable even though the 3 per cent ceiling was not reached, cohesion payments would be withheld. Spain saw this as a double jeopardy involving the loss of both cohesion payments and the benefits of the Stability Pact (*El País*, 9 March 1998). The Commission DG for Regional Policy, Eneko Landáburu, echoed the arguments of the Spanish government: EMU required the retention of the structural funds, particularly the cohesion fund, since there was no other way to adapt the economy and reduce economic inequality (Landáburu, 1999: 67). Economists warned that the EMU requirements on domestic fiscal policy might prevent states from performing their traditional redistribution of wealth, and might also exacerbate the tendency towards uneven development in the EU heartlands (Sevilla and Golf, 1999).

Spain argued that the role of the cohesion fund should not be affected by a country's access to EMU. The target should be real, not nominal, convergence. The Commission's legal services, when asked to examine whether the Stability Pact could be linked to the cohesion fund, threw their weight behind Spain and the Commission: on 26 October 1998 they ruled that a member state that had reached the third stage of EMU could still benefit from the cohesion fund, since the TEU established no link between accession to EMU and payments from the fund. On the other hand, the Stability Pact had effectively replaced the convergence programmes, so cohesion payments should be conditional on its fulfilment. A favourable vote in the European Parliament further strengthened Spain's position.

Cohesion was saved, but Spain's troubles were not over. Having ruled out rebates and the elimination of cohesion, the Commission was compelled to present alternative proposals that might satisfy net contributors. These new proposals focused, first, on national co-funding of agricultural expenditure: national governments would be asked to provide 25 per cent of farmers' direct income. The second option was to freeze contributions at the 1993–99 level. Both of these proposals were against Spanish interests and Spain argued that national co-funding would run counter to the principle of sufficiency of means, it might contaminate other policies and, most importantly, it would bear hardest on the weakest member states (Elorza, 1999:

13). Indeed, if co-funding of the CAP had been introduced this would have hit Spain as hard as a suppression of the cohesion fund: a memo prepared by the Ministry of the Economy estimated that it would cost Spain around €530 million (*El País*, 22 Nov. 1998). Spain wanted to avoid any link between CAP reform and enlargement, budgetary settlements or World Trade Organization (WTO) reforms. The principles of the CAP should remain economic and social cohesion, community preference and financial solidarity. Fortunately for Spain, the Commission's proposal was also seen as detrimental to French interests and so did not prosper.

Freezing contribution levels, then, became the more credible option. The Austrian presidency wanted to include this proposal in the conclusions to the Vienna Summit in December 1998, but Spain threatened to use her veto and even to paralyse the internal market. In the Spanish view, the Commission's proposal would merely shift the notion of 'progressive' payments from the revenue to the expenditure side. Spain invoked some of the provisions of the TEU, particularly the Protocol on Economic and Social Cohesion, which required the Own Resources System to take account of the relative prosperity of each country and to consider ways of amending the current system to the advantage of the poorer member states. Thus the Spanish proposal sought to correct a regressive tendency that had crept into the system: the richer countries would pay more in proportion to their relative wealth and the poorer countries less. The criterion would be per capita GDP. By that time, Spanish arguments had been reinforced by a report to the European Parliament by Paolo Cecchini, author of the famous White Paper that paved the way for the 1992 programme. Cecchini proposed that all member states – except, of course, cohesion countries – should help bear the cost of budgetary readjustment.

Stabilization remained top of the budgetary agenda owing to the determination of the German presidency during the first half of 1999. In practical terms, stabilization would mean a budget reduction of €20 billion a year. Spain rejected this as well as the proposal to cap the budget at 1.27 per cent of EU GDP, which was deemed insufficient to finance enlargement.

Although the Spanish government wanted to restrict discussions to the proposals outlined in the official document Agenda 2000, which was more favourable to Spanish interests, she had to recognize the existence of a 'German question' for the sake of general harmony. Spain's strategy was to highlight the discrepancy between Germany and other net contributors which, with similar or even greater per capita GDP than Germany, made smaller contributions in relative terms (Cordero, 1999). Furthermore, Spain recalled that between 1989 and 1993, some member states with above-average per capita GDP had been net recipients of EU funds (specifically Luxembourg and Denmark). To redress this unfairness, Prime Minister Aznar suggested that member states' contributions should depend on relative prosperity. This was a concession to Germany and was also directed against countries such as Italy and Denmark. It was further suggested that the burden of contributions to the EU budget (as a proportion of GDP) was heavier for Spain (and of course Germany) than for other rich member states. Thus, Germany contributed 0.63 per cent of GDP, the UK 0.33 per cent, France 0.20 per cent and Italy 0.12 per cent. Spain contributed 0.56 per cent of GDP and its share of the overall budget was 7.1 per cent, even though its GDP was only 6.6 per cent of the EU total (Martín Rodríguez, 1999).

At this stage in the negotiations, Spain put forward two specific proposals that would avert the need to generalize the British rebate and were specially designed to suit the needs of Germany (though not all the net contributors): first, a programme to provide financial support for the countries with the largest influxes of refugees and asylum seekers; second, a programme to address the development of regions bordering on applicant countries. Together, these would net Germany around €1.355 billion per annum. The Spanish negotiators were of course also aware that the former programme would be likely to benefit Spain in due course, since she was receiving large numbers of immigrants from North Africa.

In the end, these proposals were not adopted, since they would have demanded even larger financial contributions. The Berlin summit, in March 1999, settled the dispute. The Spaniards talked tough, threatening to veto any agreement and forcing the German presidency to negotiate right up to the last minute and abandon many of its original objectives. Germany had already agreed to preserve the cohesion fund, with a reassessment of eligibility in the middle of the budgetary period: if any beneficiary should cross the threshold of 90 per cent of average EU per capita income, payments would be reduced. This was directed not so much against Spain as against Ireland, which at the time was enjoying unprecedented economic growth.

In a quid pro quo, Spain accepted the 1.27 per cent ceiling, subject to a possible revision after enlargement. She also had to accept a reduction in the total amounts received: having supported the

Commission's €239 billion proposal for the structural funds as a bargaining position, Spain's real target was €218 billion but the figure finally agreed was €213 billion. Of this, Spain would receive around €6.565 billion per annum, as against an average €6.253 billion between 1993 and 1999. The cohesion fund would be €18 billion instead of the €15 billion proposed by Germany. But Spain's chief gains were from the internal redistribution of the fund: instead of the 55 per cent that it received between 1993 and 1999, it was now to receive 62 per cent of the total cohesion fund. On the income side, Spain successfully held out against the introduction of GDP-related ceilings and the generalization of rebates. In addition, the agreement maintained the existing level of agricultural expenditure.

Spain's main focus in the negotiations had always been the structural funds. But this should not hide the fact that EAGGF transfers have consistently accounted for about 40 per cent of Spain's EU receipts (see Figure 8.1). It was the introduction of the cohesion fund which took her benefits from the structural funds to a higher level than those from the CAP. Spain's enthusiasm for structural funds is due to the fact that maintaining other sources of revenue (such as agriculture) can remain a secondary consideration, since a large number of member states have an interest in sustaining them and so Spain does not have to take the lead in negotiations. Furthermore, the structural funds serve the main objective of Spanish EU membership, which is to achieve real convergence.

Budgetary concerns during the enlargement negotiations

Spain's claims for a larger share of the budget resurfaced in a 2001 Memorandum on regional policy and enlargement, in which the Spanish government endorsed the continuation of the cohesion policy after enlargement, on the grounds that it had proven so successful. Spain, it pointed out, had repeatedly endorsed the official view that structural policies should apply to new members from the very moment of accession. However, enlargement posed a problem: even in the EU as then constituted there was a considerable imbalance between the different regions, the most backward of which would continue to need financial support. But such regions might be excluded from structural funds and policies without ever having achieved real convergence, owing to what was called '*statistical* convergence'. Since the per capita

GDP of the applicant states was so much lower, the EU's overall average income would decrease in proportion, and this would make the current members and regions look richer by comparison. Thus, the inclusion of the new members when calculating parameters of wealth and eligibility would exclude current 'poor' regions without making them any less poor. Spain even went so far as to link the issue to the German proposal for a transition period on the free movement of labour; it threatened a veto if these two issues were jointly settled. Naturally, the majority of the member states, not to mention the candidate countries, were affronted by the Spanish stance.

The Laeken summit soothed Spanish fears. First, the Council's decision to delay the accession of Bulgaria and Romania meant that six Spanish regions would continue to qualify even after the accession of the other 10 candidates. In addition, the Spanish negotiators revised their calculations and discovered that most Spanish regions would be over the 75 per cent per capita EU average income threshold by 2007, when the next phase of enlargement would be negotiated. Spain itself was also moving closer to the 90 per cent threshold of the cohesion fund, and was assured that territorial cohesion would remain an explicit principle in the Treaties. Finally, the Commission had submitted a new report on the impact of enlargement on cohesion policy, which repeated the conclusions of its previous investigation. Four possible mechanisms for distributing funds after 2006 were identified:

- Retain the existing threshold (75 per cent).
- As above, plus temporary phasing out of regions above the threshold, with two levels of coverage: lower for those that were 'naturally converging' and higher for those which were 'statistically converging'.
- Set a new threshold higher than 75 per cent (but lower than that already attained by 'naturally converging' regions).
- Fix two thresholds for eligibility, one for current members and the other for new ones (this option gained little support because it was clearly discriminatory).

The impact of structural funds: achieving real convergence?

Spain's main aim on joining the EU was to reach a par with the most advanced European countries (see Chapter 1). This was not only a political aim. Despite Spain's political isolationism, international economic comparisons, which revealed Spain's economic backwardness, had provided both a criterion and a challenge since the nineteenth century (Velarde, 1995: 384). Membership brought the point of reference much closer and provided a mechanism for measuring it. Inevitably, convergence became an obsession with Spanish politicians. Some even argued that it had been the sole justification for joining the EU (Fuentes Quintana, 1995: 69, 120; Rato, 1995/6: 23).

Spanish economic policy had singled out (through both practice and theory) three main instruments for achieving convergence. Two of these were internally oriented: the development of a more competitive economy and the adoption of an orthodox economic paradigm geared towards nominal convergence. As discussed in Chapter 7, liberalization and investment in human and physical capital were the main elements in the competitiveness strategy Spain had pursued from the early stages of membership. Later on, the achievement of nominal convergence became the cornerstone of the push towards real convergence. The third instrument was financial transfers from the EU budget, providing structural investments that complemented these internal policies. Thus, the rhetoric of 'competition' developed for domestic consumption was matched by the discourse of 'solidarity' used when appealing to Spain's European partners.

In this section we assess to what extent EU structural policies have contributed to the achievement of real convergence. Before the creation of the cohesion fund, some analysts had argued that the resources committed to achieve real convergence could not be expected to remove existing inequalities in income, productivity and employment (Belloni, 1994: 32). It may therefore be instructive to review Spain's record on real convergence, and on this basis assess the impact of the funds.

'Real convergence' refers to the equalizing of those macroeconomic parameters that measure welfare. Per capita GDP is the usual criterion for convergence as far as general welfare is concerned, but on its own provides only a partial measure. Other indicators normally used, such as unemployment levels and trade balance, supply additional evidence and, occasionally, analysts also refer to more qualitative indicators such as human capital, stock of technological capital or share of GDP allocated to social expenditure and infrastructure. Within the EU, however, per capita GDP remains the most frequently used indicator. However, while the results for Spain look reasonable insofar as convergence can be measured solely in GDP terms, other more qualitative data suggest a somewhat less rosy picture. Many analysts have pointed out that Spain's failure to achieve real convergence is due to:

(a) Significant differences in human capital: despite increasing convergence with other member states, supply and skills bases remain low (Alberola, 1998: 51).
(b) Low levels of technological development: in 1996 Spain's techno-logical capital was estimated to be 34 per cent of the EU average (Martín, 1997).
(c) Unemployment: analysts agree on Spain's difficulties in creating employment at times of economic expansion and inability to preserve it in times of recession (Alberola, 1998: 48; Fuentes Quintana, 1995: 132).

These are doubtless the main impediments to economic convergence; indeed, future advances will depend on Spain's ability fully to exploit her economic resources and increase productivity (Raymond, 1995). On the other hand, if more complex indicators are used (for instance, the UN's Human Development Index), Spain's position *vis-à-vis* the other member states looks quite different. The figures in Table 8.2 show that between 1986 and 2002 Spain's per capita GDP as a percentage of the EU average rose from 69.9 per cent to 84.3 per cent. But using a longer time span, from 1970 to 1995, Martín (1995) has argued that there was no real convergence: in 1975, Spain's per capita GDP was around 79 per cent of the EU average, a level not reached again until 1997. Taking the longer period, it could be argued that Spain has maintained its relative wealth in comparison with the EU, but not progressed.

This seems to reveal a particular model of convergence in the Spanish economy, with the following characteristics. On the one hand, Spain (unlike the UK, for example) is in tune with the economic cycle of the leading EU states and thus benefits from growth in the larger EU economies. But, on the other hand, there is widespread agreement that the Spanish economy tends to overreact to external stimuli (Fuentes Quintana, 1995: 117). More specifically, it converges strongly on the EU average in times of international economic growth, but diverges sharply in times of recession (Ruesga, 1993: 12; Alberola, 1998: 48; Raymond, 1995: 517).

Using the period 1975–99 as a frame of reference, the first recession was between 1975 and 1985; that is, just before Spain's accession. GDP diminished from around 79 per cent to 69 per cent of the EU

Table 8.2 *Indicators of real convergence*

Year	GDP Growth		GDP per capita (% of EU average)	Unemployment rate	
	Spain	EU	Spain	Spain	EU
1986	3.2	2.9	69.9	20.98	10.7
1987	5.6	4.3	71.8	20.46	10.3
1988	5.2	4.3	72.4	19.48	9.7
1989	4.8	3.5	74.2	17.28	8.9
1990	3.6	3.0	75.4	16.25	8.4
1991	2.4	1.5	79.8	16.34	8.8
1992	0.8	1.1	77.5	18.5	9.6
1993	−1.0	−0.4	77.8	22.8	10.7
1994	2.0	2.6	76.1	24.1	11.2
1995	2.3	1.6	76.2	22.9	10.7
1996	2.2	1.7	78.7	22.0	10.8
1997	3.7	2.5	80.5	20.8	10.6
1998	4.0	2.6	81.1	18.8	9.9
1999	3.7	2.3	82.5	15.9	9.2
2000	4.1	3.4	83.1	14.1	8.5
2001	2.6	1.5	83.8	13.1	7.8
2002	2.0	1.0	84.3	11.3	7.7

Sources: Data from INE, Banco de España and Eurostat. GDP per capita: Dirección General de Análisis y Programación Presupuestaria, Ministerio de Economía y Hacienda (Lázaro; 1997).

average, leaving a larger gap to be closed through the effects of membership. A second period of recession occurred between 1992 and 1996. In periods of strong economic growth following entry into the EU (1986–91 and 1996–2002), Spain's convergence accelerated. In fact, the Spanish economy grew faster than that of any other EU country except Ireland. Thus, the Spanish model of convergence could be described as 'convergence through above-average growth'. Some analysts have argued that it will therefore always be difficult to bring Spain up to the European average, or even that convergence will stop short at around 80 per cent (Alberola, 1998: 48; Fuentes Quintana, 1995: 124, 132). Despite these pessimistic forecasts, however, some 1999 projections estimated that, assuming similar growth rates, Spain would eventually catch up with the EU average per capita income, though this might take another 25 years (Fundación BBV, 1999).

In any case, it is clear that Spain has slowly converged with EU member states over the whole membership period, with a brief setback between 1992 and 1996 (see Table 8.2). However, there remains dispute over the actual impact of membership. Some argue that convergence resulted from strong economic growth, which in turn was the result of the liberalization promoted by EU membership. This view is supported by the fact that periods of convergence in the Spanish economy appear to coincide with times of active liberalization (Alberola, 1998: 47). On the other hand, Martín (1995: 6) has claimed that there is no evidence that integration has favoured real, as opposed to nominal, convergence.

How has EU funding helped? The budgetary balance between 1986 and 1999 was enormously favourable to Spain. Between 1989 and 1999, Spain was the main recipient of EU structural funds. The Delors I package provided the initial impetus, but from 1994 to 1999, Spain received three times more than between 1989 and 1993 (Landáburu, 1998: 30). In qualitative terms, there can be no doubt that the relative improvement in the economic position of the four cohesion countries has been a major success for the EU (Begg, 1999: 105). As far as Spain is concerned, the evaluation of the net impact of structural funds differs depending on the sources (since the statistics are subject to political manipulation), though all show a net positive impact.

The Commission's calculations differ from those of the Spanish authorities (and of private institutions) regarding the net impact on the most important parameter: growth of GDP. The Commission's view is that structural funds contributed an extra 0.8 per cent to Spain's GDP between 1989 and 1993, and 1.7 per cent between 1994 and 1999 (see Table 8.3). Spanish estimates, though, are lower – particularly for the second period.

Most Spanish officials and analysts (see Morata and Muñoz, 1996: 196) agree that structural funds have had a smaller impact on Spain than on the other cohesion countries, and this has been used as an argument to justify the continued huge influx of funds. Table 8.4 outlines Spain's account of the comparison between the four cohesion countries, based upon two criteria: per capita resources spent by the EU and share of EU transfers as a percentage of GDP.

The criteria selected reflect Spain's anxiety to divert attention from the fact that she was, in absolute terms, the main beneficiary of structural funds. Thus, Ireland received 2.8 times more money per capita

Table 8.3   *Economic impact of the structural and cohesion funds*

	Greece	Ireland	Spain	Portugal	EUR4
Growth of GDP (%)					
1989–93	2.6	2.5	0.7	3.0	1.4
1994–99	3.0	1.9	1.5	3.3	2.0
2000–06	2.8	0.6	1.3	2.9	1.6
Gross fixed capital formation (%)					
1989–93	11.8	15.0	2.9	12.4	5.5
1994–99	14.6	9.6	6.7	14.2	8.9
2000–06	12.3	2.6	5.5	11.4	6.9

Note: Structural and Cohesion Funds: commitment data up to 1999, forecast for 2000–06.

Source: Data from European Commission, estimates based on Eurostat data and projections for 2000–06.

Table 8.4   *Resources by inhabitant and as share of GDP from structural funds*

	Criteria				
	Resources by inhabitant*			Resources as share of GDP	
	1986–88	*1989–93*	*1994–99*	*1989–93*	*1994–99*
Spain	101	197	240	0.7	1.4
Ireland	580	650	480	2.6	2.8
Greece	280	440	410	2.6	3.6
Portugal	150	360	400	3.0	3.9

* As percentage of EU average.
Source: Data from INE, Banco de España and Eurostat.

than Spain between 1989 and 1993, and 1.4 times more between 1994 and 1999. As a share of GDP, EU transfers represented 1 per cent of Spain's GDP in 1989 against 2.1 per cent of Ireland's; in 1993 the figures were 1.3 per cent and 3.1 per cent respectively (Lázaro, 1997).

The impact of membership and structural funds on Spanish regional cohesion

It is generally preferable to assess convergence on a regional rather than national basis, because the effects of inter-state convergence may mask a lack of convergence within states (or regions). If regional convergence proceeds hand in hand with economic integration, it is necessary to look at how the latter is affecting the former. Some analysts have argued that disparities in per capita GDP *between* member states were significantly reduced during the period 1955–99 whilst disparities *within* member states increased significantly (Martín Rodríguez, 1999). This seems not to have been the case in Spain. Figures indicate that in 1955 the ratio between richest and poorest regions was 3.49, whereas in 1999 this ratio had diminished to 2.24, clearly demonstrating an evening out of economic disparities (*ibid.*).

The picture looks slightly different if we subdivide this 35-year period. Thus, rapid economic convergence took place between 1955 and 1979, when the per capita GDP of the Spanish regions became progressively more similar (Raymond, 1995: 535). But in the 25 years since then, regional disparities have remained more or less unchanged, and convergence slowed markedly in the 1980s (Raymond, 1995: 541). In other words, any judgement on whether or not there has been regional convergence must relate to a specific time period, during which particular factors will have been in operation. The real question is this: if, during the 1980s and 1990s – with Spain in the EU – the evidence shows a slowdown in Spanish regional convergence, how far (if at all) was this due to EU membership? To answer this question we have to measure the Spanish regions both against each other and against the EU average.

In absolute terms, both in 1986 and 1996, one Spanish region (Extremadura) was included among the 10 poorest in Europe. In 1986, three more were among the 25 poorest (Andalusia, Castile-La Mancha and Galicia), although Andalusia and Galicia had risen a few places in this ranking by 1996 and Castile-La Mancha had moved outside altogether (Commission, 1999b). No Spanish region has ever been ranked among the 25 richest. But whilst in 1986 hardly any Spanish regions reached the EU average, in 1999 three *autonomías* had a per capita GDP above the EU average: the Balearic Islands (119.12 per cent), Madrid (110.27 per cent) and La Rioja (100.96 per cent). Thus, if the EU is taken as the point of reference, the overall disparity between the Spanish regions and the EU average has clearly been reduced. The Commission estimated that only one Spanish region, Murcia, was failing to converge with the EU average (Commission, 1999b).

When we focus on the poorest regions – that is, those included under Objective 1 of EU regional policy – we can get a fuller picture. Nine Spanish regions (Andalusia, Asturias, the Canary Islands, Castile and León, Castile-La Mancha, Valencia, Extremadura, Galicia and Murcia), plus the cities of Ceuta and Melilla, have had Objective 1 status during the budgetary periods between 1989 and 2006. A tenth region, Cantabria, was included between 1994 and 1999 and for the budgetary period 2000–06 will receive transitional assistance since it has passed the threshold of 75 per cent of the EU average. If we were to look no further than these statistics, we might conclude that there has been no convergence, since the number of Spanish regions under Objective 1 remains static.

However, when we use figures from sources other than the EU and Spain (which both have a political interest in manipulating the statistics), the picture changes significantly. Table 8.5 adds figures provided by independent organizations listing Spanish regions below the Objective 1 threshold criterion of 75 per cent of EU per capita GDP.

The following conclusions may be drawn. First, average GDP in the Spanish regions seems to be higher than the official figures show. Secondly, the figures appear to vindicate the Commission's argument that the convergence of Spain's poorest regions with the EU has progressed steadily, whether we focus on those included in Objective 1 or those that are *really* below 75 per cent of the EU average. According to this second criterion, the per capita income of these Spanish regions in 1986 amounted to 61 per cent of the EU average; in 1998, 65.22 per cent; and in 1999, 66.03 per cent. In 13 years the income of these regions has risen 5.03 percentage points, clearly demonstrating that the less-developed Spanish regions have indeed converged with the EU average.

The picture is very different, however, if we look at interregional convergence. Comparing 1986 and 1999, only two regions (Galicia and Extremadura) have improved substantially, whilst in two other cases the improvements have been very small and in the remaining cases the situation has actually worsened. Altogether, regions under 75 per cent of the EU average reached 86.2 per cent of the Spanish average in 1986, but only 80.11 per cent in 1998. In other words, the differences among the Spanish regions have remained. More significant, it appears that

Table 8.5 *Evolution of regional GDP per capita, 1986–99*

	1986		1996		1997		1998		1999	
	Index Spain=100	Index EU=100	Index Spain=100	Index EU=100	Index Spain=100	Index EU=100	Index Spain=100	Index EU=100	Index Spain=100	Index EU=100
Andalucía	75.6	53.5	72.7	57.2	72.37	57.93	72.26	58.86	68.79	59.73
Asturias	100.8	71.3	93.5	73.6	85.93	68.79	85.38	69.54	81.32	67.98
Canarias	99.3	70.2	94.4	74.3	97.31	77.90	97.52	79.43	96.21	82.18
Castilla y León	93.0	65.8	96.5	75.9	90.57	72.50	91.67	74.67	90.36	78.26
Castilla-La Mancha	78.0	55.2	83.7	65.9	80.11	64.13	79.98	65.14	78.92	71.12
C. Valenciana	101.4	71.7	93.7	73.8	100.53	79.67	99.75	79.43	101.53	84.47
Extremadura	63.3	44.8	69.3	54.6	73.42	58.77	73.26	59.67	68.26	62.45
Galicia	78.2	55.7	80.0	63.0	83.79	67.07	84.40	68.54	83.28	71.19
Murcia	96.4	68.1	85.3	67.2	80.98	64.82	79.96	65.13	81.24	69.51
Ceuta y Melilla*	91.0	64.4	91.8	72.3	75,98	60.82	73.97	60.25	76.59	n.a.
CCAA Objective 1	86.2	61.0								
CCAA under 75%	86.2	61.0	84.7	66.7	80.39	64.35	80.11	65.22	76.91	66.03
Spain	100.0	70.7	100.0	78.7	100	80.05	100	81.45	100	83.1

*Data for Ceuta and Melilla for 1997, 1998 and 1999 result from the average of data for each city.

Sources: Data from Ministry of Economy. *El País* 24 July 1999. Data for 1997 and 1998 from Fundación BBV. *Estudio sobre la renta nacional de España* (1955–98). Data 1999 FUNCAS (El Pais; 7 May 2000 p. 23).

most of the convergence among Spanish regions took place before Spain's entry into the EU, and was due to particular historical circumstances. For instance, the least developed regions lost population during the industrialization of the 1960s and 1970s. In addition, when the recession began to bite, rural areas did not face problems of reindustrialization and so their growth was above the national average. This might help explain why interregional convergence tended to take place before Spain entered the EU. Alberola (1998: 49–50) has observed that since 1986, the Spanish model of regional convergence, in which there is an inverse relationship between income and growth rate (that is, poorer regions grow faster), has ceased to apply.

The above data show two processes – inter-EU convergence and interregional divergence – functioning side by side. How can we explain this? First, EU structural policy has clearly benefited the least developed regions, and this goes a long way towards explaining their improvement in relation to the EU average. Growth in Spain's Objective 1 regions increased by an average of 0.25 per cent annually between 1989 and 1993, half of this (0.12 per cent) being a direct result of structural funding. The impact of such funding cannot be ignored. Between 1994 and 1999, Spain received around 23 per cent of the total EU budget for structural funds (€32 billion). For the ten *autonomías* included in Objective 1, these funds made up a significant share of their budgets: around 5 per cent on average and in some cases (such as Asturias) as much as 14 per cent (Ordóñez Solís, 1996). The Commission estimated that these funds boosted growth at an average of 0.7 per cent annually, of which 0.4 per cent resulted directly from EU funds (Commission, 2000). More directly, the Commission reported that the growth in per capita GDP for these regions was 3 per cent faster between 1989 and 1999 than it would have been without the structural funds (Commission, 2000; Landáburu, 1998: 30).

In addition, as we saw in Chapter 4, EU structural policies acted as a spur to Spain's regional policy. The funds committed under the national Regional Development Plans also affected growth in the less-developed regions: additional funds allocated by Spain amounted to 0.8 per cent of GDP between 1989 and 1993, and 1.7 per cent between 1994 and 1999 (Commission, 2000). It has been forecast that the impact of the 2000–06 Plan will lead to an extra 0.48 per cent annual growth in GDP for these regions. The combined effect of national plus EU funds can be seen from the figures on family incomes (that is, adding public transfers to per capita GDP) in the Spanish regions. As Figure 8.3 shows, family incomes in the poorer regions

Figure 8.3 *Regional* per capita *GDP and family incomes, 1999*

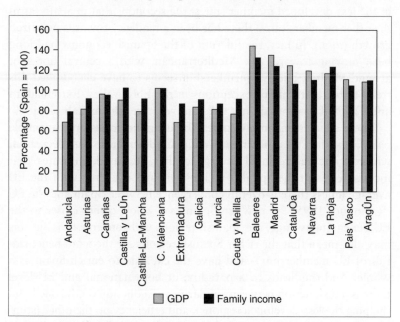

Source: Data from FUNCAS, *Magnitudes económicas provinciales años 1985 a 1999* (Madrid: Funcas, 1999).

have grown substantially, and the differences between the poor and richer regions have diminished greatly.

The figure shows that family incomes increased faster than per capita GDP in the poorer regions, an improvement that reflects the increased welfare spending in the regions (as well as price differentials) (Raymond, 1995: 532). As a general conclusion, it can be said that redistributive measures (stemming both from the EU and from the Spanish government) have had a very positive impact on regional inequalities (Martín Rodríguez, 1999).

There is another side to the coin, however. Paradoxically, while Spain's poorest regions have converged with the EU average, and EU structural (as well as national) funds have played an essential part in achieving this, the gap between Spain's poorest and her richest regions remains unbridged. In fact, rapid convergence by a few areas (such as Catalonia) contrasts with the very marginal improvement of the less-developed regions (Begg, 1999: 105). There are two possible reasons for this (Martín Rodríguez, 1999). The first is that creation of the single market has given a particular fillip to the most dynamic regions in the less-developed member states; the second is that in Spain (as in the other member states) there has been a tendency towards polarized growth (*ibid.*). In fact, the fulcrum of the Spanish economy had long been moving towards the Mediterranean, with a central hot spot around Madrid, and EU membership seems to have encouraged this trend (albeit with minor exceptions in the Ebro Valley, Extremadura and Castile-León that do not substantively alter the overall picture).

These conclusions imply some difficult policy decisions. In simple terms, the fact that interstate regional divergence has decreased, whereas internal regional divergence has increased, indicates that income levels in the Spanish regions will not converge with the EU average unless there is overall convergence between Spain and the EU (Raymond, 1995: 545). When Spain as a whole comes closer to the EU per capita average, the Spanish regions will converge too. But this may also mean that the richer Spanish regions are the main beneficiaries of EU membership – and have the capacity to enrich Spain as a whole. And this leads to a paradox: at both national and EU level there is a disjunction between solidarity and cohesion on the one hand (helping the less-developed regions), and efficiency on the other (stimulating economic activity in the more developed regions) (Martín Rodríguez, 1999). Some analysts even argue that an excessive emphasis on redistribution could hamper the global growth of the Spanish economy (Raymond, 1995: 549) – which would endanger its overall convergence.

Distribution of cohesion funds between different sectors

Cohesion funds were invested in two politically important areas – transport and the environment. In both of these, Spain (like the other cohesion countries) lagged far behind the other EU member states and huge public investment was required. Moreover, EU policies required compliance with certain standards on environmental policy as well as the development of trans-European transport networks. Table 8.6 illustrates the distribution of cohesion funds by sector.

It is worth pointing out that the main priority of the Spanish central government was infrastructure, particularly roads. In fact, the Commission and the Spanish government repeatedly clashed over the

Table 8.6   *Dristribution of cohesion fund grants by sectors*

	Spain: commitments 1993–98	
	(€millions)	%
Environment		
Drinking water	951.6	12.7
Wasted water	1500.1	20.0
Solid waste	419.7	5.6
Erosion and deforestation	529.6	7.1
Other	328.1	4.4
Total	3729.1	49.8
Transport		
Roads	2531.8	33.8
Railroads	1134.1	15.1
Airports	73.2	1.0
Harbours	25.3	0.3
Total	3764.4	50.2
Total grants	7493.5	100

Source: Data from EU Commission, *Annual Report on Cohesion Fund*, COM (1999) 483 final.

definition of the 'priority axis of intervention' in relation to structural policy. While the former stressed the need to encourage new business initiatives, the Spanish government focused exclusively on general infrastructure projects in order to close the gap between Spain and the more developed member states (Morata and Muñoz, 1996: 207). Moreover, where infrastructure projects were concerned, the Commission and the European Parliament heavily criticized the lavish investment in roads (Commission, 1999). After 1988, investment in rail transport began to increase, as the Commission urged the cohesion countries (and particularly Spain) to pay more attention to this area.

Two main reasons account for the Spanish government's preferences. First, it could use EU funding to pay for its existing programme of public investment in infrastructure. Second, responsibility for environmental policy had been devolved to the regions, and the central government was not particularly eager to hand over control of funds too, despite pressure from regional parties. Some analysts have argued that the cohesion fund has actually strengthened Spain's central government, since it does not impose the heavy institutional and administrative burdens that characterize the structural funds, and can be easily be channelled into central government programmes (Morata and Muñoz, 1996: 216).

Nevertheless, in 1994 the government agreed that control of cohesion resources should be devolved to the regions, and from 1998 (apparently as a consequence of combined pressure from the Commission and the Autonomous Communities) the number of environmental projects began to increase. Investment was mainly concentrated on water – both supply and waste recycling. Another strong boost to the development of environmental projects came from EU regulations. Spain had approved the National Plan for treatment of waste water, but it was only in 1998, under pressure to comply with the EU Directive, that waste-water projects began to absorb a large share of resources (55 per cent of the total environmental budget). The two other main areas of environmental activity have been reforestation and coastal conservation.

Chapter 9

Intergovernmental Cooperation: Foreign Policy and Home Affairs

The EU Treaty is organized around three main 'pillars', designed to respect the wish of member states to preserve areas of 'sovereignty' against Community interference. But the very existence (and expansion) of such pillars suggests they offer an effective means of organizing new forms of cooperation among member states. On second and third-pillar issues (foreign and security policy and justice and home affairs), Spain's preference has been for closer convergence and harmonization, backed by a transfer of powers to the EU. As regards foreign and security policy, Spain has backed a general and progressive development of a common policy, but one linked to national priorities. In general terms, Europeanization has been marked in Spain, and European policy institutions have had a decisive influence on both outcomes and preferences (Torreblanca, 2001b). As regards justice and home affairs, Spain has actively backed the development of European-level policies to tackle specific domestic problems. Indeed, Spain's own concerns have had a clear influence on a number of intergovernmental mechanisms and policies. In the case of both pillars, the EU has become an enlarged arena for Spanish national interests, which are increasingly tending to merge with those of the Union itself.

Foreign and security policy: seeking status as a medium-sized power

In general terms, the EU has offered Spain an ideal means by which to develop its new status as a medium-sized power. Torreblanca (2001b) has laid much emphasis on this 'instrumental' use of the EU, which has provided the opportunity to enhance the foreign policy capacity and the national goals of a country which, in its pre-EU days, was not only saddled with a wide-ranging and problematic foreign policy agenda, but also lacked the economic resources and foreign affairs experience to match ambitions to policies, as well as being short on international prestige.

The precondition to achieve credible medium-power status was the modernization of Spain's foreign policy. Basically, this meant eliminating the Francoist inheritance (Grasa, 1997: 30). On account of the Franco regime, Spain was slow to join the international community and somewhat out of place in it: her security policy had been dictated by the army; her relationship with the USA was one of distinct inferiority; and Spanish public opinion, unlike that in most of Europe, was strongly anti-American rather than anti-Soviet. Spanish foreign policy in the 1970s was largely driven by concerns about security. Modernization was eased by the fact that the two main post-Franco political parties, the Unión de Centro Democrático (UCD) and the Partido Socialista Obrero Español (PSOE), broadly agreed on priorities (Grasa, 1997; Alonso Zaldívar and Castells, 1992: 206). UCD governments formulated the basic objectives of foreign policy and PSOE governments implicitly accepted them. However, not all analysts agree that there was such consensus over foreign policy, whilst nonetheless accepting that constitutional consensus did spill over into foreign and security policy (Rodrigo, 1995: 52–3). The one real exception to the general consensus on foreign policy was the question of security, which came to a head over the single issue of NATO.

At the beginning of the post-Franco era, Spanish governments strove to normalize their foreign relations. Normalization implied converging with European modalities and casting off the Francoist inheritance, especially as regards security, where further clarification was urgently needed if Spain's foreign policy agenda was not to remain dominated, to the point of distortion, by the security issue. The key points of debate were Spain's membership of NATO, her security relationship with the USA, and her nuclear status. Spain had become a NATO member almost by default in 1981, mainly for external reasons: by 1980 the Spanish government had come to realize that there was in practice a close link between membership of NATO and membership of the EU, and between NATO membership and the defining of a new security relationship with the USA (Rodrigo, 1995: 57).

The PSOE was at the time wholly opposed to NATO membership and made a political commitment to call a referendum on the issue.

But having gained power in 1982, the PSOE changed its position – this being the price of EU membership and, in particular, German support (Powell, 2001). Thus the PSOE accepted NATO membership on three conditions: Spain would not form part of the military structure; would not build or store nuclear weapons nor allow them on her soil; and there must be a negotiated reduction in the US military presence. The dramatic and long-delayed referendum of 1986, in which the government won support for Spain to remain in NATO but outside the military structure, left the country in a unique position within the organization. However, settlement of the NATO issue reduced its importance in the eyes of the public and its status as a bone of political contention. Both were essential to the normalization of Spanish foreign policy, which in turn was a prerequisite for the Europeanization of that policy.

'Europeanization' means the assumption of the EU's foreign policy concerns (Grasa, 1997), as well as its legislative and decision-making mechanisms as encompassed in the *acquis*. Before Spain's accession, patterns of European political cooperation (EPC) had conflicted in particular with two trends that dominated Spain's agenda: relations with the developing world, and Gibraltar (Barbé, 1999: 186, note 21). On the eve of accession, however, Spain was pressured to adapt to mainstream European policies on the specific issues of Israel and the Soviet Union (Story and Grugel, 1991). In regard to the former, the Netherlands demanded that Spanish accession should be conditional on her recognizing Israel and establishing diplomatic relations with her. As to the Soviet Union, NATO membership would anyhow oblige Spain to align herself with the other EU Atlantic allies.

After accession, a favourable international context helped the Europeanization of Spanish foreign policy. Between 1986 and 1989, no major international crisis threatened to create a divergence between Spain's priorities (Latin America and the Arab world) and the wishes of the majority in the EU. This meant that Spain could assume the Community *acquis* without sacrificing any of her special relationships, unlike during the Malvinas/Falklands War, for example, when Spanish public opinion had sympathized with Argentina and the Spanish government had opposed NATO involvement. So long as no similarly conflictive situations arose, Spain – like Portugal – could be a 'mainstreamer' under the terms of EPC and the Common Foreign and Security Policy (CFSP). Indeed, in most areas and on most issues Spain went along with the majority view, with only minor divergences (Diedrichs and Wessels, 1996). In fact, EU membership removed

Spain's freedom of choice in such areas as disarmament and non-proliferation, multilateral trade and investment, international financial cooperation, human rights, and so forth (Torreblanca, 2001b). From an EU viewpoint, Spain's accession did not alter any important existing trends, or open up any new areas for consideration under the EPC framework or, subsequently, the CFSP (Diedrichs and Wessels, 1996: 324).

Spain's assumption of the EU presidency in 1989 has been defined as the second 'Big Bang' in her post-Franco foreign policy, the first being entry into NATO and the EU (Fernández Ordóñez, 1989). It was a turning point in the integration of Spanish foreign policy within the prevailing structure of EPC. However, despite an ambitious programme, the achievements of the presidency were minor: a declaration on Latin American debt, calling on public creditors to voluntarily reduce interest payments and seeking further loan facilities from international organizations; an increase in the share of EU development aid allocated to Latin American countries; and the splitting of DGI (External Relations) into two divisions, responsible for Asia and Latin America respectively. In addition, Spain pushed through a declaration on the Middle East which reflected traditional EU policy. Even in these achievements the role of the Spanish government was secondary: Spain was merely building on foundations already laid by the EPC *acquis*. Advances in such important areas as the Middle East and Latin America owed much to the development of preexisting EU agendas, and in practice Spain failed to ensure further EU economic concessions to Latin America.

After the first phase of intense Europeanization, the fall of the Berlin Wall and the resulting change in the geopolitical landscape led to a redefinition of Spanish foreign policy, again described by some analysts as 'normalization' (Ortega, 1995: 193; Barbé, 1996: 10). But this time 'normalization' meant that Spain had her own interests, which did not always coincide with mainstream EU ones. Spain now began to suffer from 'periphery syndrome' owing to the EU's increased orientation towards Eastern Europe. This syndrome had two consequences. First, Spain began to assert her own priorities more stridently (for instance, as regards the Maghreb). Secondly, Spain adopted a more pragmatic approach to security policy (Barbé, 1996: 11), paying more attention to the economic aspects of foreign relations (related to growing overseas investment in areas such as Latin America). In the new context, Spain shifted from a 'bilateral' (or, at best, 'regional') concept of foreign relations to a global and multidisciplinary one, combining bilateral and multilateral instruments (Elorza, 1997: 28). Spain was seeking a new international role as a medium-sized power – both as an objective in itself and as a way of overcoming 'peripheral' status. The process of Europeanization in Spain has been conditioned by the ideological stance of ruling governments. The PP administration which took office in 1996 adopted a 'neo-realist' stance and displayed a discourse which cast Spain as a medium-sized power whose strength derives from its 'assets': its economic development (tenth in the world in terms of GNP), open economy (reflected in direct foreign investment, where it ranked sixth in the world), and the global importance of the Spanish language (Barbé, 2001). Success in EU internal policies strengthened José María Aznar's conception of international politics as a competition whose outcome depends entirely on the strength of each player (Rodrigo, 1998: 30). Conservative policy diverged from that of the outgoing Socialists in at least three areas: relations with the USA, meaning fuller support of American policies (most notably, in the case of the 2003 invasion of Iraq); a new model of full participation in NATO; and more hostile relations with Cuba. While the change to Spain's status within NATO was an inevitable result of the new geopolitical climate, the changed relationships with both the USA and Cuba mirror Conservative tastes and a process defined as the 'Atlanticisation' of Spanish foreign policy (Barbé, 1999:149). In 1998, for example, Aznar was the only continental European leader publicly to support the Anglo-American bombing of Iraq (shortly after a visit by the American Secretary of State to Madrid). Subsequently, Aznar adopted a certain unilateralism, showing himself to be receptive to the American Strategic Defense Initiative despite the reticence of other governments and before the development of any common position.

Three main reasons explain Aznar's strongly pro-US stance and his support for the war in Iraq, despite the huge scale of opposition among the Spanish public. First, he was a strong advocate of the global antiterrorist campaign of the Bush administration after September 11, believing that the US administration had a more realistic perception of the immediacy of the terrorist threat than did Spain's EU partners. Secondly, he saw support for the USA as part of a wider strategic goal to align Spain with the UK and Italy as part of the 'new Europe' which would act as a counterweight to the traditional Franco–German axis. Aznar's concern was to avoid the development of a 'fortress Europe' as a rival pole of power to the USA, and also to ensure that Spain's interests in Latin America were defended (see below). Thirdly, Aznar wanted to present Spain as playing a key international role as a country with a privileged position in transatlantic dialogues, and with a voice that would command respect. Thus, the war in Iraq and close association with the USA was seen as a means by which Spain might effect a shift from being a middle power to becoming a major player within the EU, able to stand alongside the 'big four' of France, Germany, Italy and the UK (Heywood, 2003).

These developments suggest that the USA represents, at the very least, a complementary model to the European one for Aznar and for certain sections of his party. Europeanization nonetheless remains the key to most aspects of Spain's foreign policy, though she has retained a margin of autonomy. This Europeanization has two interlinked dimensions: Spain's own security and foreign relations, and the definition of common instruments and procedures for the implementation of a common security and defence policy.

The Europeanization of Spain's foreign policy: the Mediterranean and Latin America

Apart from the general drive towards convergence with mainstream European policies, Spain has Europeanized her foreign policy through the additional mechanism of policy transfer – that is, the attempt to impose a Spanish agenda on the EU (Torreblanca, 2001b). Spain has endeavoured to steer EU policy in two key geographical areas, Latin America and the Mediterranean. In both, Spain has cast the EU as paymaster and supplier of the political clout needed to back up Spanish-designed strategies and concepts. This has enabled Spain to enhance her international role *vis-à-vis* third parties, which in turn feeds back into the formulation of EU policies (Barbé, 1999). Spain does not have an identical attitude towards the two areas: Latin America is perceived as a prestige area, the Mediterranean in contrast as more of a risk area (Barbé, 1996: 23). The slogan 'peace in the Mediterranean and democracy in Latin America', as formulated by one of Felipe González's foreign policy advisers, effectively encapsulates this dichotomy (Gillespie, 2000: 175).

The Mediterranean and the Middle East

Spain's policy of cultivating the Arab world started in 1946 as a consequence of international hostility to the Franco regime. This policy suited the requirements of an economy highly dependent on imported energy supplies, although it was mainly rhetorical and never developed into a coherent project based on increasing cooperation (Gillespie, 1995: 160; Salomon, 1996: 93; Bataller and Jordán, 1997: 138). When Spain joined the EU she had to reconcile two divergent objectives: first, to keep the traditional links of friendship with the Arab world whilst seeking to conform to Western interests (Salomon, 1996: 94); secondly, to protect her direct security interests in one particular part of the Arab and Mediterranean world, the Maghreb. Other member states did not have such a sense of immediate potential threat; in fact, NATO defines the Maghreb as out-of-area, highlighting a rather different conception of security risk in the region.

Developing an overall global policy that would cater for both objectives was further complicated because of the duality of interests involved in the Maghreb. Spain's primary concern was security, which was perceived initially in territorial and strategic terms, but this basically military approach was subsequently replaced by concern over Islamic fundamentalism, immigration pressure and population growth in North Africa (Gillespie, 2000: 159; Bataller and Jordán, 1997: 139). Solving these problems would require a combination of financial, commercial and political cooperation.

But economic and trading interests were diametrically opposed to these security concerns. Agricultural products from the southern Mediterranean countries had traditionally competed with Spanish ones on the EU market, and some of those countries had historically received a better deal from the EU (see Chapter 6). In fact, Algeria was part of the Common Market when it was created in 1957, and Morocco was receiving special treatment within the French market by the time Spain signed its 1970 Preferential Agreement. Spanish relations with these countries, especially Morocco, were therefore complicated by Spain's accession. In particular, Spain wanted yet more preferential treatment for its Mediterranean agricultural products (Gillespie, 1995: 168; Tovias, 1995: 100). Thus, the natural competition between Spain and the southern Mediterranean (agricultural products being the strongest element in the Arab economies) severely restricted Spanish headroom when it came to political initiatives.

The existence of these two contradictory objectives led to an equally contradictory policy – as seen through Arab eyes, at least (Gillespie, 2000: 175). But Spanish governments could easily explain the contradiction as part of normal EU schizophrenia, which saw a separation between Community policies and the structure of EPC. Thus Spain could take a lofty moral stance by defending the 'just cause' of the Arabs, whilst pursuing her own interests in the Maghreb

(Salomon, 1996). To a certain extent, Spain became the leader, within the EPC framework, of a 'progressive block' that included France, the UK, Ireland and Greece (Salomon, 1996: 98). In point of fact, the EPC structure lacked the necessary clout to influence the direction of world politics. Spain steered through the 1989 Madrid Declaration on the Middle East which updated that backbone of EU policy, the Venice Declaration. She also initiated several 'Troika' missions in Arab countries, believing that the international climate favoured this course. Spain also introduced her 'principled' stance on the Sahara conflict (a very sensitive issue for Spain) on to the EPC agenda – an example of how her interests were Europeanized (Barbé, 1996: 15; 1999: 24).

Community policies, on the other hand, fit well with Spanish interests. Thus, the immediate effect of Spanish accession was to change the EU's attitude to the Mediterranean region. To begin with at least, Europeanization meant subsuming Spanish interests into broader EU policies or, more precisely, unloading Spain's problems on the EU (Torreblanca, 2001b). The Renovated Mediterranean Policy (RMP) – implemented in 1992, allegedly under heavy pressure from the two Spanish commissioners (Tovias, 1995: 103) – brought about a shift from a relationship based on trade concessions towards a policy based on financial transfers from the EU. Spain also ensured that the Maghreb fell within the sphere of EU involvement, and, most important of all, strove to get Morocco a much better deal than hitherto as part of the EC's evolving Mediterranean policy. Partly as a result of Spanish diplomacy during 1992, the Community was persuaded that of all the Maghreb countries, Morocco was the most worthy of a special partnership agreement, with the potential for a gradual move towards free trade (Gillespie, 1995: 169). Spain's contribution to European policy in this area has thus been to convince her EU partners, first that the Maghreb is a European problem (Gillespie, 1995 173), and second that this problem has to be solved through trade, improved communications and generous hand-outs. The main obstacle to Spanish policy within the EU stems from powerful economic interests (for instance, fishing agreements with Morocco, the gas pipeline from Algeria), though Gillespie (2000: 159) has argued that immediate economic gain has never been of prime importance to Spain's Mediterranean policy. Nonetheless, Spanish interests have turned fishing and agriculture into permanent stumbling blocks in the relationship between the EU and Morocco (see Chapter 6).

From the beginning of the 1990s, realism has pushed the Mediterranean higher up Spain's foreign policy agenda. The end of the Cold War prompted the Spanish government to redesign its Mediterranean policy with a stronger orientation towards security. Fear of marginalization is another factor in Spain's insistence on putting the Mediterranean at the top of the EU agenda (Barbé, 1999: 161). Also, Spanish diplomats gradually realized that Spain's interests in the western Mediterranean and other regions would be best served by espousing an EU-backed strategy rather than a purely national one (Baixeras, 1996: 154). Spain simply could not afford, in purely financial terms, to go it alone.

This new global approach did not mean renouncing fundamental Spanish interests; on the contrary, the new goal was to redirect EU Mediterranean policy (traditionally concentrated in the Middle East) towards the Maghreb (Baixeras, 1996: 151), which simply meant channelling Community resources towards that region. The Dezcallar report, compiled by Spanish diplomats, underlay the 1992 Lisbon Declaration that singled out the western Mediterranean as a priority area for EU security interests (Baixeras, 1996: 155). The communiqué of the European Council meeting at Lisbon in 1992 listed the Maghreb as one area of possible joint action under the CFSP, and approved a Declaration on the Maghreb (Salomon, 1996: 105).

The most innovative aspect of Spain's revamped policy was her new assertiveness in the eastern Mediterranean, as part of a global definition of the region. Felipe González had argued at the start of the 1990s that the Middle East conflict was at least as important to the EU as to the USA, and that Europe should be involved in the debate as a logical consequence of the long European presence in the region (González, 1992: 19). Spain did not seek to replace the USA as protagonist; indeed, throughout the 1990s Spain called for both EU and US involvement in Mediterranean security initiatives (Gillespie, 2000: 170). But Spanish support for the USA in the Gulf War was repaid by Washington's acquiescence in greater Spanish involvement in Mediterranean politics. As a further reward for Spanish support, the USA government accepted Madrid as the venue for the October 1991 conference on the Middle East peace process. This alignment with the USA did not arise from a sudden bout of pro-Americanism: as Gillespie (2000: 172) has noted, it served Spain's commercial interests and need for modernization as well as being a logical consequence of Europe's failure to develop an independent response to the security crises in the Mediterranean.

Spain was also able skilfully to exploit the failure of a French initiative. France had proposed a '5 + 5' process, backed by Spain and Italy, which aimed to set up a permanent sub-regional dialogue between northern and southern Mediterranean countries. The 5 + 5 initiative failed because of the implications of Libya's participation in the wake of the terrorist attack over Lockerbie. Its replacement, the Mediterranean Forum (again led by France and including Egypt and Turkey) had a looser structure that was never consolidated.

Spain then stepped into France's shoes and, in partnership with Italy, proposed a much wider framework for dialogue: the model for the Conference on Security and Cooperation in Europe (CSCE) should be adapted for the Mediterranean by setting up a Conference on Security and Cooperation in the Mediterranean (CSCM) to cover the same three areas as the CSCE: security, economics and human rights. A number of factors dogged the CSCM project from the outset: insufficient cooperation between Madrid and Rome, a lukewarm response by France (who saw it as a challenge to her own leading role in the Mediterranean in an area of special national interest) and, most important, the reluctance of the USA to become involved (Gillespie, 2000: 171), which Spain had wanted but France had not (Baixeras, 1996: 161).

Despite its failure, some important elements of the CSCM proposal were retained in what became the Barcelona process. The Euro–Mediterranean Partnership, with 27 participants, was established on a more practical scale than the CSCM, but retained the same three policy areas (Gillespie, 2000: 173). The Euro–Mediterranean Dialogue, as presented by Spanish and Italian foreign ministers, would become the third axis of a full relationship – the other two being the development and strengthening of bilateral links (mainly through association agreements) and the gradual construction of a free trade zone combined with EU financial transfers to southern Mediterranean countries (Solana and Agnelli, 1995).

As before, Spain's intention was to bend EU policy towards her own concerns – this time involving a whole region. She managed to convince her European partners that it was impossible to safeguard Europe against the unstable south by maintaining a *cordon sanitaire* supplemented by the threat of military intervention (Gillespie, 2000: 169). Any alternative mechanism should be based on strong financial commitments and trade concessions. Spain believed that the success of the Barcelona meeting depended on securing financial commitments and the government was also aware that this was likely to be a final opportunity, since a number of Eastern European countries were about to join the EU, thereby limiting its capacity to provide foreign aid (Barbé, 1996: 21).

Thus, by 1995 Spain was pressing hard for an increase in EU aid to the Mediterranean region. At the Cannes summit and during the French presidency, Spain persuaded Germany to agree to a 22 per cent increase in the resources allocated to that region. The money was, of course, the carrot being dangled before the southern Mediterranean countries to ensure their commitment to the process, but Spain also had a direct interest in channelling the whole financial package, or at least the lion's share of it, towards the Maghreb (Baixeras, 1996: 160).

Despite the grand design and financial package which was secured to bolster it, several factors undermined the efficiency of the Barcelona process (Menéndez del Valle, 2001). First, the Palestinian–Israeli conflict continues to bedevil any attempt to achieve progress on political cooperation. Secondly, there is a fundamental trade imbalance of 34:1 in favour of the northern countries. The conclusions of the Euro–Mediterranean conference had to be very cautious about preferential access to EU markets for Mediterranean products because of pressure from agricultural lobbies (Bataller and Jordán, 1997: 143) – although the evidence suggests that trade concessions on fruit and vegetables have not destabilized EU markets or affected Spanish agriculture.

To sum up, Spain has been Europe's most committed proponent of an EU policy of political, social and economic cooperation with the Mediterranean (Baixeras, 1996: 150). The main weaknesses in its leadership derive from a mismatch between the number of ideas emanating from Madrid and the extent to which it is willing to pay for them – the assumption usually being that the most prosperous EU countries will foot the bill (Gillespie, 2000: 174). The model of Europeanization has meant that Spanish interests have been subsumed within broader EU policies, but Europeanization has also been extremely useful in 'blame avoidance'. For instance, the introduction of visas for Maghreb countries in 1991 was blamed on the EU, although Madrid had quite clearly opposed demands from high-immigration countries to extend mobility rights to non-EU nationals (Gillespie, 2000: 168).

Latin America

Expectations ran high as regards the potential impact of Spanish accession to the EU on relations with Latin America, given Spain's historic links with the region. The rationale of cooperation suited not only Spain and Latin America, but also the EU. From a Spanish perspective, many of the benefits of EU members' joint activities in Latin America would be reaped by Spain alone (Grugel, 1996: 74). As far as the Latin American countries were concerned, their relationship with Spain lacked any real content in most areas, including diplomatic, financial and commercial relationships and development cooperation. They had everything to win and very little to lose as far as potential damage to bilateral relations was concerned. Finally, for the EU itself, Latin America was a potential terrain for establishing the Community as a world player, to prevent paralysis or 'Euroesclerosis' from threatening its external role (Grugel, 1996: 75).

Two factors characterize the Spanish/EU policy towards Latin America. Firstly, the area includes a large number of countries unified by a common Spanish (or Portuguese) heritage but sharply differentiated internally by their economic and political structures. Additionally, Spain's economic presence has grown steadily over the years. Both factors have progressively transformed the model of Spanish involvement and, hence, of Spanish-influenced EU policy.

Initially, when Spain joined the EU in 1986, she tried unsuccessfully to obtain a special status for Latin American countries along the lines negotiated by Britain and France for their former colonies. Spain obtained only a vague 'Common Declaration regarding the development and strengthening of the relationship with Latin American countries'. Moreover, Spain's adoption of the common external trade policy threatened some of her own trade connections with Latin America (Salmon, 1995: 74). Spain did, however, obtain a number of minor concessions from the EU, such as the extension of the System of General Preferences to several Latin American crops (for example, coffee and cocoa) of which Spain was a large importer; increased loans from the European Investment Bank (EIB); the inclusion of the Dominican Republic in the Lomé Convention; and agreements with Mercosur and Mexico (Elorza, 1997).

Arguably the biggest impact was through EPC, whose Latin American agenda expanded after 1986 to cover four areas (Grugel, 1996):

1 Pacification of Central America.
2 Support for democratization.
3 Support for moves towards Latin American integration.
4 Institutionalized interregional dialogue.

Observers have stressed that Spain cannot take all the credit for recent increases in cooperation. Rather, Spain became part of a bloc of countries interested in extending the EU presence in Latin America and, supported by Portugal, made clear her aspiration to lead that bloc (Grugel, 1996: 77). The goal was to deepen contacts between the two regions following the existing guidelines, and, as with the Mediterranean, the EU was expected to pay for it all. Whether or not this can be considered the result of Spanish action, EU financial assistance to Latin America rose from €37 million in 1985 to €367 million in 1995. Spain had at last found a plaster for her Achilles' heel – her poor record on economic assistance to Latin America (Grugel, 1996: 81).

Perhaps Spain's most significant contribution was to call for an EU policy on Latin America which clearly diverged from that of the USA. This meant that EPC, and sometimes Spain herself, ran counter to the views of individual member states over (for instance) the American invasion of Panama in 1989 and the Contra affair in Nicaragua.

The progressive democratization of the continent reduced the need for political initiatives in support of democracy and ultimately left Cuba as the only country resistant to this general trend. In fact, Cuba provided a test-case for the strength of Europeanization. Under the PSOE, Spain had adopted a gradualist approach and the European Council, meeting in Madrid during the Spanish presidency, agreed to continue dialogue and cooperation with Cuba. The Commission was asked in 1996 to prepare a draft agreement on trade and economic cooperation, a policy which served Spanish interests as it ensured EU protection against the US Helms–Burton Act for investments in Cuba while offering carrots to encourage a liberalization of the regime. When the conservative PP assumed power in Spain in 1996, there was a changed attitude towards Cuba, which had been a fulcrum of Spanish foreign policy since Franco's day (Barbé, 1999: 123). Aznar adopted a tougher position that led in December 1997 to the adoption of a common EU position on Cuba: cooperation was made conditional on progressive democratization and respect for human rights (Rodrigo, 1998: 40). Torreblanca (2001b) has argued, however, that these attempts to reverse policy were severely curtailed: paradoxically, while the EU's policy on Cuba is wholly of Spanish origin, the very fact that it is now a *European* policy has constrained the Spanish government's freedom of manoeuvre.

Spanish policy has changed as a consequence not only of democratization but also of the change in her links with Latin America. It had been argued in the 1990s that Spain's lack of economic weight was hampering some of the proposals for improving trade since the costs would have to be borne by other member states (Grugel, 1996: 88). However, during the mid-1990s, the presence of Spanish firms grew significantly in all Latin American countries, and in some of them Spain became the leading foreign investor and a primary trade partner. Democratization in Latin America, coupled with greater financial clout thanks to the EU, brought about a subtle change in Spanish strategy. The new objective was to achieve economic agreements between Latin American countries and the EU that would secure and increase Spanish economic penetration in the region.

Mexico offers a good illustration of this policy. Spain was the leading advocate of the Association Agreement between EU and Mexico signed in May 2000. This was in reaction to the NAFTA agreement, the direct effect of which was to reduce trade between Mexico and the EU (from 11 per cent in 1990 to 6 per cent in 2000). Spanish trade followed this pattern: it received 1.8 per cent of Mexico's exports in 1993, but only 0.9 per cent in 1999. Spain is the fourth largest EU investor in Mexico in terms of direct investment (after the UK, the Netherlands and Germany), but the first by number of companies (Blanco, 2000: 38). Spain is Mexico's third largest customer, whilst Mexico is Spain's eighth largest (Ceceña, 2000; Riva, 2000). Thus, the trade agreement is reactive rather than proactive, though it is also an attempt to access the much larger US market through the back-door of Mexico. In turn, Mexico was keen to diversify a risk that was formerly, under NAFTA, very much concentrated in the USA. Institutionally, the agreement includes a consultative organism, the Joint Council, made up of ministers and presidents plus the Commission. But the EU did not achieve its target of ensuring parity with the trade tariff applied by NAFTA. Nonetheless, the agreement paves the way for forthcoming ones with Mercosur and Chile, both areas where Spanish firms have a strong presence.

Spain's increased prosperity thanks to her EU membership has further modified her traditional relations with Latin America in fields such as immigration. In 1995, the Spanish Permanent Representative sought to reshape the Schengen Agreement to better serve Spanish interests. This meant squaring it with the dual nationality agreements between Spain and the Latin American countries. Only two of these (Cuba and the Dominican Republic) appeared on the existing agreed list of countries whose nationals required visas to visit Spain (Elorza, 1995b). But in 2001 Spain agreed to demand visas for Colombians, provoking outrage among both Spanish and Colombian intellectuals and politicians. The Spanish government protested that it had only yielded in order to facilitate the new agreement, but opponents did not fail to notice that the new measures coincided with a hardening of Spanish immigration law.

Decision-making on foreign and security policies

Spain's approach to decision-making could be defined as cautiously mainstream. When the Common Foreign and Security Policy (CFSP) was being drawn up at the 1991 IGC, Spain – with other member states – rejected the Dutch plan to integrate the CFSP within the Community, preferring to establish it as another 'pillar'. Spain also supported the idea that decision-making in all areas of foreign policy should be by consensus, leading to qualified majority voting at some point in the future. The paper that Spanish representatives submitted to the IGC broadly followed the Franco–German line. However, Spain's attitude can be seen as ambiguous: whilst in favour of a more efficient Union, she is also anxious to defend national interests – meaning North Africa and Latin America – and therefore does *not* want majority voting to apply in those areas (Rodrigo, 1996: 32; Barbé, 1999: 35).

Spain's aim is to keep to her own agenda while Europeanizing certain parts of it. She would like to square the circle by supporting the principle of a common foreign policy, but with strong intergovernmental organs and decision-making by consensus. Rather than adopting full-scale federalism, Spain has adopted a Europeanist attitude based on gradual implementation and realistic decision-making mechanisms (Barbé, 1999: 160). She has therefore advocated exploring *ad hoc* arrangements such as 'unanimity with positive or constructive abstention', 'unanimity minus one', 'super qualified majority', and so forth (Rodrigo, 1996: 32).

Security and defence policy

The foundations of Spain's security and defence policy during the 1980s and the first half of the 1990s were included in the 1984 'Decalogue' or Declaration drafted by the PSOE government prior to joining NATO. While accepting NATO membership, the Socialist government called for a Europeanization of security (Alonso Zaldívar and Castells, 1992: 213). This strategy started within NATO itself with Spain's participation in the European Projects Group, and was further pursued when Spain assumed the status of observer member at the Western European Union (WEU) in 1988, followed by full membership in 1990. Spanish governments at the time spoke of 'wearing two hats' and being 'separable but not separate' (Ortega, 1995: 189) – meaning that the creation of multinational units within NATO should not prevent the WEU from setting up its own forces, nor should it prevent any country from assigning the same units to NATO and the WEU. In parallel, Spain has advocated the progressive integration of the WEU into the EU. She is strongly in favour of the steady development of an autonomous European security and defence identity and has argued that the military dimension of the CFSP should be improved (Rodrigo, 1996: 33).

The reinforcement of the WEU provided Spain with a shortcut to involvement in collective defence activities. The Gulf War, meanwhile, marked the end of a century of Spanish isolationism (Barbé, 1999: 48). It provided the opportunity for active involvement in collective security organizations, showing that Spain was willing to support her allies (mainly the USA) despite hostile domestic public opinion. From the beginning of the war Spain strove to collaborate with her EU partners and put all military activities under the WEU umbrella. The disappearance of bipolarism facilitated Spain's participation in the European security debate (Barbé, 1999: 50). By 1991, the Spanish government had formulated the theory of an EU defence organization comprising three complementary bodies: the Conference on Security and Cooperation in Europe (CSCE), NATO and the WEU (Barbé, 1999: 50).

The Conservative government which came to power in 1996 made no changes to the main guidelines of security and defence policy, and maintained the Socialists' emphasis on building a European system. This inspired the objectives of the main policy instrument, the 1996 National Defence Directive, by which Spain sought:

- to help define a common European security and defence policy;
- to contribute to collective defence through NATO, whilst supporting the development of a specifically European security and defence identity; and
- to participate in European multinational forces constituted for the implementation of 'Petersberg tasks' (Article 17 of the TEU).

While keeping Europeanism as a target, the profound change in NATO owing to its enlargement eastwards forced a revision of Spain's previous attitude. Fear of marginalization imposed an 'end to eccentricity' (Barbé, 1999: 126) and led the government to seek full incorporation into NATO's military structure in 1997. Geostrategic changes informed this change of attitude, which was hardly in tune with Conservative ideology. In fact, all political parties except the United Left (which had been created as a result of the 1986 referendum) endorsed this decision. Spain demanded a regional command covering the Iberian peninsula, but this was rejected by the UK (to keep Gibraltar out of Spanish control) and Portugal (which did not want a Peninsular command that would subordinate her forces to Spain's).

The PP government continued to prioritize the European dimension. The White Paper on Defence (2000) stated that Spain supported the development of a European Initiative on Security and Defence within NATO and the progressive development of a common European defence policy in accordance with the Washington and Cologne summits (Ministerio de Defensa, 2000: 59). However, Spain had not participated in the design of the new CFSP agreed in Helsinki in 1999. Spain's view, as outlined by Aznar, focused instead on how it should be institutionalized through defence committees and a Council of Ministers of Defence. The Prime Minister announced the commitment of 6000 troops (10 per cent of the Spanish total) to the newly created Rapid Intervention Force (expected to be operative by 2003), and also suggested the coordination of defence purchasing and a convergence programme (akin to EMU) to decide each member state's contributions towards an autonomous common European defence system.

This latest Spanish policy appeared driven by fears of marginalization. During the Nice negotiations, Spanish representatives voiced a preference for a gradual and collective approach rather than bilateral initiatives such as the Franco–British declaration at St Malo. They submitted a proposal for greater cooperation on second-pillar issues, allowing any member state to contribute to EU initiatives if it so wished. This would prevent the emergence of cliques. Spain proposed integrating bilateral initiatives (such as Eurocorps, which Spain joined in 1993) within the EU framework, where they would act as catalysts to encourage the development of a future European defence system.

Most of Spain's earlier initiatives make sense from this integrative and gradualist viewpoint. Spain's Europeanism has been translated into, first, a ready involvement in multilateral forces, and, secondly, the creation of a pan-European defence industry. Regarding the first point, in December 1993 Spain assigned forces to Eurocorps, a joint division comprising troops from Germany, France, Belgium, Spain and, subsequently, Luxembourg. The Mediterranean states (France, Italy, Spain and Portugal) have also developed some military cooperation under the WEU umbrella: EUROFOR (joint land forces) and EUROMARFOR (naval forces), ratified in the Lisbon Declaration of 1995. In 1997, Spain and Italy set up a Spanish–Italian amphibian force. Finally, Spain forms part of the European Air Group (created to reinforce the NATO European Initiative), along with Italy, France, Germany, Belgium, Holland, Sweden and the UK. This group has no permanent forces assigned to it, however.

In regard to the defence industry, Spain has been committed to participation in European-based initiatives. Examples include Spanish participation in the European Air Defence System (EADS) consortium via CASA, and, jointly with Germany and the UK, in the Euro-fighter project (for the EFA EF-2000, of which Spain is to purchase 57). She has also contributed to the Helios I (military observation satellite) programme. Spain again demonstrated her interest in a pan-European defence industry in 1998 by signing, along with Germany, UK, Italy, France and Sweden, the *Charter of Intent on the Re-structuring of the European Defence Industry* – a joint endeavour that could form the basis for a European defence industry.

The PP government's 2000 White Paper on Defence laid down the guidelines for Spain's defence industry. It combined the liberal approach already adopted on market issues with a policy of 'national champions': the government promised to fund R&D in leading industries that might contribute to the development of a 'common European defence'. But, at the same time, it encouraged free competition in the purchase and use of commercial products according to civil rules and standards. In point of fact, some decisions seemed to pay more heed to this liberal attitude than to strategic considerations. This certainly applied to the armaments manufacturer, Santa Bárbara SA, which was sold to the US company General Dynamic. Certainly General Dynamic's offer was higher than that of its competitor, the German Krauss-Maffei. But tactical and political reasons favoured the German company: it had sold tanks to the Spanish army for a token price; it had a joint manufacturing agreement with Santa Bárbara for the Leopard tank; it was preferred by the Spanish army; and it was strongly supported by the German government. The sale underlined how far Aznar's foreign policy had turned in the direction of deeper cooperation with the USA, even at the expenses of European allies.

The 'third pillar': the Europeanization of Spanish problems

The 'third pillar' offers an example of policy transfer triggered by domestic concerns: it is driven chiefly by concern over immigration and, in particular, terrorism. Domestic politics also explain the enthusiastic integrationist stance that has resulted in Spain making a significant contribution to shaping EU policies in various different ways. On immigration, the EU provides the Spanish government with a useful means of 'blame avoidance' and a way to legitimize Spanish domestic policies. In the fight against terrorism, meanwhile, the EU provides a wider arena and a wider range of instruments.

Tailoring EU instruments and policies

Spain's most important impact in this area has been her contribution to an improved design for policies and instruments. In 1990, Spain became a participant in the Schengen Agreement: the government proclaimed this as conclusive proof that Spain belonged to the inner core of the EU. But, far from being satisfied with the status quo, successive Spanish governments have consistently sought further improvements to international police co-operation and extradition mechanisms among EU member states.

The drive for Europeanization stems from a domestic issue: the struggle against the Basque separatist group ETA. Spain's problems were compounded by the tolerant (and occasionally, even sympathetic) attitude towards ETA terrorists in some other EU member states. On several occasions French (1989 and 1995) and Italian (1990) courts rejected extradition claims against ETA members on the grounds that their alleged offences were politically inspired (Fungairiño, 1995: 100), and at times ETA terrorists have found shelter in other EU member states. While no democratic government accepts ETA's argument that it is the army of a nation oppressed by the Spanish state, ETA terrorists have found the openness of some states towards asylum seekers extremely convenient. Thus, in 1993 two ETA members asked for political asylum in Belgium, and again, in 1996, an ETA member sought similar status from the Portuguese authorities. Both applications were ultimately rejected but they did delay Spanish requests for the extradition of alleged terrorists and also provided fodder for terrorist propaganda. Messages about the 'romantic' army of a nation without a state were not without an audience in Flemish-speaking parts of

Belgium. In Portugal, a group of intellectuals and politicians signed a manifesto in support of ETA activists which caused intense outrage among Spanish politicians. Both the Belgian *Conseil d'Etat* and the Portuguese Supreme Court refused to extradite ETA members, though the Belgian application was thrown out on a technicality.

These experiences help explain Spain's desire for an EU-wide reformulation of the domestic application of asylum and extradition. Spain's initial proposal was to replace general international instruments regulating asylum and extradition by EU-designed ones. In practice, some EU member states were not even parties to the European Convention on Extradition (Belgium, for instance, signed up only in 1995). Several policy initiatives under the umbrella of EU intergovernmental cooperation and, more recently, under third-pillar provisions have sought to commit member states to EU-defined objectives that reflect Spanish priorities.

In 1995, the EU approved a resolution on minimum guarantees for asylum procedures; implicitly targeted against third-country nationals. Although this resolution created a fast-track examination procedure, Spain complained that delaying tactics (appeals on technicalities, and so forth) can be used spin out this 'fast' procedure over several years. She therefore pressed for the rapid introduction of additional instruments, and in September 1996 the Council agreed a new convention supplementing an earlier one in order to simplify extradition procedures among EU member states. This new convention aimed to remove the main limitations of the Council of Europe's European Convention on Extradition. First, extradition was not limited to nationals of the requesting state; it also applied to nationals of the state receiving the request (in the latter case, or if extradition is forbidden under the state's constitution, that state can unilaterally enter an objection for a renewable period of five years). Secondly – the most important point, as far as Spain was concerned – there was a significant reduction in the number of cases in which extradition could be refused between member states. Specifically, the state receiving a request could not describe a terrorist offence as 'political' (Art. 5). In the opinion of the Spanish justice ministry, the effective elimination of the notion of 'political' offences meant that no person can be prosecuted in another member state for political reasons.

However, in Spanish eyes a broad, if rather technical, aspect that had underlying political implications weakened the new Convention. Possible objections to an extradition procedure by an EU signatory state include the principles of legal identity and reciprocal punishments for criminal offences. The importance of this issue can be seen when we recall that the Belgian courts had rejected a Spanish extradition claim on the grounds that collaboration with terrorists was not a crime in Belgian law. How this issue will be resolved will depend on how national parliaments interpret the Convention during the ratification process.

A second, practical, weakness concerned the conditions required for the Convention to be effective. It would not come into force, for example, until all EU member states had ratified it. Foreseeing long delays which might detract from its effectiveness, the Spanish government secured a 'fast-track' procedure to resolve pending problems, which entailed the possibility of immediate bilateral application between two EU member states as long as both agreed to the procedure (Art. 18.4). The Spanish government wasted no time in negotiating such a bilateral application of the Convention with Belgium: on 24 September 1996 both justice ministries signed a Declaration. Spain went on to hold bilateral summit conferences with certain other countries (Germany, France, Portugal and Italy) to agree advanced application of the 1995 and 1996 Extradition Conventions.

Shaping EU policies: Spain takes the lead

After 1996 Spanish governments became much more assertive in the definition of a global policy for third-pillar issues. Spanish officials defined the new third pillar EU objective included in the Treaty of Amsterdam as 'creating a space of freedom, security and justice', and under this bold heading they included several concrete policy proposals that aimed at shaping the third pillar to suit Spanish interests. Most importantly, they proposed eliminating the right of asylum for EU citizens. This had a twofold purpose: first, to prevent extradition requests being delayed or paralysed by a parallel application for asylum; secondly, to undermine any ETA propaganda arising from asylum claims by its members. Such claims, according to Spain, were an abuse of the right to asylum; moreover, asylum applications by EU nationals might induce member states to mistrust each other's democratic systems. The proposal provoked a heated debate and it was finally watered down owing to mounting pressure from NGOs and several governments (Closa, 1998).

Spanish negotiators submitted several other proposals: operational powers should be given to Europol; there should be direct judicial cooperation between judges of different member states; and Conventions should come into force once ratified by a majority of member states (instead of all of them). The new Treaty incorporated only the Europol proposal; as one official wrote, Spain's over-ambitious third pillar objectives were scarcely consonant with the current state of European integration (Dastis, 1999: 226). But the PP administration was deliberately trailing agenda items that could be picked up again later on.

The Spanish government did not concentrate all its negotiations on the constitutional reforms stemming from IGCs. On the contrary, Spain's approach was pragmatic: she wanted results, not fine words. At the 1996 Florence summit, Aznar had proposed holding a special summit on the creation of a European space of freedom, security and justice (Arístegui, 2000: 10), and he repeated the proposal in 1998 at the Extraordinary Summit in Pörtstach. Spain called for an extraordinary summit on justice and internal affairs of which the main focus would be the fight against terrorism. Accordingly, Spanish officials and politicians claimed most of the credit for the October 1999 Tampere summit which drew up the guidelines for the EU policy on third-pillar issues (Arístegui, 2000; Aznar, 1999; Matutes, 1999).

A number of issues in the summit agenda clearly reveal the Spanish hand. For instance, Spain favoured a 'global approach'; which would include criminal behaviour, people-smuggling, police cooperation and money-laundering in addition to the usual topics of immigration and asylum. Some of the summit conclusions also reflected Spanish initiatives, in particular those relating to terrorism. On immigration, the Spanish government claimed that the conclusions reflected Spain's threefold approach to immigration: maximum rigour against people-smugglers; strict control of external borders; and full integration of legal immigrants. The government claimed that these points justified and legitimized the most restrictive aspects of its own 2000 Immigration Law. This new law focused on the control of immigration flows and made a sharp distinction between legal and illegal immigrants and the rights granted to each group – all of which, according to the government, stemmed from EU policy.

Two other specific issues reflected long-standing Spanish objectives: the principle of mutual recognition of judicial rulings and sentences, and the idea that extradition proceedings could be short-circuited by an immediate handing over of suspects (Conclusion 35). Spanish representatives also claimed that the Spanish law of 'solidarity with the victims of terrorism' inspired the items relating to access to justice for victims of crime, and the principle that the state should be responsible for paying compensation and legal aid.

On other issues, however, Spain did not get what she wanted, though some of these remained on the agenda. At the conceptual level, Spain continued to press for the suppression of the concept of political crime in relations among EU member states. Institutionally, she demanded the creation of a permanent secretary for European justice; and at the domestic level she called for immigration and asylum procedures to be harmonized throughout the Union.

The Tampere summit was tantamount to an official blueprint for Spain's strategy of creating Europe-wide instruments for pursuing ETA terrorists throughout the EU. In other words, she aimed to transform the EU into ETA's political antagonist. The declarations were very important in view of the attitudes previously adopted by certain other member states. The clearest EU commitment to the struggle against ETA came in December 2000, when the Council for Home Affairs declared that ETA was a threat to the whole of Europe. The European Parliament's Committee on Public Liberties then drafted a report that called for a common legal basis to regulate search and arrest warrants for terrorist crimes throughout the EU. Spain's strategy of seeking EU support was also pursued outside the EU institutions; the January 2001 Congress of the European People's Party (EPP) condemned ETA terrorism and endorsed the creation of the European Warrant Order.

Apart from such declarations of support, Spain wanted practical solutions. The 2002 presidency set a target for the submission of a number of policy initiatives to implement the Tampere conclusions. Immigration and asylum were the two main priorities of the presidency, and approval was sought for directives on the harmonization of asylum policies and the status of long-stay immigrants. It also attempted to develop a common policy on drug trafficking. An Asia–Europe Ministerial Conference on Cooperation for the Management of Migratory Flows between Europe and Asia took place in Lanzarote on 4 and 5 April 2002 to pursue cooperation on immigration.

The priority of the 2002 Spanish presidency was to replace extradition by the immediate transfer of suspects, and in preparation for this, Spain concluded bilateral agreements with some other member states. The first of these, in November 2002, was a bilateral agreement between Spain and Italy for the mutual recognition of sentences of imprisonment for terrorism, organized crime, drug trafficking, people-smuggling, child sex abuse and arms dealing. The large number of Mafia members living on the Spanish coast, under the protection of Spanish extradition laws, explains Italy's interest in this instrument. The Treaty involved mutual recognition of judicial decisions and an undertaking to implement them. In practice, this meant the effective elimination of extradition proceedings.

Spain took this agreement as a model and sought to extend it to Germany, the UK, France, Belgium and Portugal, with uneven results. In November 2001 the UK and Spain signed a similar treaty committing them to a rapid hand-over of persons accused or convicted of serious crimes (terrorism, organized crime and people-smuggling), thus rendering extradition obsolete. Spain has studied the possibility of achieving agreement with Germany on the issues of extradition, reciprocal acceptance of criminal investigators and a joint approach to the training of examining magistrates. Progress was less positive with Spain's nearest neighbours, Portugal and France. Portugal refused to suppress extradition proceedings, saying that this would require an amendment to her constitution; she proposed a common EU regulation instead. France was willing to co-operate with Spain on these issues, but the agreement came up against resistance from the judicial system.

The Commission followed Spain's lead and adopted some of her initiatives. Specifically, the Commission initiated a study of three measures:

1 A common definition of the crime of terrorism.
2 An agreement for a fast-track extradition procedure (taking the Hispano–Italian agreement as the model for a possible EU-wide agreement).
3 Suspects would be sent for trial in the country where they had allegedly committed their most serious terrorist crime, regardless of the country in which they had been detained.

The events of 11 September 2001 were taken as a vindication of Spain's long-standing strategy against terrorism. Scarcely a month later the European Council, meeting in Ghent, committed itself to drafting a European list of terrorist organizations, and in November the Council of Ministers accepted the European Warrant Order which was to apply to some 30 crimes. The new context also stimulated bilateral cooperation (often a first step towards EU-wide cooperation): in

October, Spain signed a far-reaching agreement with France which included the handing over of terrorist suspects, the principle of judging terrorists in the country in which they had committed their most serious crime, and the creation of joint investigating teams and the immediate disclosure of documents.

Chapter 10

Conclusion: The EU as Spain's National Project

This book has argued that the story of Spain's membership of the European Union (EU) has been one of progressive 'normalization'. Put another way, we can analyse Spanish patterns of activity, preferences and choices in regard to the EU in terms which are equally applicable to any other member state. Whereas Spain could initially be seen as a singular case, in which the need to defend her nascent democracy was paramount, the country is now a fully integrated, mainstream member of the EU on a par with other established states. Although Spanish idiosyncrasy retains some explanatory value – particularly in regard to the drive for membership – such an observation is equally true for all member states, each of which has its own distinctive features. Indeed, the argument presented in this study calls into question the continued analytical utility of notions such as 'Mediterranean Europe', or the idea that Southern Europe should be seen as distinctive (apart from the obvious fact of geographical location), characterized by political corruption, corporatism, illiberal economic practices, and generally lower levels of development. Instead, we argue that comparative studies of the EU and its member states should be built around robust classificatory principles, rather than rely on potentially flawed categories derived from historical developments and trajectories.

In this study, we have adopted a neo-institutionalist analytic framework. Naturally, the evidence presented also offers support for some of the claims which underpin the two other principal approaches identified in the introduction: the structural view, rooted in studies of interdependence, which analyses state policy in terms of determinants imposed by the international environment; and the intergovernmentalist argument that the position adopted by member states within the EU is an extension and/or projection of domestic politics. In regard to the structural approach, we have shown how Spain's position in the EU has undergone clear and substantive changes. Initially, Spain was very much a minor power in a 12-member EU which, in the context of the Cold War and under the lead of the Franco–German partnership, was pushing strongly for increased integration. In these circumstances, the adoption of a clearly federalist rhetoric was able to deliver substantial pay-offs by bringing Spain closer to the European mainstream. Over time, Spain has both modernized and become substantially richer, seeking to reconcile a significantly enhanced role within the EU with a commitment to retaining support through structural funds.

The transformation in Spain's position has taken place against the background of the massive geo-political changes of the 1990s which brought to an end the Cold War division of Europe and led the EU to focus eastwards. Moreover, these changes also contributed to a much less favourable macroeconomic situation in the early 1990s, involving substantial restructuring and tight budgetary constraints. Thus, it would be easy to deduce that Spain's policy options were indeed determined by developments in the international arena. Indeed, several analyses of Spain's economic development and foreign policy coincide in linking them directly to the international conjuncture (Bernardos and Aznar, 1996; Barbé, 1999). In particular, scholars working in the field of international relations have emphasized the role of external factors in what they identify as a series of reactive changes in Spain's position. The drive towards enlargement and the end of bi-polarism, together with worldwide economic recession, led to the EU taking a new direction which no longer coincided with Spain's original perceptions of her role within it. In fact, 1992 – the so-called 'Year of Spain' on account of the Olympic Games in Barcelona, Expo in Sevilla, and Madrid as European City of Culture – marked the peak of Spanish influence within the orthodox project of European integration.

After 1992, domestic political turmoil associated with corruption scandals linked mainly to the ruling Socialist Party, the Partido Socialista Obrero Español (PSOE) followed by victory for the right-wing Partido Popular (PP) of José María Aznar in the general elections of 1996, led to a change in Spain's political landscape. The EU itself also underwent significant shifts in this period, with a change in the composition and direction of the Commission under the Presidency of Jacques Santer, who in 1995 replaced the forceful and long-serving Jacques Delors. Under Santer, the Commission's agenda included a series of measures which Spain saw as potentially threatening. First, the gathering pace of moves towards Economic and Monetary Union (EMU) posed major challenges for Spain, which feared not making the 'first cut' of qualifying countries and thereby being perceived as an economic 'laggard'. Secondly, moves towards eastern enlargement of the EU reinforced these fears of being relegated to a secondary rank. Thirdly, the institutional reorganization of the EU that would have to follow enlargement also threatened to reduce Spain's relative strength and influence. Finally, the downturn in global economic circumstances led a tougher stance in negotiations over the EU budget, marked by a more assertive rhetoric over the need to meet the targets for EMU.

In Spain, meanwhile, these structural shifts were reflected in a cooling of public opinion towards the benefits of EU membership and the adoption of a more nationalist rhetoric by the PP government, which did not enjoy the same sense of common purpose with the new Commission as the PSOE had done with its predecessor. As a result of these various changes, a more distinctive Spanish discourse on Europe has emerged. Naturally, all member states seek to steer the EU in a direction which coincides with their national interests, and Spanish governments have been no exception. However, there has been a marked divergence in styles between the periods before and after the mid-1990s. Initially, Spain's historic experience of exclusion from the EU, together with the widespread political consensus over European integration, helped shape a shared perception that national interests were neither radically different from, nor incompatible with, the integration project. Rather, each Community policy was assessed in terms of how it could be made to fit with Spain's domestic interests. During the 1990s, however, Spanish governments adopted a more assertively nationalist rhetoric in which defence of domestic interests became more overt. Three interconnected reasons account for this shift, two internal and one wholly external. The external driver was the emergence of a more cautious approach throughout the EU towards federalist models of integration. The internal drivers (explored in depth in Chapter 2) were the increasingly instrumentalist view of the EU expressed in public opinion polls, and the election of a right-wing PP government with a markedly less enthusiastic attitude towards integration than that of the PSOE administrations.

Thus, it would appear that Spain's relationship with the EU has indeed been conditioned by a combination of structural international factors on the one hand, and domestic political developments on the other. However, to draw such a conclusion would mean leaving out of account one of the most significant impacts of Spain's membership of the EU, namely the process of Europeanization. In short, membership has brought about far-reaching changes in the Spanish political system, which has had to adapt to EU demands. Whilst formal decision-making processes appear relatively autonomous of any direct shaping influence by the EU, the fact of membership nonetheless provides an implicit framework within which the domestic political process is conducted. That Spain is part of the EU has a continuing impact both on public opinion and on the positions adopted by political parties. Although we have argued that normalization has been reflected in public opinion taking a more instrumental view of the benefits of membership, as well as in governments adopting a more nationalist discourse, this should not be allowed to disguise the fact that there has been a striking degree of integration between Spanish and European identities. The EU does not provide a basis for any serious political cleavages in Spanish politics, and is not an issue around which a 'Eurosceptic' political grouping could seek to organize.

In their comparative study of the impact of EU membership, Wessels and Rometsch (1996: 356) concluded that the Spanish polity (its national government, parliament, and the Autonomous Communities) had reached a 'medium' level of Europeanization. Such a finding is consistent with the argument of sociological institutionalists that domestic institutional structures manifest considerable robustness and resilience in the face of EU membership. We should not expect institutions to change easily or rapidly, other than under extraordinary circumstances (Olsen, 2001: 25). The Spanish case confirms that it is difficult to discern a dramatic change in formal institutional structures as a result of EU membership. However, rather than conclude that there has therefore been no such impact, we should look at more subtle, though still meaningful, alterations that may in the long run appear to be the result of fundamental underlying transformations. There is evidence – admittedly impressionistic – that EU membership has indeed brought about such subtle organizational changes through a process of institutional mimesis. Spain's bureaucratic culture has internalized the fact of EU membership through the acquisition of knowledge, its ongoing process of learning, and a certain appropriation of EU institutional culture. In this regard, it can be argued that the Spanish polity has indeed become more Europeanized.

Europeanization has also had a marked impact on system outputs in terms of policy formulation. In particular, the requirements of the single market and especially of EMU have provided the framework for Spanish macroeconomic policy. Spain's wholehearted adoption of market-oriented competition owes much to participation in the single market and in EMU. At regional level, too, similar impacts can be seen: indeed, it could be argued that the EU's regional policy acted as a stimulus to Spain adopting a regional policy of its own, particularly in respect of its redistributive dimension. Other policy areas, such as environmental policy, also provide evidence of the impact of Europeanization. Of course, it is the case that other factors than membership of the EU have also had an impact on Spain's policy framework, notably a more generalized interdependence in what is routinely referred to as an increasingly globalized world. However, the notion of globalization can be seen as even more contestable than Europeanization, and it is our belief that the EU remains the single most obvious source with transformative potential over its member states.

Naturally, the relationship between the EU and member states does not move in only one direction. Spain has also been able to use the EU as an effective arena for the resolution of specific domestic issues, in part by transferring competencies to the EU level – as has been the case, in part, with fishing policy, immigration and anti-terrorist initiatives. Of maybe more significance to Spain's national interests in the long run is the fact that successive Spanish governments have been able to develop a range of arguments, ideas and concepts that are now embedded into EU policies. Paradoxically, governments which seek resolutely to pursue their own interests may end up contributing to the creation of a 'logic of appropriateness' which conditions or shapes their own future behaviour. Spain has often made play of the importance of defending the *acquis communautaire* during negotiations on key issues, a principle established long before Spanish membership of the EU. Nonetheless, Spain has also played an important role in ensuring that essential principles such as European citizenship, or social and economic cohesion, have been incorporated into the *acquis*. Such interactions point to a very subtle process of institutionalization at work.

On balance, it is hardly open to argument that Spain's membership of the EU has contributed to a deep and far-reaching modernization of the country, leading to a recuperation of national self-esteem. Some analysts have argued that European integration has actually rescued (Milward, 1992) or reinforced (Moravcsik, 1994) the nation-state. In the case of Spain, it is difficult to equate the recovery of a national project with such arguments, since the rescue or reinforcement in question refers to a concept of the nation-state which is no longer clearly identifiable with the classic Westphalian model – of which Spain was one of the first. EU membership may have reinforced the Spanish 'state', but at the expense of deep changes which make it difficult to locate the contemporary Spanish political system within classic conceptions of 'stateness': questions of national identity remain powerful around symbols such as the '*ñ*', but appear almost irrelevant in regard to replacing the peseta with the euro. Meanwhile, high levels of autonomy for the regions induce less tension with the central state when placed within the context of EU membership, with its inherent structure of multi-level governance. What can be said with certainty is that any recovery of a Spanish national project will have to take place as part of a complex wider system which is itself undergoing a process of ongoing transformation.

On the tenth anniversary of the signing of the Accession Treaty, the leading Spanish newspaper, *El País* (11 June 1995), declared that the Community ideal had

> resulted in the rediscovery of a truly national project and the fixing of Spain's destiny firmly with that of the rest of Europe. In spite of occasional differences which may lead to splits between Spanish and European interests, no Spanish project has any meaning outside of its natural European framework in the current era of transnationalism, market liberalisation, and high-speed communication. There can be no serious Spanish national project outside Europe.

In short, EU membership is itself the Spanish national project.

Bibliography

Abad Balboa, C., García Delgado, J. L. and Muñoz Cidad, C. (1994) 'La agricultura española en el último tercio del Siglo XX: Pautas evolutivas', in J. M. Sumpsi (ed.), *Modernización y cambio en la agricultura española* (Madrid: Secretaría General Técnica, MAPA), pp. 69–125.

Abellán, J. L. (1988) 'El significado de la idea de Europa en la política y en la historia de España', *Sistema*, vols. 86–7, pp. 31–45.

Agh, A. (1993) 'The "comparative revolution" and the transition in Central and Southern Europe', *Journal of Theoretical Politics*, vol. 5(2), pp. 231–52.

Agüero, F. (1995) *Soldiers, Civilians, and Democracy* (Baltimore, Md.: Johns Hopkins University Press).

Alberola Ila, E. (1998) *España en la Unión Monetaria. Una aproximación a sus costes y beneficios*. Banco de España. Servicio de Estudios, *Estudios Económicos*, vol. 62 (Madrid: Banco de España).

Alberola Ila, E. (2001) 'Europeización de la política macroeconómica', in C. Closa (ed.), *La europeización del sistema político español* (Madrid: Istmo), pp. 330–349.

Alonso, A. (1985) *España en el Mercado Común. Del Acuerdo del 70 a la Comunidad de los Doce* (Madrid: Espasa Calpe).

Alonso Zaldívar, C. and Castells, M. (1992) *España, fin de siglo* (Madrid: Alianza).

Alonso, J. A. and Donoso, V. (1999) 'Sector exterior: apertura económica y líneas de especialización', in J. L García Delgado (ed.), *España, economía: ante el siglo XXI* (Madrid: Espasa Calpe).

Álvarez-Miranda, B. (1994) 'Integración europea y sistemas de partidos en el sur de Europa: despolarización y convergencia', *Revista de Estudios Políticos*, vol. 85, pp. 143–67.

Ansell, C. K., Parsons, C. A. and Darden, K. A. (1997) 'Dual networks in the European Regional Development Policy', *Journal of Common Market Studies*, vol. 35(3), pp. 347–75.

Arce Janáriz, A. (1997) 'Unión Europea y Parlamentos regionales', *Parlamento y Constitución*, vol. 1, pp. 77–107.

Arias Salgado, R. (1995) 'La política europea de España y la conferencia intergubernamental de 1996', *Política Exterior*, vol. 47(IX), pp. 38–46.

Arias Salgado, R. (1997) 'El Partido Popular y la Presidencia española de la UE', in A. Matutes *et al. Los dos pilares de la Unión Europea* (Madrid:Fundación Cánovas del Castillo/Colección Ventiuno), pp. 61–70.

Atienza, L. (1994) 'Con el vino en el corazón', *El País*, 24 June.

Aznar, J.M. (1994) *Address to the European Democratic Union* (EDU) Prague, December 1994.

Aznar, J.M. (1995) 'La reforma de la Unión Europea', *Política Exterior*, vol. 9(43), pp. 76.

Aznar, J. M. (1999) 'Europa, libertad y justicia', *El Mundo*, 13 June.

Aznar, J. M. (2000) Conference at the Instituto Francés de Relaciones Internacionales (París, 26 September 2000) http://www.la-moncloa.es/ inicio.htm.

Aznar, J. M. and Blair, T. (2000) 'El crecimiento, objetivo esencial para Europa', *El Mundo*, 13 June. http://www.elmundo.es/2000/06/13/opinion/ 13N0025.html.

Axt, H.-J. (1992) 'Liberalization and cohesion. Southern Europe's development and prospects within the European Community', *International Journal of Political Economy*, vol. 22(1), pp. 23–40.

Baixeras, J. (1996) 'España y el Mediterráneo', *Política Exterior*, vol. 51(X), pp. 149–62.

Balfour, S. (1997) *The End of Spanish Empire* (Oxford: Clarendon Press).

Banco de España (1997) *La Unión Monetaria Europea* (Madrid: Banco de España).

Barbé, E. (1993) 'La política española de seguridad en la Nueva Europa: dimensión mediterránea e instrumentos europeos', *Revista CIDOB d'Afers Internacionals*, no. 26, pp. 77–96.

Barbé, E. (1996) 'De la ingenuidad al pragmatismo: 10 años de participación española en la máquina diplomática europea', *Afers Internacionals*, vol. 34–5, pp. 9–29.

Barbé, E. (1999) *La política europea de España* (Barcelona: Ariel).

Barbé, E. (2001) 'La política europea de España 2000–2001', IUEE Working Paper no. 2/2001 http://selene.uab.es/_cs_iuee/catala/obs/ m_presentacion.html.

Barceló, L. V. (1993) 'Política de reestructuración de la agricultura española', in MAPA (ed.), *Agriculturas y políticas agrarias en el sur de Europa* (Madrid: Secretaria General Técnica, MAPA).

Barea, J. (1995a) 'Convergencia europea y déficit público español', *Política Exterior*, vol. 44(IX) pp. 135–53.

Barea Teijeiro, J. (1995b) 'El sector público español ante la integración europea', in E. Fuentes Quintana (ed.), *Problemas económicos españoles en la década de los 90* (Madrid: Galaxia Gutemberg/ Círculo de Lectores) pp. 229–80.

Barreiro, B. and Sánchez Cuenca, I. (2001) 'La europeización de la opinión pública española', in C. Closa (ed.), *La Europeización del sistema político español* (Madrid: Istmo).

Barroso, C. and Rodero, A. (1996) 'La política regional en España en el contexto de la integración europea: síntesis y valoración', in J. J. Romero and A. Rodero (eds), *España en la CEE: del Acta Única al Tratado de Maastricht* (Madrid: ETEA).

Bassols, R. (1995) *España en Europa. Historia de la adhesión 1957–1985* (Madrid: Política Exterior).

Bastarreche, C. (1999) 'España y la Agenda 2000', *Cuadernos del CERI*, nos 3–4 (Madrid: CERI).

Bataller Martín, F. and Jordán Galduf, J. M. (1996) 'España y su acción Mediterránea: ¿Abogado o competidor?', *Información Comercial Española*, 759, pp. 137–52.

Begg, I. (1999) 'Previsiones sobre convergencia regional en la Unión Europea', *Papeles de Economía Española*, vol. 80, pp. 100–21.

Belloni, F. P. (1994) *The Single Market and Socio-Economic Cohesion in the EC: Implications for the Southern and Western Peripheries*. Centre for Mediterranean Studies, University of Bristol. CMS-Occasional Paper no. 8.

Bernárdez, J. (1995) *Europa. Entre el timo y el mito* (Madrid: Ediciones Temas de Hoy).

Bernardos, G. and Aznar, P. (1996) 'El sector exterior de la economía española (1986–1995)', *Afers Internationals*, vols. 34–5, pp. 31–46.

Bilbao Arrese, J. and López Vázquez, J. (1994) 'El poder de las naciones en la Unión Europea', *Política Exterior*, vol. 8(4).

Birkelbach, M. W. (1962) *Rapport fait au nom de la Commission européenne sur 'les aspects politiques et institutionnels de l'adhésion ou de l'association à la Communauté*. Assemblée Parlementaire Européenne, Documents de Séance, 1961–1962, no. 122, 15 January.

Blanco, H. (2000) 'Relaciones hispano-mexicanas y el acuerdo de asociación con la UE', *Economía Exterior*, vol. 12, pp. 33–9.

Boix, C. (1999) *The Process of European Integration and Spanish Social Democracy*. ARENA Working Paper no. 17/99.

Börzel, T. and Risse, T. (2000) *When Europe Hits Home: Europeanization and Domestic Change*. EUI Working Papers RSC no. 2000/56.

Borras-Alomar, S., Christiansen, T. and Rodríguez-Pose, A. (1994) 'Towards a "Europe of the Regions"? Visions and reality from a critical perspective', *Regional Politics and Policy*, vol. 4(2), pp. 1–27.

Borrás, S., Font, N. and Gómez, N. (1998) 'The Europeanization of National Policies in Comparison: Spain as a case study', *South European Society and Politics*, vol. 3(2), pp. 23–44.

Brugué, Q., Goma, R. and Subirats, J. (2001) 'Multilevel Governance and Europeanization: The Case of Catalonia', in K. Featherstone and G. Kazamias (eds), *Europeanization and the Southern Periphery* (London: Frank Cass).

Bullmann, U. (1997) 'The Politics of the Third Level', in C. Jeffery (ed.), *The Regional dimension of the European Union. Towards a third level in Europe?* (London: Frank Cass), pp. 3–18.

Bulmer, S. (1983) 'Domestic politics and the European Community policy-making', *Journal of Common Market Studies*, vol. 21(4), pp. 349–63.

Bulmer, S. (1986) *The domestic structure of European Community policy-making in Germany* (London: Garland).

Bulmer, S. (1994) 'The governance of the European Union: a new institutionalist approach', *Journal of Public Policy*, vol. 13, pp. 351–80.

Camilleri, A. (1986) *La agricultura española ante la CEE* (Madrid: Instituto de Estudios Económicos).

Carderera, F. (1995) 'La pesca y la ampliación', *Boletín Económico de ICE*, vol. 2442, pp. 3819–24.

Cascajo Castro, J. L. (1997) 'La participación de las Comunidades Autónomas en las decisiones comunitarias del Estado: la Conferencia para Asuntos relacionados con las Comunidades Europeas', in A. Pérez Calvo (ed.), *La participación de las Comunidades Autónomas en las decisiones del Estado* (Madrid: Tecnos/ Instituto Navarro de Administración Pública), pp. 81–8.

Cazorla, L. M. (1997) 'Doce años de revolución jurídica silenciosa y paulatina tras la incorporación de España a la hoy Unión Europea: una visión general', *Información Comercial Española*, no. 766, pp. 49–58.

Ceceña, C. (2000) 'Comercio bilateral entre España y México', *Economía Exterior*, vol. 12, pp. 77–87.

CES (1999) *La política de convenios pesqueros de la Unión Europea*, Colección informes 3/1999 (Madrid: Consejo Económico y Social).

Chari, R. S. (1999) 'Spanish Socialists, Privatising the Right Way?', in P. Heywood (ed.), *Politics and Policy in Democratic Spain: No Longer Different?* (London: Frank Cass), pp. 163–79.

Cienfuegos, M. (1996) 'El control de las Cortes Generales sobre el gobierno en asuntos relativos a las Comunidades Europeas durante la década 1985–1995', *Revista de las Cortes Generales*, no. 38, pp. 47–99.

Cienfuegos, M. (1997) 'La Comisión Mixta para la Unión Europea: Análisis y balance de una década de actividad en el seguimiento de los asuntos comunitarios', *Gaceta Jurídica de la CE* D-27, pp. 7–69.

Cienfuegos, M. (1997b) 'La intervención de las Comunidades Autónomas en asuntos relativos a las Comunidades Europeas a través de la Comisión General de las Comunidades Autónomas y la Conferencia para Asuntos relacionados con las Comunidades Europeas', *Autonomies. Revista Catalana de Derecho Público*, vol. 22, pp. 155–204.

Cienfuegos, M. (2000) 'La coordinación de los asuntos europeos en las administraciones autonómicas', *Revista de Estudios Políticos*, vol. 108, pp. 103–42.

CIRES (1993) *La situación social en España* (Madrid: CIRES).

Clavera, J. (1996)'Diez años en el camino de la integración monetaria', *Afers Internationals*, nos. 34–5, pp. 47–66.

Closa, C. (1995) 'La ampliación de la Unión Europea', *Revista de Estudios Políticos*, vol. 90, pp. 147–71.

Closa, C. (1995a) 'National interest and convergence of preferences: a changing role for Spain in the EU?', in S. Mazey and C. Rhodes (eds), *The state of the European Union*, Vol. III (Boulder, Co.: Lynne Rienner, 1995), pp. 293–316.

Closa, C. (1996) 'Spain: The Cortes and the EU – A growing together', in P. Norton (ed.), *National parliaments and the European Union* (London: Frank Cass), pp. 136–50.

Closa, C (1996a) 'El nuevo papel de España en la Unión Europea', *Política y Sociedad*, pp. 111–24.

Closa, C. (1998) 'International Limits to National Claims in EU Constitutional Negotiations: The Spanish Government and the Asylum Right for EU Citizens', *International Negotiations*, vol. 3(3), pp. 389–411.

Closa, C. (2000) 'La política pesquera común', in F. Morata (ed.), *Políticas públicas en la Unión Europea* (Barcelona: Ariel), pp. 121–42.

Closa, C. (ed.) (2001) *La europeización del sistema político español* (Madrid: Itsmo).

Closa, C. (2001b) 'National plurality within single statehood in the European Union', in F. Requejo (ed.), *Democracy and national pluralism* (London: Routledge), pp. 105–27.

Colino, C. (2001) 'La integración europea y el estado autonómico: europeización, estrategias y cambio en las relaciones intergubernamentales', in C. Closa (ed.), *La europeización del sistema político español* (Madrid: Istmo), pp. 225–62.

Colino, J. and Noguera, P. (1999) 'La difícil convergencia de las agriculturas europeas', in J. L. García Delgado (ed.), *España, economía: ante el siglo XXI* (Madrid: Espasa Calpe), pp. 11–28.

Comisión Europea (1995) *Eurobarómetro: La opinión pública en la Unión Europea*. Eurobarómetro Mega 45 (Luxemburgo: Oficina de Publicaciones Oficiales de la Unión Europea).

Comisión Mixta (1995) *Consecuencias para España de la ampliación de la Unión Europea y sus reformas institucionales* (Madrid: Congreso de los Diputados).

Commission of the EC (1977) *Statement by the President of the Community* EC-Bull. 10–1977.

Commission of the EU (1996) *Annual Report of the Cohesion Fund 1996* COM (96).

Commission of the EU (1999) *Annual Report of the Cohesion Fund 1998* COM (1999).

Commission of the EU (1999b) Sixth periodic report on the social and economic situation and development of the regions of the European Union (http://www.europa.eu.int/comm/regional_policy/sources/docoffice/official/reports/toc_en.htm).

Commission of the EU (2000) *Spain's stability programme update (1999–20003). An assessment*, Brussels, 14 February ECFIN/117/00-EN.

Commission of the European Communities (2001) *Ninth Survey on State Aid in the European Union* COM (2001).

Conde Martínez, C. (1998) 'El proceso de convergencia y la europeización de las administraciones nacionales (Estudio comparado de los casos francés y español)', *Revista de Derecho Comunitario Europeo*, vol. 2(4), pp. 683–720.

Cordero, G. (1999) 'La financiación de la UE: el debate sobre la Agenda 2000', *Meridiano CERI 25*, pp. 4–8.

Crespo MacLennan, J. (2000) *Spain and the Process of European Integration, 1957–85* (Basingstoke: Palgrave).

Dastis, A. (1995) 'La administración española ante la Unión Europea', *Revista de Estudios Políticos*, vol. 90, pp. 323–50.

Dastis, A. (1999) 'Un espacio de libertad, seguridad y justicia', in J. M. de Areilza (ed.), *España y las transformaciones de la Unión Europea* (Madrid: Fundación para el Análisis y los Estudios Sociales), pp. 207–40.

Díaz Eimil, C. (1997) 'Diez años de construcción de la Unión Europea y de la PAC', *Información Comercial Española*, vol. 766, pp. 69–76.

Díaz Torres, A. (1999) 'La Agenda 2000: su incidencia en España', in C. Bastarreche *et al.*, *España y la agenda 2000* Cuadernos CERI 3/4 (Madrid: CERI).

Diedrichs, U. and Wessels, W. (1996) 'From newcomers to mainstreamers: Lessons from Spain and Portugal', in F. Algieri and E. Regelsberger (eds), *Synergy at Work. Spain and Portugal in European Foreign Policy* (Bonn: European Union Verlag), pp. 315–30.

Diez Hochleitner, J. (1995) 'La flota española entra en la Europa Azul', *Meridiano CERI*, no. 2, pp. 14–20.

Díez Picazo, L. M. (1998) 'El derecho comunitario en la jurisprudencia constitucional española', *Revista Española de Derecho Constitucional*, vol. 18, no. 54, pp. 255–72.

Díez Peralta, E. (2001) 'La adaptación judicial: jueces y derecho comunitario', in C. Closa (ed.), *La europeización del sistema político español* (Madrid: Itsmo), pp. 263–96.

Easton, D. (1965) *A systems analysis of political life* (New York: Wiley and sons, Ltd.).

Elorza Cavengt, F. J. (1992) 'Cohesión económica y social', *Gaceta Jurídica de la CE* D-17, pp. 155–91.

Elorza, F. J. (1995) 'La negociación institucional', *Boletín Económico ICE*, vol. 2442, pp. 33797–804.

Elorza, F. J. (1995b) 'Schengen, España y la inmigración', *El Pais* (6 July).

Elorza, F. J. (1997) 'Reflexiones y balance de diez años en la Unión Europea', *Información Comercial Española*, vol. 766, pp. 15–29.

Elorza Cavengt, F. J. (1998) 'El Consejo: la ponderación de votos, la mayoría cualificada y mejoras de funcionamiento', in *España y la negociación del Tratado de Amsterdam* (Madrid:Política Exterior), pp. 251–70.

Elorza, F. J. (1998b) 'El Tratado de Amsterdam: Una evaluación española', in *España y la negociación del Tratado de Amsterdam* (Madrid: Política Exterior), pp. 35–48.

Elorza, J. (1999) 'La agenda 2000 y España', *Información Comercial Española*, no. 776. pp. 9–23.

Farrell, M. (2001) *Spain in the EU. The Road to Economic Convergence* (Basingstoke: Palgrave).

Featherstone, K. (1989) 'The Mediterranean challenge: cohesion and external preferences', in J. Lodge (ed.), *The European Community and the challenge of the future* (London: Pinter), pp. 186–201.

Feito, J. L. (1997) 'Política económica del PP y acceso a la moneda única', *Política Exterior*, vol. 57(XI), pp. 73–85.

Fernández Martínez, P. (1997) 'Los Fondos Estructurales Europeos y el desarrollo regional: Balance de una década desde la perspectiva española', *Información Comercial Española*, vol. 766, pp. 135–45.

Fernández Martínez, P. (1999) 'Los nuevos reglamentos de los fondos estructurales y el fondo de cohesión para el período 2000–2006', *Información Comercial Española*, no. 776, pp. 73–83.

Fernández Ordóñez, F. (1989) 'The EC Presidency experiences of Spain', *European Affairs*, vol. 3, pp. 18–20.

Fernández Ordóñez, M. A. (1999) 'Privatización, desregulación y liberalización de los mercados', in J. L. García Delgado (ed.), *España, economía: ante el siglo XXI* (Madrid: Espasa Calpe), pp. 661–82.

Foro Agrario (2000) *La reforma de la PAC de la Agenda 2000 y la agricultura Española* (Madrid: Foro Agrario).

Franco, F. (1975) *Pensamiento político de Franco*, vol. II (Madrid: Ed. del Movimiento).

Franquesa, R. (1997) 'Estrategias estatales y política común en la pesca europea', *Papeles de Economía Española*, vol. 71, pp. 167–81.

Fuentes Quintana, E. (1995) 'El modelo de economía abierta y el modelo castizo de desarrollo económico en la España de los años 90', in E. Fuentes Quintana (ed.), *Problemas económicos españoles en la década de los 90* (Galaxia Gutenberg/ Círculo de Lectores), pp. 63–175.

Fundación BBV (1999) *Renta nacional de España y su distribución provincial* (Bilbao: Fundación BBV).

Fungairiño Bringas, E. (1995) 'La Cooperación judicial. El Convenio Europeo de Extradición', *Cuadernos de la Guardia Civil*, vol. 14, pp. 3–104.

Fusi, J.P. and Palafox, J.(1997) *España 1808–1996. El desafío de la modernidad* (Madrid: Espasa).

Galera, S. (1996) 'Consideraciones sobre la Constitución económica', in C. Molina del Pozo ed.), *España en la Europa comunitaria. Balance de diez años* (Madrid: Editorial Centro de Estudios Ramón Areces), pp. 95–115.

Gallastegui, M. C. (1992) 'Los acuerdos de Maastricht y el Plan de Convergencia: una visión crítica', *Información Comercial Española*, vol. 710, pp. 101–14.

Gamir, L. (1998) 'Dos escenarios: dentro o fuera de la Unión Económica y Monetaria', in J. Colino Sueiras and A. García Sánchez (eds), *España y Maastricht: ventajas e inconvenientes* (Madrid: Civitas), pp. 193–205.

García, C. (1995) 'The autonomous communities and external relations', in R. Gillespie, F. Rodrigo and J. Story (eds), *Democratic Spain. Reshaping external relations in a changing world* (London; Routledge), pp. 123–40.

García Delgado, J. L. and García Grande, M. J. (1999) 'La agricultura: una profunda transformación estructural', in J. L. García Delgado (ed) *España, economía: ante el siglo XXI* (Madrid: Espasa Calpe), pp. 83–110.

Gil Ibáñez, A. (1992) 'Spain and European political union', in F. Laursen and S. Vanhoonacker (eds), *The Intergovernmental Conference on Political Union* (Maastricht: EIPA), pp. 99–114.

Gillespie, R. (1996) 'The Spanish socialists', in J. Gaffney (ed.), *Political parties and the European Union* (London: Routledge), pp. 155–69.

Gillespie, R. (2000) *Spain and the Mediterranean. Developing a European Policy towards the South* (Basingstoke: Palgrave).

Gillespie, R., Rodrigo, F. and Story, J. (eds) (1995) *Democratic Spain. Reshaping external relations in a changing world* (London; Routledge).

Goetz, K. H. (1995) 'National governance and European integration: inter-governmental relations in Germany', *Journal of Common Market Studies*, vol. 33(1), pp. 91–115.

Goma Torres, J. (1995) 'La cooperación policial en la UE: Especial referencia al Acuerdo de Schengen y a su Convenio de Aplicación', *Cuadernos de la Guardia Civil*, vol. 14, pp. 83–92.

Gómez Castañeda, J. (1994) 'La economía de la democracia española 1975–1993', in R. Calduch (ed.), *La política exterior de España en el siglo XX* (Madrid: Ediciones de Ciencias Sociales), pp. 169–99.

González, F. (1988) 'La cohesión y la solidaridad en la construcción europea', *Sistema*, no. 86–7, pp. 11–20.

González, F. (1992–1993) 'La Europa que quiere España', *Política Exterior*, vol. 30(VI), pp. 7–20.

González, F. (1992) '¿Qué podemos esperar de Maastricht? España ante la Unión Europea', *Tiempo de Paz*, vol. 22, pp. 18–25.

González, F. (1995/6) 'Pilotar Europa hacia su rumbo', *Política Exterior*, vol. 48(IX), pp. 14–21.

González Alemán, H. (1999/2000) 'España y el sector agroalimentario frente a la ampliación', *Economía Exterior*, vol. 11, pp. 101–9.

González-Páramo, J. M. and Melguizo Esteso, A. (1999) 'Reforma tributaria y política fiscal', in J. L. García Delgado (ed.), *España, economía: ante el siglo XXI* (Madrid: Espasa Calpe), pp. 579–612.

Gourevitch, P. (1978) 'The second image reversed: the international sources of domestic politics', *International Organization*, vol. 32(4), pp. 881–911.

Granell, F. (1995) 'Los acuerdos de adhesión de Austria, Finlandia y Suecia a la Unión Europea y los intereses de España', *Afers Internationals*, vols. 29–30 pp. 117–37.

Grant, C. (1994) *Delors: Inside the house that Jacques built* (London: Nicholas Brealy Publications).

Grasa, R. (1997) 'Política exterior y de seguridad en un año de tránsito', *Anuario Internacional CIDOB 1996* (Barcelona; CIDOB), pp. 29–47.

Grugel, J. (1996) 'Spain: Latin America as an ambiguous topic', in F. Algieri and E. Regelsberger (eds), *Synergy at work. Spain and Portugal in European foreign policy* (Bonn: European Union Verlag), pp. 73–90.

Hall, P. and Taylor, R. (1994) 'Political science and the three new institutionalisms', *Political Studies*, vol. 44(5), pp. 936–57.

Hanley, D. (1996) 'The European People's party: towards a new party form', in D. Hanley (ed.), *Christian Democracy in Europe: A comparative perspective* (London: Pinter).

Hernando Moreno, J. M. (1997) 'El comercio exterior español: Balance de una década en la Unión Europea', *Información Comercial Española*, vol. 766, pp. 147–61.

Herrador, F. (2001) 'El proceso de europeización del diálogo social en España', in C. Closa (ed.), *La Europeización del sistema político español* (Madrid: Istmo), pp. 85–109.

Heywood, P. (1993) *Spain and the European Dimension: The Integrated Market, Convergence and Beyond.* Strathclyde Papers on Government and Politics, no. 94.

Heywood, P. (1995) *The Government and Politics of Spain* (London: Macmillan).

Heywood, P. (1997) 'From dictatorship to democracy: changing forms of corruption in Spain', in D. Della Porta and Y. Mény (eds), *Democracy and Corruption in Europe* (London: Pinter), pp. 65–84.

Heywood, P. (1999) 'Power Diffusion or Concentration? In Search of the Spanish Policy Process', in P. Heywood (ed.), *Politics and Policy in Democratic Spain: No Longer Different?* (London: Frank Cass), pp. 103–23.

Heywood, P. (2000) 'Spanish Regionalism: A Case Study', in A. Smith and P. Heywood, *Regional Government in France & Spain* (London: The Constitution Unit), pp. 20–40.

Heywood, P. (2003) 'Desperately seeking influence: Spain and the war in Iraq', *European Political Science*, vol. 3(1).

Heywood, P. and I. Molina (2000) 'A quasi-presidential premiership: administering the executive summit in Spain', in B. G. Peters, R. A. W. Rhodes and V. Wright (eds) *Administering the Summit* (Basingstoke: Palgrave), pp. 110–33.

Holman, O. (1996) *Integrating Southern Europe: EC expansion and the transnationalization of Spain* (London: Routledge).

Hooghe, L. (ed.) (1996) *Cohesion policy and European integration: Building multilevel governance?* (Oxford: Oxford University Press).

Hooghe, L. (1998) 'Consociationalists or Weberians? Senior Commission Officials and the Role of Nationality' *ARENA Working Paper* (University of Oslo), no. 98/20.

IFREMER (1999) *Evaluation of the fisheries agreements concluded by the European Community* Summary Report http://europa.eu.int/comm/fisheries/doc_et_publ/liste_publi/studies/rsen.pdf.

Jáuregui, P. (1999) 'National pride and the meaning of 'Europe': a comparative study of Britain and Spain', in D. Smith and S. Wright (eds), *Whose Europe? The turn towards democracy* (Oxford: Blackwell), pp. 257–87.

Jáuregui, F. and Vega, P. (1985) *Crónica del antifranquismo (3)* (Barcelona: Argos Vergara).

Jones, R. (2000) *Beyond the Spanish State. Central government, domestic actors and the EU* (Basingstoke: Palgrave).

Jupille, J. and Caporaso, J. (1999) 'Institutionalism and the European Union: beyond international relations and comparative politics', *Annual Review of Political Science*, vol. 2, pp. 429–44.

Kassim, H. and Wright, V. (1991) 'The role of national administrations in the decision-making processes of the European Community', *Rivista trimestrale di diritto pubblico*, vol. 3, pp. 832–50.

Kassim, H., Peters, G., and Wright, V. (eds) (2000) *The national co-ordination of EU policy. The domestic level* (Oxford: Oxford University Press).

Kassim, H. and Peters, G. (2001) 'Conclusion', in H. Kassim, A. Menon, G. Peters and V. Wright (eds), *The national co-ordination of EU policy. The European level* (Oxford: Oxford University Press).

Kay, A. (1998) *The reform of common agricultural policy: the case of the MacSharry reforms* (New York: CAB International).

Keating, M. (1993) *Regionalismo, autonomía y regímenes internacionales* (Barcelona: Institut de Ciènces Politiques i Socials), Working Paper 1993/66.

Kirchner, J. (1992) *Decision Making in the European Community. The Council Presidency and European Integration* (Manchester: Manchester University Press).

Ladrech, R. (1994) 'Europeanization of domestic politics and institutions: the case of France', *Journal of Common Market Studies*, vol. 32(1), pp. 69–88.

Laffan, B. (1999) 'Becoming a Living Institution: The European Court of Auditors', *Journal of Common Market Studies*, vol. 37(2), pp. 251–68.

Laitin, D. (1997) 'The cultural identities of a European State', *Politics and Society*, vol. 25(3), pp. 277–302.

Lamela, M. (2000) Intervención del Subsecretario de Agricultura en la inauguración del seminario 'Nuevos tiempos, nueva agricultura: ante la PAC', in MAPA (ed.) *Reforma de la PAC y Agenda 2000. Nuevos tiempos, nueva agricultura* (Madrid: Secretaría General Técnica, MAPA), pp. 5–30.

Lamo de Espinosa, J. (1999) 'La reforma de la reforma: la nueva PAC', in J. M. de Areilza (ed.), *España y las transformaciones de la Unión Europea* (Madrid: Fundación para el Análisis y los Estudios Sociales), pp. 149–205.

Landáburu, E. (1998) 'España y la política de cohesión europea', *Política Exterior*, vol. 65(XII), pp. 29–40.

Landáburu, E. (1999) 'España, la agenda 2000 y la política europea de cohesión económica y social', *Información Comercial Española*, vol. 776, pp. 63–72.

Lázaro Araujo, L. (1997) 'España y la UEM. Economía, política e ideología', *Política Exterior*, vol. 59(XI), pp. 37–52.

Liedtke, B. (1998) *Embracing a Dictatorship. US Relations with Spain, 1945–53* (London: Macmillan).

Llamazares, I. and Reinares, F. (1998) 'Identificaciones territoriales, ciudadanía europea y opinión pública española', in I. Llamazares and F. Reinares (eds), *Aspectos políticos y sociales de la integración europea* (Valencia:Tirant lo Blanch), pp. 179–99.

López Castillo, A. (1998) 'La jurisprudencia iuscomunitaria del Tribunal Constitucional a doce años de la integración española en las Comunidades Europeas', *Revista de Estudios Políticos*, vol. 99, pp. 189–215.

López Escudero, M. and Cuesta, F. (1999) 'Aplicación judicial del derecho comunitario en España durante 1998', *Revista de Derecho Comunitario Europeo*, vol. 3(6), pp. 395–418.

Magone, J. (1993) *The Iberian Members of the European Parliament and European integration*, Centre for Mediterranean Studies University of Bristol. Occasional Paper no. 7.

Mangas, A. (1994) 'El nombramiento de los miembros del Comité de las Regiones: el caso español', *Noticias VE*, no. 117.

MAP (1997) 'La necesaria y continua adaptación de la administración española al proceso de integración europea (la consolidación de un nuevo marco de actuación)', in *Contribución al análisis de la Administración general del Estado: Ideas para un plan estratégico* (Madrid: Ministerio para las Administraciones Públicas).

MAPYA (2001) *Facts and figures 2000* http://www.mapya.es/portada/pags/indice.asp?arriba=/indices/pags/info/inforsup.htm&izq=/indices/pags/info/inforizq.htm&der=/info/pags/public/publicaciones1.htm.

March, J. G. and Olsen, J. P. (1989) *Rediscovering institutions: The organizational basis of politics* (New York: Free Press).

Marichal, J. (1988) 'La europeización de España (1898–1936)', *Sistema*, pp. 53–60.

Marks, G. (1993) 'Structural policy and multilevel governance in the European Community', in A. Cafruny and G. Rosenthal (eds), *The State of the European Community*, vol. 2 (New York: Lynne Rienner), pp. 391–416.

Marks, G. (1997) 'An actor-centred approach towards multilevel governance', in C. Jeffery (ed.), *The Regional dimension of the European Union. Towards a third level in Europe?* (London: Frank Cass), pp. 20–39.

Marks, G. and Llamazares, I. (1995) 'La transformación de la movilización regional en la Unión Europea', *Revista de Estudios Políticos*, vol. 22(1), pp. 149–70.

Marks, G., Nielsen, F., Salk, J., and Ray, J. (1996) 'Competencies, cracks and conflicts: Regional mobilization in the European Union', in *Comparative Political Studies*, vol. 29(2), pp. 164–93.

Martín, C. (1995) 'La convergencia real en Europa: un referente clave para la política económica española', *Papeles de Economía Española*, vol. 63, pp. 2–17.

Martín, C. (1999) 'La situación tecnológica: cambio técnico y política tecnológica', in J. L. García Delgado (ed.), *España, economía: ante el siglo XXI* (Madrid: Espasa Calpe), pp. 355–76.

Martín, C. (2000) *The Spanish economy in the new Europe* (Houndmills, Basingstoke: Macmillan). Spanish original, C. Martín (1997) *España en la nueva Europa* (Madrid: Alianza Editorial).

Martín Rodríguez, M. (1999) 'Disparidades regionales: perspectiva histórica y europea', in J. L. García Delgado (ed.) *España, economía: ante el siglo XXI* (Madrid: Espasa Calpe), pp. 483–506.

Martínez Serrano, J. A. (1999) 'Fluctuaciones, desequilibrios y políticas macroeconómicas', in J. L. García Delgado (ed.) *España, economía: ante el siglo XXI* (Madrid: Espasa Calpe), pp. 683–707.

Matutes, A. (1999) *Los logros de Tampere* Mimeo (Madrid: MAE).

Méndez de Vigo, I. (1997) 'El proyecto nacional del PP ante la Conferencia Intergubernamental de 1996', in A. Matutes *et al. Los dos pilares de la Unión Europea* (Madrid:Fundación Cánovas del Castillo/Colección Ventiuno), pp. 49–59.

Menéndez del Valle (2001) 'Fallos en la cooperación Euro-Mediterránea', *El País*, 17 Marzo.

Miguel, R. de (1999/2000) 'Problemas políticos de la ampliación y soluciones posibles', *Economía Exterior*, vol. 11, pp. 7–15.

Milward, A. (1992) *The European Rescue of the Nation State* (London: Routledge).

Ministerio de Defensa (2000) *Libro blanco de la defensa* (Madrid: Ministerio de Defensa).

Molina, I. (1997) 'La respuesta administrativa española a la integración europea' Paper for the III Congreso de la Asociación Española de Ciencia Política y de la Administración (Salamanca, October).

Molina, I. (1999) 'The Impact of EU Membership on Domestic Policy-Making Processes: Multi-level policy-networks and central co-ordination in Spain.' Paper for the Center for European Studies, Harvard University, 26–28 February.

Molina, I. (2001a) 'La adaptación a la Unión Europea del poder ejecutivo español', in C. Closa (ed.), *La Europeización del sistema político español* (Madrid: Istmo), pp. 162–97.

Molina, I. (2001b) 'La liberalización de la economía española (por efecto de la pertenencia a la Unión Europea)', in C. Closa (ed.), *La Europeización del sistema político español* (Madrid: Istmo), pp. 298–328.

Molina del Pozo, C. (1995) 'El control parlamentario nacional sobre los actos normativos emanados de las instituciones europeas', in C. Molina del Pozo (ed.) *España en la Europa comunitaria. Balance de diez años* (Madrid: Editorial del Centro de Estudios Ramón Areces), pp. 149–64.

Molins, J. and Casademunt, A. (1998) 'Pressure groups and the articulation of interests', *West European Politics*, vol. 21(4), pp. 124–46.

Molins, J. and Morata, F. (1993) 'Spain: rapid arrival of a latecomer', in R. M. van Schendelen (ed.), *National public and private EC lobbying* (Aldershot: Darmouth), pp. 113–30.

Montes, P. (1994) *La integración en Europa: del Plan de Estabilización a Maastricht* (Madrid: Editorial Trotta).

Morán, F. (1980) *Una política exterior para España* (Barcelona: Planeta).

Morán, M. L. (1995) 'La cultura política y la interpretación de las transiciones a la democracia. (Notas sobre el caso español)', *Política y Sociedad*, no. 20, pp. 97–110.

Morata, F. (1996) 'Spain', in D. Rometsch and W. Wessels (eds.), *The European Union and its member states. Towards institutional fusion?* (Manchester: Manchester University Press), pp. 134–54.

Morata, F. (1998) *La Unión Europea. Procesos, políticas, actores* (Barcelona: Ariel).

Morata, F. (1998) 'Spain: modernization through integration', in K. Hanf and B. Soetendorp (eds), *Adapting to European integration: small states and the European Union* (London: Longman), pp. 100–15.

Morata, F. (2000) 'La política regional y de cohesión', in F. Morata (ed.), *Políticas públicas en la Unión Europea* (Barcelona: Ariel), pp. 143–87.

Morata, F. and Muñoz, X. (1996) 'Vying for European funds: Territorial restructuring in Spain', in L. Hooghe (ed), *Cohesion Policy and European Integration, building multilevel governance* (Oxford: Clarendon Press), pp. 95–218.

Moravcsik, A. (1993) 'Preferences and power in the European Community: A liberal intergovernmentalist approach', *Journal of Common Market Studies*, vol. 31(4), pp. 473–524.

Moravcsik, A. (1998) *The choice for Europe. Social purpose and state power from Messina to Maastricht* (London: UCL Press).

Moreno Juste, A. (1998) *España y el proceso de construcción europea* (Barcelona: Ariel).

Moreno, J. and Bonmati, M. (1999) 'La apuesta, más Europa', *El País*, 28 de junio.

Moyano, E. (1997) 'Acción colectiva y organizaciones profesionales agrarias en España', in C. Gómez Benito and J. J. González Rodríguez (eds), *Agricultura y sociedad en la España contemporánea* (Madrid: CIS), pp. 773–95.

Moyano, E. and Entrena, F. (1997) 'Cooperativismo y representación de intereses en la agricultura española', in C. Gómez Benito and J. J. González

Rodríguez (eds), *Agricultura y sociedad en la España contemporánea* (Madrid: CIS), pp. 797–815.

Muñoz Machado, S. (1993) *La Unión Europea y las mutaciones del Estado* (Madrid: Alianza).

Muñoz Cidab, C. (1999) 'Consumo y nivel de vida', in J. L. García Delgado (ed.) *España, economía: ante el siglo XXI* (Madrid: Espasa Calpe), pp. 527–45.

Myro, R. (1999) 'España en la Unión Europea: etapas y efectos de la integración', in J. L. García Delgado (ed.), *España, economía: ante el siglo XXI* (Madrid: Espasa Calpe), pp. 241–72.

Niedemayer, O. (1995) 'Trends and contrasts', in O. Niedemayer and R. Sinnot (eds), *Public opinion and internationalized governance* (Oxford: Oxford University Press), pp. 53–72.

Núñez Villaverde, J. A. (2001) 'The Mediterranean: A Firm Priority of Spanish Foreign Policy?', in R. Gillespie and R. Youngs (eds), *Spain: The European and International Challenges* (London: Frank Cass), pp. 129–47.

Olsen, J. P. (1997) 'European challenges to the Nation State', in B. Steunenberg and F. van Vaught (eds) *Political institutions and public policy* (Dordrecht: Kluwer), pp. 157–88.

Olsen, J. P. (2001) 'The many faces of Europeanization', *ARENA Working Papers* (University of Oslo), no. 01/2.

Ordóñez Solís, D. (1994) *La ejecución del derecho comunitario en España* (Madrid: Fundación Universidad Empresa/ Civitas).

Ordóñez Solís, D. (1997) *Fondos estructurales europeos. Régimen jurídico y gestión administrativa* (Madrid: Marcial Pons. Ediciones Jurídicas y Sociales).

Ortega, A. (1994) *La razón de Europa* (Madrid: El País/ Aguilar).

Ortega, A. (1995) 'Spain in the post-Cold war', in R. Gillespie, F. Rodrigo and J. Story (eds), *Democratic Spain. Reshaping External relations in a Changing World* (London: Routledge).

Ortega, L. (1988) 'La articulación España-Europa' *Sistema*, vols. 86–7, pp. 157–73.

Ortúzar, L. *et al.* (1995) *La participación de las Comunidades Autónomas en los asuntos comunitarios europeos* (Madrid: MAP).

Oyarzun, R. (1961) *Informe del Ministerio de Asuntos Exteriores sobre las relaciones con la CEE (12-XII-1961)* Archivo del Ministerio de Asuntos Exteriores (AMAE), leg. R-6415 E 26.

Page, E. (1997) *People who run Europe* (Oxford: Clarendon Press).

Payno, J. A. (1984) 'España: características de la economía y motivos para la adhesión', in J. A. Payno and J. L. Sampedro (eds), *La segunda ampliación de la CEE: Grecia, Portugal y España ante la Comunidad* (Madrid: Servicio de Estudios Económicos, Banco Exterior de España).

Pérez, S. (2000) 'Exchange rate rules and economic policy choices: lessons from the Spanish and Italian experiences of the ERM', *South European Society and Politics*, vol. 5(3), pp. 1–32.

Pérez Tremps, P. (1991) 'Il raforzamento dell'esecutivo come conseguenza della integrazione nella Comunitá Europea', in G. Rolla (ed.), *Le forme di governo nei moderni ordinamenti policentri* (Milan: Giuffré).

Pérez Tremps, P. (1999) 'El Tratado de Amsterdam y la Constitución Española', *El País*, 5 de marzo de 1998.

Pérez Tremps, P., Cabellos Espiérrez, M. A. and Roig Moles, E. (1998) *La participación europea y la acción exterior de las Comunidades Autónomas* (Madrid/ Barcelona: Generalitat de Catalunya/Marcial Pons).

Peters, B.G. (1998) *Institutional Theory in Political Science. The 'New Institutionalism'* (London and New York: Pinter).

Pierson, P. (1996) 'The path to European integration. A historical institutionalist analysis', *Comparative Political Studies*, vol. 29(2), pp. 123–63.

Pierson, P. (2000) 'Path Dependence, Increasing Returns, and the Study of Politics', *American Political Science Review*, vol. 94(2), pp. 251–67.

Piqué, J. (2002) Intervención del Ministro de Asuntos Exteriores, Josep Piqué, en el Instituto de España, 'La ampliación a la Europa del Este' (Madrid, 7 de marzo de 2002) http://www.futuroeuropa.es/declar.html.

Pollack, M. (1995) 'Regional actors in an intergovernmental play: the making and implementation of EU structural policy', in S. Mazey and C. Rhodes (eds), *The state of the EU* (Boulder, Co.: Lynne Rienner), pp. 361–90.

Pollack, B. with Hunter, G. (1987) *The paradox of Spanish foreign policy: Spain's international relations from Franco to democracy* (London: Pinter).

Powell, C. T. (1993) 'La dimensión exterior en la transición española' *Afers Internationals*, vol. 26, pp. 37–64.

Powell, C. T. (1995) 'Spain's external relations 1898–1975', in R. Gillespie, F. Rodrigo and J. Story (eds), *Democratic Spain. Reshaping external relations in a changing world* (London: Routledge), pp. 11–29.

Powell, C. T. (2001) 'Fifteen years on: Spanish membership of the European Union revisited', Paper presented at the Conference 'From isolation to integration: 15 years of Spanish and Portuguese membership in Europe', Minda de Gunzburg Centre for European Studies, Harvard University, 2–3 November 2001.

Preston, P. (1986) *The Triumph of Democracy in Spain* (London: Methuen).

Preston, P. (1993) *Franco* (London: HarperCollins).

Preston, P. and Smyth, D. (1984) *Spain, the EEC and NATO* (London: Routledge).

Pridham, G. (1991) 'The politics of the European Community, transnational networks and democratic transition in Southern Europe', in G. Pridham (ed.), *Encouraging democracy: The international context of regime transition in Southern Europe* (London: Leicester University Press/Pinter).

Puchala, D. (1972) 'Of blind men, elephants and international integration', *Journal of Common Market Studies*, vol. 10(3), pp. 267–84.

Putnam, R. D. (1988) 'Diplomacy and domestic politics: the logic of two-level games', *International Organization*, vol. 42(3), pp. 427–60.

Ramírez, M. (1996) *Europa en la conciencia española y otros estudios* (Madrid: Trotta).

Ramos, E. (2000) 'Retos del mundo rural ante la Agenda 2000', in MAPA (ed.), *Reforma de la PAC y Agenda 2000*. *Nuevos tiempos, nueva agricultura* (Madrid: Secretaría General Técnica, MAPA), pp. 77–103.

Rato, R. (1995/6) 'Un nuevo horizonte para la economía española', *Política Exterior*, vol. 48(IX), pp. 23–39.

Raymond Bara, J. L. (1995) 'Convergencia real de España con Europa y disparidades regionales en España', in E. Fuentes Quintana (ed.), *Problemas económicos españoles en la década de los 90* (Madrid: Galaxia Gutemberg/Círculo de Lectores), pp. 517–52.

Richards, M. (1998) *A Time of Silence. Civil War and the Culture of Repression in Franco's Spain, 1936–1945* (Cambridge: Cambridge University Press).

Riva, A. de la (2000) 'Asociación política y libre comercio entre la UE y México', *Economía Exterior*, vol. 12, pp. 63–7.

Romero, J. (1993) 'Problemas estructurales de la agricultura española en el contexto comunitario', in MAPA (ed.), *Agriculturas y políticas agrarias en el sur de Europa* (Madrid: Secretaria General Técnica, MAPA), pp. 415–38.

Rodrigo, F. (1995) 'Western alignment: Spain's security policy', in R. Gillespie, F. Rodrigo and J. Story (eds), *Democratic Spain. Reshaping external relations in a changing world* (London: Routledge), pp. 50–65.

Rodrigo, F. (1996) 'The Spanish debate', in *The 1996 IGC-National debates (2). Germany, Spain, Sweden and the UK* (London: The Royal Institute of International Affairs), pp. 22–36.

Rodrigo, F. (1998) 'La política exterior española en 1997', in *Anuario Internacional CIDOB 1998* (Barcelona: CIDOB), pp. 29–41.

Roldán Barbero, J. and Hinojosa Martínez, L. (1997) 'La aplicación judicial del derecho comunitario en España (1996)', *Revista de Derecho Comunitario Europeo*, vol. 1(2), pp. 549–80.

Rosa, A., Blanco, F., Díaz, F., de Castro, R. (1998) 'Europe as a discursive resource for Spanish national identity', in U. Hedetoft (ed.), *Political symbols, symbolic politics. European identities in transformation* (Aldershot: Ashgate), pp. 105–131.

Ruesga, S. (1993) 'España ante el Mercado Único Europeo y reflexiones desde una perspectiva económica', *Sistema*, vols. 114–15, pp. 113–28.

Ruiz-Jarabo Colomer, D. (1993) 'El juez nacional como juez comunitario. Valoración de la práctica española', in G. C. Rodríguez Iglesias and D. Liñán Noguera (eds), *El derecho comunitario europeo y su aplicación judicial* (Madrid: Civitas), pp. 653–75.

Rupérez, J. (1996) *Continuidad y cambio en la política exterior española* (Madrid: INCIPE).

Sabá, K. (1986) 'The Spanish foreign-policy decision-making', *The International Spectator*, vol. 26(4), pp. 24–33.

Sahagún, F. (2000) 'La política exterior española en 1999', *Anuario Internacional CIDOB 2000* (Barcelona: CIDOB), pp. 29–46.

Salmon, K. (1995) 'Spain in the world economy', in R. Gillespie, F. Rodrigo and J. Story (eds), *Democratic Spain. Reshaping external relations in a changing world* (London: Routledge), pp. 67–87.

Salomon, M. (1996) 'Spain, Scope Enlargement towards the Maghreb and the Arab World', in F. Algieri and E. Regelsberger (eds), *Synergy at Work. Spain and Portugal in European Foreign Policy* (Bonn: Europa Union Verlag), pp. 91–109.

Sánchez Mateos, E. (1999) 'La política exterior española en 1998', *Anuario Internacional CIDOB 1998* (Barcelona:CIDOB), pp. 29–40.

Saro, G. (2001) 'La política industrial', in C. Closa (ed.), *La europeización del sistema político español* (Madrid: Istmo), pp. 421–565.

Scharpf, F. (1994) 'Community and autonomy: multilevel policy-making in the European Union', *Journal of European Public Policy*, vol. 1.

Schmitter, Philippe C. (1993) 'The International Context of Contemporary Democratization', *Stanford Journal of International Affairs*, vol. 2(1), pp. 1–34.

Senante Berendes, H. C. (1999) *La opinión pública española ante el Tratado de la Unión Europea* (Valencia: Institut de Cultura Juan Gil-Albert).

Serra Rexach, E. (2000) 'La nueva defensa, la defensa de Europa', *El País*, 6 January, p. 11.

Sevilla, J. (1997) *La economía española ante la moneda única* (Madrid: Ediciones Debate).

Sevilla, M. and Golf, E. (1999) 'Política fiscal y convergencia regional', *Papeles de Economía Española*, vol. 80, pp. 185–202.

Sidjanski, D. (1989) 'Les groupes d'intérêt de l'Europe du sud et leur insertion dans la CE', *Revue du Marché Commun*, p. 325.

Smith, D. and Wanke, I. (1993) '1992: who wins? Who loses?', in A. Cafruny and G. Rosenthal (eds), *The state of the European Community vol.2 The Maastricht debates and beyond* (Boulder, Co.: Lynne Rienner), pp. 353–72.

Smyrl, M. (1997) 'Does European Community regional policy empower the regions?', *Governance*, vol. 3, pp. 287–309.

Solana, J. (1993) 'España-Europa', *Sistema*, vols. 114–15, pp. 13–23.

Solana, J. and Agnelli, S. (1995) 'Una estrategia hispano – italiana', *El País* (10 May).

Solbes, P. (1993) 'La adhesión española a la CEE: principales repercusiones sobre el sector agrario valenciano', in MAPA (ed.), *Agriculturas y políticas agrarias en el sur de Europa* (Madrid: Secretaria General Técnica, MAPA), pp. 15–30.

Solbes, P., Arias Cañete, M. and Aldecoa, F. (1988) *La presidencia española de las Comunidades Europeas* (Madrid: CEC).

Story, J. (1995) 'Spain's external relations redefined: 1975–1989', in R. Gillespie, F. Rodrigo and J. Story (eds), *Democratic Spain. Reshaping external relations in a changing world* (London: Routledge), pp. 30–49.

Story, J. and Grugel, J. (1991) *Spanish external policies and the EC Presidency*, Occasional Paper 2 Centre for Mediterranean Studies (Bristol: University of Bristol).

Sumpsi, J. M. (1994) 'La agricultura española actual. El marco de referencia', *Papeles de Economía Española*, vols. 60–1, pp. 2–14.

Szmolka, I. (1999) *Opiniones y actitudes de los españoles ante el proceso de integración europeo* (Madrid: CIS).

Tamames, R. (1978) *El Acuerdo Preferencial CEE-España y las preferencias generalizadas* (Barcelona: Dopesa).

Torcal, M. and Montero, J. R. (1999) 'Facets of social capital in new democracies: the formation and consequences of social capital in Spain', in J. W. van Deth, M. Maraffi, K. Newton and P. F. Whiteley (eds), *Social Capital and European Democracy* (London: Routledge), pp. 167–91.

Torreblanca, I. (1998) 'Overlapping games and cross-cutting coalitions in the European Union', *West European Politics*, vol. 23(2), pp. 134–153.

Torreblanca, I. (1999/2000) 'España y la ampliación: mito y realidad', *Economía Exterior*, vol. 11, pp. 111–18.

Torreblanca, I. (2001a) 'Política exterior e identidades colectivas', in C. Closa (ed.). *La Europeización del sistema político español* (Madrid: Itsmo), pp. 483–511.

Torreblanca, I. (2001b) 'Ideas, preferences and institutions: Explaining the Europeanization of Spanish foreign policy', *ARENA Working Paper*, no. 01/26.

Torrero Mañas, A. (1998) 'Consecuencias del esfuerzo de convergencia nominal para el conjunto de la economía española', in J. Colino Sueiras and A. García Sánchez (eds), *España y Maastricht: ventajas e inconvenientes* (Madrid: Civitas), pp. 155–73.

Tovias, A. (1995) 'Spain in the European Community', in R. Gillespie, F. Rodrigo and J. Story (eds), *Democratic Spain. Reshaping external relations in a changing world* (London; Routledge), pp. 88–105.

Tsoukalis, L. (1981) *The European Community and its Mediterranean enlargement* (London: George Allen & Uwin).

Valle, A. and Fajardo del Castillo, C. (1999) 'La aplicación judicial del derecho comunitario en España', *Revista de Derecho Comunitario Europeo*, vol. 3(5), pp. 109–28.

Velarde Fuertes, J. (1995) 'Evolución del comercio exterior español: del nacionalismo económico a la Unión Europea', in E. Fuentes Quintana (ed.), *Problemas económicos españoles en la década de los 90* (Madrid: Galaxia Gutemberg/Círculo de Lectores), pp. 383–414.

Viñas, A. (1999) 'Breaking the shackles from the past: Spanish foreign policy from Franco to Felipe González', in S. Balfour and P. Preston (eds), *Spain and the Great Powers in the Twentieth Century* (London: Routledge), pp. 245–67.

Viñas, A. (2001) 'Spaniards in the service of the European Commission', *South European Society and Politics*, vol. 6(2).

Widgrén, M. (1994) 'Voting power in the EC decision-making and the consequences of two enlargements', *European Economic Review*, vol. 38, pp. 1153–70.

Wessels, W. and Rometsch, D. (1996) 'Conclusion: European Union and national institutions', in D. Rometsch and W. Wessels (eds), *The European Union and its member states. Towards institutional fusion?* (Manchester: Manchester University Press), pp. 328–65.

Westendorp y Cabeza, C. (1995) 'España y la ampliación de la Unión Europea', *Boletín Económico de ICE*, vol. 2442, pp. 3763–7.

Whitehead, L. (1991) 'Democracy by convergence and Southern Europe: a comparative politics perspective', in G. Pridham (ed.), *Encouraging democracy: The international context of regime transition in Southern Europe* (London: Leicester University Press/Pinter).

Whitehead, L. (1996) 'Democracy by Convergence: Southern Europe', in L. Whitehead (ed.), *The International Dimensions of Democratization* (Oxford: Oxford University Press).

Wright, V. (1996) 'The national coordination of European policy-making', in J. Richardson (ed.), *European Union: power and policy-making* (London: Routledge), pp. 147–69.

Xunta de Galicia (1993) *A política pesqueira de Galicia no contexto comunitario* (Santiago de Compostela: Xunta de Galicia).

Yáñez, J. A. and Viñas, A. (1992) 'Diez años de política exterior del gobierno socialista (1982–1992)', in A. Guerra and J. F. Tezanos (eds), *La década del cambio. Diez años de gobierno socialista 1982–1992* (Madrid: Editorial Sistema), pp. 85–133.

Zapico Goñi, E. (1995) 'La adaptación de la administración española a la Unión Europea: un proceso de evolución y aprendizaje permanente', *Gestión y Administración de Políticas Públicas*, vol. 4, pp. 47–65.

Zaragoza, J. A. (1990) 'El resurgimiento de la política regional: la nueva política comunitaria y la política regional española', *Información Comercial Española*, vol. 679, pp. 27–37.

Index

ADVERTISEMENT

Make sense of the European Union

European Voice, the weekly newspaper published by The Economist Group in Brussels, is where thousands of politicians, administrators and business people look to get the inside story on what is happening in the European Union. Packed with news and analysis, *European Voice* is now available to readers of this book at a special discounted subscription rate. (Please quote ref MCM01)

Subscribe now for 20% off the normal annual rate:

❐ Please enter my annual subscription at £89 (BEF 4,518) **EURO 112**

Name

Company (if applicable)

Address

Postcode/City   Country

❐ Please charge my

❐ Visa   ❐ Mastercard   ❐ American Express   ❐ Diners Club

Card Number   Expiry Date M❐❐ Y❐❐

Signed   Date

❐ I enclose a cheque made payable to *European Voice*

To subscribe today,

☎ Call now on:
+44 (0) 20 8402 8499,
or fax this form to:
+44 (0) 20 8249 4159

✉ Or post this form to:
European Voice,
c/o Publishing Power,
Garrard House,
2-6 Homesdale Road,
Bromley, BR2 9WL
United Kingdom
www.european-voice.com

Registered in the UK under the Data Protection Act.
From time to time we may allow certain reputable
companies to send you information. Please tick here
if you prefer not to receive such mailings ❐

EuropeanVoice

Euro force to be armed
with uranium weapons

M
C
M
0
1